Kids These Days

Kids These Days

Facts and Fictions About Today's Youth

Karen Sternheimer

ROWMAN & LITTLEFIELD PUBLISHERS, INC.
Lanham • *Boulder* • *New York* • *Toronto* • *Oxford*

ROWMAN & LITTLEFIELD PUBLISHERS, INC.

Published in the United States of America
by Rowman & Littlefield Publishers, Inc.
A wholly owned subsidary of The Rowman & Littlefield Publishing Group, Inc.
4501 Forbes Boulevard, Suite 200, Lanham, Maryland 20706
www.rowmanlittlefield.com

PO Box 317
Oxford
OX2 9RU, UK

British Library Cataloguing in Publication Information Available

Library of Congress Cataloging-in-Publication Data

Sternheimer, Karen.
  Kids these days : facts and fictions about today's youth / Karen Sternheimer.
    p. cm.
  Includes bibliographical references and index.
  ISBN-13: 978-0-7425-4667-7 (cloth : alk. paper)
  ISBN-10: 0-7425-4667-5 (cloth : alk. paper)
  ISBN-13: 978-0-7425-4668-4 (pbk. : alk. paper)
  ISBN-10: 0-7425-4668-3 (pbk. : alk. paper)
  1. Teenagers—United States—Life skills guides. 2. Teenagers—United States—
Conduct of life. I. Title.
HQ796.S82685 2006
305.2350973—dc22   2005037155

Printed in the United States of America

∞™ The paper used in this publication meets the minimum requirements of
American National Standard for Information Sciences—Permanence of Paper
for Printed Library Materials, ANSI/NISO Z39.48-1992.

Contents

Acknowledgments

This book may have a single author, but it could not have been written without the support and encouragement of many people. I am grateful for the enthusiasm of Matthew Hammon, Alan McClare, Alex Masulis, Lea Gift, and the staff at Rowman and Littlefield for making the publication of this book possible. Alex provided many excellent suggestions that doubtlessly made the book stronger. I also acknowledge those who provided early support and feedback for this project, in particular Jill Rothenberg, Kristi Long, Ed Parsons, and Mike Males, as well as several anonymous reviewers.

The continued support of the members of the Sociology Department at the University of Southern California, has been invaluable to my personal and professional development for the past thirteen years. In particular, Mike Messner, Barry Glassner, and Elaine Bell Kaplan have been and remain wonderful mentors. I am also grateful for the ongoing help of the department's staff, Patricia Adolph, Stachelle Overland, Monique Thomas, and Alicia Guzman.

Many USC undergraduate students contributed to the research for this book. Jessica Bertain, Kathi Cipriaso, Kimberly Grether, Nicole Gutierrez, Michael Karpeles, Wendy Koo, Malinda Lin, Patricia Nicolas, and Tyler Rodde all provided assistance by combing through thousands of newspaper and magazine articles. I also acknowledge the students in my courses for providing enthusiasm and inspiration for this book's subject matter, and an opportunity to discuss the ideas in their early stages. I am also indebted to the many graduate students who have provided teaching assistance over the past several years, and whose help gave me the time to research and write this book.

I am thankful for the ongoing friendship and support of Sally Raskoff, Carmela Lomonaco, Elisabeth Burgess, Monica Whitlock, Janis Prince, Portia Cohen, Molly Ranney, and Jean Summer throughout this process. Additionally, I am eternally grateful for the unconditional support of my family, without whom none of this would be possible. My grandmother, Frieda Fettner, continues to be a source of inspiration and wisdom. I have also been blessed with many extended family members who have been informal PR agents for me; thanks especially to Barbara Cohen, Saul Fettner, and Nancy and Larry Friedman. I am particularly grateful for my sisters, Laura and Linda; brother-in-law, Jacob; and parents, Toby and Lee, who have always been there for me.

Introduction

Kids These Days

What the devil's wrong with these kids today?
Who could guess that they would turn out that way!
Why can't they be like we were,
Perfect in every way?
What's the matter with kids today?

—"Kids," from *Bye Bye Birdie*, Charles Strause and Lee Adams, 1960

Kids snatched from their bedrooms, shot at in school, fatter than ever, prone to risk-taking and cruelty . . . is childhood today as scary as the news accounts would have us believe? Is this generation headed for disaster?

Many of us seem to think that they are. We complain that kids today are pop-culture clones, shallow, self-centered, greedy, lazy, and sometimes violent. A 1999 poll by the Public Agenda Foundation found that 71 percent of the general public described teenagers negatively as rude, wild, or irresponsible.[1] In a 2001 *Time*/CNN poll, 80 percent of parents agreed with the statement that kids are more spoiled today than they were ten to fifteen years ago.[2] A 2002 survey found that adults most often used words like *selfish* and *materialistic* to describe today's youths compared with youths of twenty years ago, and used words like *idealistic* and *patriotic* to describe kids of the past.[3]

This book critically examines the hottest news stories of the past few years to see if the truth about today's young people is really as bad as it sounds. *Kids These Days* looks at the stories that made headlines and goes deeper to explore overall trends and statistics and to compare the hype to reality. For instance, is kidnapping by strangers really a bigger threat now than in the past? Are disputes at school now settled with guns instead of fists? And are

1

kids, especially girls, becoming bigger bullies than ever before? The truth is, kids today do face unique obstacles and challenges, but their situation isn't nearly as dire as the compelling news accounts would have us believe.

I decided to write *Kids These Days* while working on my first book, *It's Not the Media*. In researching the first book, I read hundreds of newspaper and magazine articles and was struck by their negative narrative about the state of youths today, something we seem to take for granted as a sad but unquestionable fact. Bad news about greedy, fat, promiscuous, self-centered, lazy, and violent kids was all over the headlines. If I weren't familiar with data to the contrary, I might believe the hype myself. This bad-news theme motivated me to want to tell the other side of the story, the side not cranked out by our news media machine that seeks to excite at any cost.

My goal here is to provide a much-needed alternative to the perennial belief that young people are both in danger and dangerous. We can then focus on the most important threats young people face: poverty, family violence, inadequate foster care, underfunded schools, a sped-up society, and increasingly zero tolerance for young people themselves.

Having been a teen twenty years ago, I can recall accounts equally as dire about my generation. A 1983 U.S. Department of Education report titled "A Nation at Risk" predicted an overall decline in the knowledge base of our country; our generation was allegedly too stupid to be able to fill the necessary roles to maintain the American economic powerhouse that our elders had created. Yet just a decade after this dour report, my generation was at the forefront of one of the biggest periods of economic expansion in American history. In 2004, nine-year-olds scored better in math and reading than at any time since the standardized tests were first administered in the early 1970s. Older kids also scored just as well or better than their 1970s counterparts.[4] And as of 2003, math SAT scores had reached a thirty-six-year high, and verbal scores were on the rise as well, even with more students taking the test than in past generations.[5]

Complaints about the next generation have been made for centuries. Socrates observed that children were more disobedient, had less respect for authority, and had poorer manners than his generation.[6] Much has changed since the days of ancient Greece, but the complaints have not. In 2001, 82 percent of adults also said that children's manners today are worse than when the adults themselves were young.[7]

When we're not blaming kids for not being like "we were," we fear that the world has become unsafe for children, mostly unsafe for kids from middle-class, well-manicured suburbs. We forget that for past generations high school was a luxury of the well-to-do, and that young people were often expected to work in factories and fields. We seem to suffer from generational myopia, whereby the past is always better, safer, and more innocent than the present. Seventy-one percent of those polled by the Kaiser Family

Foundation in 1996 said that they were "very concerned" that life for their children will not be better than it has been for them.[8] In a Massachusetts Mutual poll, 37 percent strongly disagreed that life is better for children now than it was when they were kids.[9]

Our fears about kids being taken from their homes, killed in school, or seduced by fast-food advertising are fed by countless news stories encouraging us to fear the outside world and the kids in it. This has led to tighter clampdowns on kids and attempts to seal young people off from the world for their—or our—protection.

Our nation's youths have been targeted as a problem population to absolve adults of responsibility for creating the often dangerous and difficult conditions many young people must endure. This book serves to offer a better understanding of the realities of the first generation to come of age in the twenty-first century, and it will hopefully help us all rethink our assumptions about kids today. Each chapter will address one or more of our common complaints about today's young people: they are rude and annoying; they are immoral; they are lazy and greedy; they are stupid; or they are at risk and in danger.

COMMON COMPLAINT NUMBER 1:
KIDS ARE RUDE AND ANNOYING

Whether they are said to be whining, running around in public, or disregarding adult social conventions, kids in restaurants, airplanes, and other places where adults may be are often the subject of complaints. *Los Angeles Times* columnist Al Martinez wrote of his experience viewing the movie *The Ring* in a local theater. Describing how he "ended up in teenage hell," Martinez complained that the other young moviegoers, whom he estimated to be between thirteen and sixteen, "were unable to keep quiet and sit still even when the movie began," and he compared the theater to an asylum.[10]

Rather than attributing the noise of the audience members to the scary nature of the film or a few loud individuals, Martinez ascribed this quality to the young people as a group, and concluded that the movie was "not half as scary as being surrounded by . . . all those raging hormones."[11] Imagine publishing a column about attending a movie with a different racial-ethnic group than your own and using a biological argument to explain their behavior. Unlikely in 2002, when this column ran, but kids today are apparently still fair game.

Earlier that year, the *Los Angeles Times* published an editorial about a seventeen-year-old who defrauded nearly a thousand investors out of about a million dollars through an Internet scheme. Instead of noting that young people with their wit and use of technology can sometimes con adults, the editors took the opportunity to condemn youths in general, calling young people "emotional mutants on a hormone driven thrill ride."[12] "On teen planets," the editors continued, "nothing is so small that it can't be blown up into a volcanic argument or a life-altering disappointment." Exactly what these observations have to do with Internet fraud is unclear, nor was the "raging hormone" explanation used for the dozens of high-profile financial scandals of the early 2000s committed by middle-aged adults.

COMMON COMPLAINT NUMBER 2: KIDS ARE IMMORAL

The seventeen-year-old's Internet scam may be used by some to justify the next complaint about kids today, that they have less moral grounding than past generations. Gary Bauer, president of the Family Research Council, charged that young people have "no standards of right and wrong," and suffer from a "value deficit."[13] Furthering this claim, a 2004 wire report suggested that "Cheating Is Widespread among Teens."[14] A closer look at the study this report was based on reveals that less than a third of twelve- to seventeen-year-olds admitted to cheating, but they think that everyone else is doing it—seven in ten surveyed said that they believe other students cheat on tests and homework.

Proof of a "value deficit"? Maybe so, but the deficit is certainly not only in young people. David Callahan, author of *The Cheating Culture: Why More Americans Are Doing Wrong to Get Ahead*, notes that to understand cheating we must look at the broader cultural context, which encourages us all to get ahead at any cost and best our competition. Gordon Gekko, the character made famous by Michael Douglas in the movie *Wall Street*, is alive and well in many of us who secretly accept that "greed is good," at least when our stocks are doing well. Many of today's business leaders, rocked by scandal, became successful by changing the rules to fit their needs as they went along.

By contrast, a 2002 University of California at Berkeley study found that young people were more religiously conservative than their elders, with 69 percent supporting prayer in school compared to 59 percent of adults age twenty-seven to fifty-nine.[15] In a 1998 poll of teens age thirteen to eighteen, 91 percent of the respondents said that they consider themselves responsible, 80 percent said that they trust others, and 64 percent described themselves as religious.[16]

If we think kids lack strong values, we have only ourselves to blame. A 2002 online survey of nearly ten thousand kids found that the vast majority viewed parents and teachers as their central role models: 86 percent said that they feel they can trust those adults, with friends coming in at 77 percent.[17] Musicians and athletes scored much lower, with only 35 and 30 percent of the kids reporting that they trust these celebrities respectively. But typically when we worry that young people are lacking morality, we are talking about other people's children: a 2000 *Newsweek* poll found that only 13 percent of parents worried a lot about *their own* children's morals.[18]

COMMON COMPLAINT NUMBER 3:
KIDS ARE LAZY, GREEDY, AND SELF-CENTERED

We try to teach young people that playing by the rules and hard work will lead to success. Of course, we ourselves don't always abide by this advice, otherwise we wouldn't play the lottery, cheat on our taxes, or be as overweight as many of us are. But we often isolate laziness as a quality of the young, and science has been studying the underlying causes of this taken-for-granted assumption of adolescence.

The Public Broadcasting System (PBS) aired a program in 2002 called "The Teenage Brain" to scientifically explain why teens are sometimes lethargic in the morning. A related study made the news in 2004; one headline claimed that "Lazy Teens May Have an Excuse."[19] An experiment compared groups of kids twelve to seventeen years old with young adults twenty-two to twenty-seven years old on a computer game where they could earn between twenty cents and five dollars. Blood flow to the part of the brain associated with motivation was higher in the older group, and thus the younger group was deemed lazy. Lack of motivation, however, is not exactly the same as laziness. Perhaps the younger group felt less motivated to earn small sums of money—a twelve-year-old probably isn't struggling to pay the electric bill as a twenty-two-year-old might be. But since we have already decided that teens are lazy, science is used to justify our preconceived belief.

We don't think that kids are lazy when it comes to satisfying their own selfish needs, though. We often view them as pleasure-seeking creatures that "care more about [file-sharing website] Napster than the plight of women and children smothered by the Taliban," as the author of a story about human rights complained.[20] Two high-school students responded to this reporter with a letter to the editor (something lazy people would never do), challenging the author's assumption about young people by pointing out that their school had a large and active human-rights club.[21]

While many see young people as apathetic, marketers see dollar signs in today's young people, causing critics to complain that kids are tricked into spending inordinate amounts of money on entertainment and fashion, especially trashy clothes. But Nordstrom has reported a widespread interest in their "modesty" fashion shows, featuring clothes for teens that Britney Spears may not have worn since her Mouseketeer days. The retail clothing industry has also taken a hit lately, as teen girls have scaled back spending. But rather than view this as a sign of more conscientious consumption, industry analysts then describe shoppers as "fickle young female consumers."[22] Sometimes kids just can't win.

COMMON COMPLAINT NUMBER 4: KIDS ARE STUPID

If kids are materialistic, self-centered, and lazy, they certainly can't be scholars. Seventeen percent of parents in a 1995 Gallup Poll admitted to calling their kids dumb or lazy.[23] News stories occasionally trigger this complaint too. A 2002 Associated Press wire report titled "Where in the World? Students Don't Know" lamented that three-fourths of high-school seniors had "only a basic grasp of geography," whatever a "basic grasp" means, and that 16 percent of eighth graders couldn't locate the Mississippi River on a map.[24] That means that 84 percent could. And in 2005, the American team of teens won the National Geographic World Championship for the fourth year in a row. And how geographically illiterate are adults? Of course, the report did not include them. Stories decrying the ignorance of youths today overlook the fact that kids today are twice as likely to graduate from high school, and three and one-half times more likely to graduate from college compared with their predecessors in 1960.[25]

Additionally, kids today seem to be smart enough to get the message that smoking is a bad idea, because rates of cigarette smoking have dropped to their lowest levels in decades, and drinking and illegal drug use are down as well.[26] Yet in a 1999 poll, only 22 percent of the respondents described children today as having positive traits, such as being curious or smart.[27] That number dropped to 15 percent when the pollsters asked specifically about teenagers.[28]

Maybe if it's kids that are stupid and lazy, we don't need to work so hard to improve some of the nation's troubled public schools. Kids aren't bright enough to appreciate all that we adults do for them, apparently. In spite of complaints about today's students, however, educational research indicates that overall school performance has been relatively stable over the past decades.[29]

COMMON COMPLAINT NUMBER 5:
KIDS ARE AT RISK AND IN DANGER

When we're not worried about how kids are performing on tests in school, our attention often turns to the danger they may face at school or in the world in general. An ad for a speaker series in the September 18, 2002, edition of the *Los Angeles Times* began ominously: "Abductions. Drug abuse. Plummeting test scores. Terrorism. School shootings. Isn't it time we asked:

Who's saving America's kids?"[30] The ad also described youths as "increasingly at risk."

The announcement focused on the unlikeliest of events; as we will see in the next chapter, the chances that someone other than a parent will abduct a child for any length of time is extremely small. Drug abuse was (and still is) a bigger problem for the baby-boom generation than it is for today's kids; test scores aren't plummeting; and a child is more likely to be struck by lightning than die in a school shooting. And by invoking terrorism in a list of supposed youth problems, post–September 11 fears are triggered and projected onto kids.

Juvenile arrest rates for violent crime have been dropping for a decade, and homicide arrest rates are lower than or on par with 1960s rates.[31] Many people erroneously perceive that violence has been steadily increasing, even though overall violent crime in the United States has been in a steep decline. This is because we see shocking acts of violence reported nightly on the evening news but rarely hear about crime rates in context. News stories promoting fear of youths grab our attention because it is an old, familiar theme, one we heard about ourselves when we were young. We often hear about the rare but tragic acts of violence by children, but seldom learn of how unusual they actually are, which leads us to believe that young people today are at a greater risk of victimization from each other.

Some of our concerns about kids today do have merit. Kids today *are* more likely to be obese than just a few years ago. Some kids *are* abducted and murdered by strangers. And some young people can be mean and make poor choices. But we seldom hear about the broader context of these issues, like the U.S. population's growing rates of obesity, the threat parents pose to their own children, or how our culture promotes bullying. We tend to blame the kids themselves or their parents rather than explore what are both individual and societal issues.

Fearing kids and fearing for kids reflects a larger sense of anxiety and not just a realistic concern for young people's health and well-being. At a time when many of us will move several times in our lives, we are less likely to know—or to trust—our neighbors than in the past when families lived in the same communities for generations. We have experienced a national trauma, and now we feel less safe within our own borders. The world feels more out of control, and we fear that childhood and children themselves will be worse off from these changes. Young people, we fear, will reflect the changes in our society that scare us the most.

OLD NEWS

Complaints about youths are part of an old tradition. But this generation *really is* worse, observers may claim. "Every generation thinks the kids of the next generation are both wilder and have more to contend with," said a North Carolina lobbyist, who argued that "these days, it's true."[32] Each generation creates an idealized view of the past to support their belief that things really were better, or simpler, in their day.

Sometimes I feel that way too. But I have to remind myself that American life in the past was far from ideal. Going through childhood in the 1970s—a period marked by massive inflation, a decline in manufacturing, an energy crisis, growing rates of crime and drug use, Watergate, and the Vietnam War—was not really as simple or as innocent as it may seem now. Life for kids today might be different in many ways than it was thirty years ago, but it is not uniformly better or worse. According to Duke University's Foundation for Child Development, the overall quality of life for children in 2003 was much the same as in 1975, the first year of data their study analyzed. Kids in 2003 were safer, and less likely to get pregnant or drink alcohol, but more likely to live in poverty or in a single-parent home than were children of my generation.[33]

Certainly there are young people—and not so young people—whose values and behavior leave much to be desired. As long as there have been youths, there have been people complaining about them. According to an observer in 1818, "parents have no command over their children."[34] Nearly two hundred years later, a 1999 CBS News/*New York Times* poll found that 91 percent of adults said that teens today need more supervision, and 86 percent said that parents watch their kids less today than when they were teens.[35] A mid-nineteenth-century issue of *Presbyterian Magazine* complained that kids were "given up to idleness, knowing no restraint . . . familiar with drunkenness, profaneness, and all the captivating focus of youthful dissipation."[36]

Throughout the twentieth century, young people were considered harbingers of trouble. As the labor of children and adolescents was needed less for a functioning household or economy, animosity grew. A 1912 *Ladies' Home Journal* article complained that "ninety-three of every one hundred children [are] . . . unfitted for even the simplest tasks of life."[37] A few years later, the Roaring Twenties was a time of economic growth, leading to increased leisure time for young people. A 1921 issue of *Century* magazine described kids as "running wild," and contended that "no age . . . has had on its hands such a problem of reckless and rebellious youth."[38] Elders were concerned that religion had lost its strong hold on regulating behavior, especially behavior pertaining to sex.

In 1929, Robert and Helen Lynd published *Middletown: A Study in Modern American Culture*, and their respondents had much to say about perceived changes in youthful mores. Much as today, adults felt that kids were growing up too fast. "Children of twelve or fourteen nowadays act just like grown-ups," an observer told the Lynds.[39] A Middletown mother complained that "girls are far more aggressive today."[40] Another stated that "girls aren't so modest nowadays; they dress differently. . . . We can't keep our boys decent when girls dress that way."[41]

Writer Pearl S. Buck noted in a 1935 issue of *Harper's Magazine* that Depression-era youths, at the time called the Lost Generation but whom we now regard as the Greatest Generation, were "completely selfish . . . so sophisticated with a sort of pseudo-sophistication which is touching in its shallowness."[42] The future heroes of World War II were described by author Maxine Davis in *Lost Generation* as a group that "accepts its fate with sheep-like apathy," and she suggested that "youth today . . . would not fight for states' rights or any rights, because they have no interest in them."[43] Of course, a few years later the same youths went on to liberate Western Europe from fascism—but hindsight is 20-20.

That group of supposed ne'er-do-wells is our elder generation now, often the leaders in complaints about kids today. But they also had much to say about their own offspring. A 1951 *Reader's Digest* article complained that kids "could not write a clear English sentence, do simple mathematics, or find common geographical locations such as Boston or New York City."[44]

The children of the Lost (or Greatest) Generation, the baby boomers, now idealize their own youth, which made famous the idea of a generation gap. The boomers were criticized in their youth for being ungrateful, selfish (the "me generation"), drug-taking, promiscuous troublemakers. A 2002 study by sociologist Elaine Bell Kaplan found that parents who were more adventurous during the 1960s became very controlling parents years later, idealizing their own experimentation with sex and drugs as more innocent and somehow safer than life is for kids today.[45]

Complaints about youths' behavior echo across the ages, as adults look at children and find them to be less than perfect. While animosity toward youths is not new, it has intensified as young people become increasingly separated from adults both socially and in the labor market. Additionally, as our population ages, kids today are increasingly outnumbered. While there are more young people in raw numbers today than ever before, they comprise a smaller proportion of the overall population. According to the U.S. Census Bureau, in 1970 there were 70.3 million Americans under eighteen, or about 35 percent of the population. In 2000 there were 72.2 million Americans under eighteen, but kids only made up 26 percent of the overall population.[46]

If each generation seems to believe that the next is worse than ever, we need to examine why. Throughout this book, I explore not only the facts and fictions about today's youths, but also why we so often invent the fictions and overlook the facts. While the reasons we feel anxiety about the next generation are numerous and complex, there are three key themes that explain the animosity that occasionally bubbles to the surface.

For one, during times of change, be they economic, political, technological, or social, our anxiety about the future is projected onto young people.

Secondly, as these changes were taking place during the twentieth century, American young people increasingly enjoyed more leisure time and less responsibility in the labor market and at home. While each generation says that they want things to be easier for their children, as childhood, adolescence, and even young adulthood have increasingly become defined as time for fun, the elders may look back at their own struggles and begrudge the young of today for avoiding them. And finally, if we can blame youths themselves for the problems that emerge from the many changes noted above, we feel absolved of responsibility or blame. Kids become a convenient scapegoat for what we refuse to see in ourselves.

Fear of and fear for youths is a rite of passage, a common lament that comes with change. Young people both represent and must deal with the consequences of these fluctuations, which stem from a changing economy, increased social fragmentation, and the growth of technology. These shifts have created new challenges, and we need to focus on supporting, rather than denigrating or overprotecting, young people today. Bad behavior stories make kids today seem unworthy of adult sympathy and in need of further restriction instead of policies to support their transition into adulthood. Negative and fear-inducing stories have led us to mourn the death of childhood innocence, something we presume was alive and well in the not-so-distant past.

For example, in the spring of 2004, comedian Bill Cosby complained in a speech at an NAACP gala that too many kids are "standing on the corner and they can't speak English."[47] He didn't only blame the kids; he criticized parents for spending money on expensive shoes but not on education, and charged that "the lower economic people are not holding up their end in this deal."

Cosby's remarks were widely criticized, but were also used by some to justify their negative beliefs about kids today, especially poor kids of color. There is a danger if we look at the problems young people face as *only* a consequence of their behavior and fail to see how schools are also responsible for failing many of these young people that Cosby says have no command of the English language. One would hope that Cosby, who holds a doctorate in education, is aware of these institutional problems, but clearly many who heard about his remarks are not.

Youth bashing is most insidious when it causes us to turn our backs on the challenges young people face and to see their failures solely as the result of their own insufferableness. For young people of color, so often demonized as illiterate, violent, and promiscuous, the stakes are even higher. Those most in need of supportive social programs are seen as the least deserving and condemned as a generation. When we focus on young people's shortcomings and overlook important environmental factors, it is easier for us to cut funding for existing programs such as subsidized meals, after-school programs, and aid for families in poverty. In the meantime we build more maximum-security prisons to hold the products of our self-fulfilling prophecy.

Kids these days do often face unique challenges that generations before did not. We often overlook the importance of broad-scale youth entitlements like the New Deal–era Civilian Conservation Corps, then later the GI Bill, which subsidized housing and education, not to mention free or extremely low-cost tuition at state colleges and universities. Young people today come out of college with far more student-loan debt than their predecessors did; between 1977 and 1996 the median student-loan debt load increased more than sevenfold.[48] Young people today are also more likely than their parents were to have to navigate life in a blended family following divorce, and to suffer the economic consequences that often follow in a single-parent household. Complaining about kids today whitewashes these challenges and prevents us from asking what we can do at the societal level to support young people in their growth and development instead of just criticizing them.

In the following chapters, I explore six topics of concern about youths today that regularly appear in the news. The first three topics, kidnapping, obesity, and school violence, focus mostly on children as potential victims. In these chapters I examine our fear that the world, including schools, neighborhoods, and even a child's bedroom, is no longer the safe haven we think it used to be. Chapter 1 focuses on how kidnapping serves as a powerful metaphor for the dangers that we perceive children face from outsiders, when statistically the danger is most potent from within. American fears of kidnapping were heightened in 2002 because we were still reeling from the trauma of September 11, when strangers attacked us at home.

Chapter 2 looks at our fears about overindulged kids and the growing number of children classified as overweight. Obesity is an outgrowth of automation and is reportedly on the rise throughout the industrialized world. Yet in press coverage about child obesity, the problem is often framed as unique to kids, their bad habits, and supposed laziness. Chapter 3 explores our fear that schools have become pits of danger and examines how our widespread response to this fear—crackdowns and so-called zero-tolerance policies—punishes individual kids for lesser and lesser infractions, at a time when school violence is actually on the decline. Meanwhile, as principals are suspending kids found with Tylenol or bread knives, many classrooms are growing more crowded and facilities are falling into disrepair.

Within our fear of dangerous schools, kids are viewed not only as victims, but also as violent threats, hazardous to both other kids and the adults that work in the schools. Chapters 4 through 6 therefore focus mainly on teens and preteens and the perceived threat that they pose to themselves, each other, and the rest of us.

Chapter 4 explores hazing and bullying among young people. Books like *Queen Bees and Wannabees* and *Odd Girl Out: The Hidden Culture of Aggression in Girls* suggest that girls in particular are in the midst of a new crisis. This chapter looks at news coverage of "mean kids" and considers the broader cultural context as well as why this theme resonates so well with adults today. By placing these threats in context, we can better understand the realities of peer culture in America today.

Chapter 5, by focusing on the "stupid-teen trick" theme in many news stories, asks whether teens and bad behavior go hand in hand. Reports of kids jumping over moving cars or lighting themselves on fire and other anecdotal stories occasionally appear in the news and make us shake our heads and wonder how anyone could have such bad judgment. In this chapter, I explore the assumption that risk-taking is a uniquely teenage phenomenon by challenging the argument that their brains make them all that way. Chapter 6 looks at the much-maligned teen driver and critically explores whether teen drivers pose the threat to public safety that we are encouraged to fear. In addition to looking at the brief history of the teen driver, the chapter examines street racing as a metaphor for both youth and danger.

Finally, the last chapter looks at why on some level we crave bad news about youths. They may have their entire future ahead of them, opportunities to look forward to that we didn't, and younger bodies, but if we tell ourselves they are fundamentally flawed, it somehow makes us feel better. I recently ran into one of my elementary-school teachers and jokingly asked if she had ever seen in her many years of teaching third graders as bright as we were. "Actually," she said, "they keep getting better and better, which is why I haven't retired." I have to admit that I was a little disappointed—I wanted to hear that we were special. I guess on some level we all want to leave our mark in the world, but we also know that eventually we will be replaced. There is probably another child living in my old bedroom now, someone else playing in what was once my backyard, and another student at my desk in that third-grade classroom.

Aside from the emotional aspects of leaving youth behind, fear of young people sells, and some of us even find bad news about kids entertaining. In 2005, ABC introduced an unscripted show about troubled teens disparagingly titled *Brat Camp*. Each episode began by featuring the participants' baby pictures followed by more recent photos of the sneering teens. Their seriously troubled lives were boiled down to a descriptive phrase that appeared below their names, such as "delinquent," "destructive," or "spoiled liar."

In the conclusion to this book, I look at the economic aspects of fearing kids today. From fingerprint fairs and fat camps to school police and higher auto insurance rates, our fears have very real financial outcomes. Fear also saves us money, at least up front, when it comes to not financing social programs that we think young people no longer deserve.

I have written this book in the hope of broadening some of the many narrow beliefs and stereotypes we hold about young people today. Some of these stereotypes are so deeply entrenched in the words *teen, child,* and *youth* that it is difficult to find terminology that does not carry its own unique set of baggage. Thus, I use these terms and others, such as *adolescent, pre-teen,* and *young people,* throughout this book with hesitation, knowing that they are each loaded constructs but still necessary to describe the perceptions and realities of people within these age groups.

"Youth is wasted on the young," we complain. Youth is at once a time we idealize and a group that we demonize. By unilaterally condemning the generation that follows us, we may be overlooking the contributions that young people have to offer today, not just sometime in the future when they are no longer kids. The next chapter explores how our fears of kidnapping are symbolic of the widespread belief that childhood itself has been stolen, and that the contemporary world is no longer a safe place for children.

NOTES

1. Public Agenda Foundation, "Proprietary Association Kids," telephone poll of 1,005 adults, 1999.

2. Nancy Gibbs et al., "Who's In Charge Here?" *Time,* August 6, 2001, 40.

3. Results cited in Laura Sessions Stepp, "Are We Giving Teens a Bad Rap?" *Los Angeles Times,* February 5, 2002, E2.

4. "Nine-Year-Olds Better in Reading, Math," *Los Angeles Times,* July 15, 2005, A28.

5. Associated Press, "Math Scores Reach 36-Year High," *CNN Student News,* August 27, 2003.

6. Frank R. Donovan, *Wild Kids: How Youth Has Shocked Its Elders—Then and Now!* (Harrisburg, Pa.: Stackpole Books, 1967), 11.

7. Rasmussen Research, "Portrait of America," telephone poll of 1,067 adults, May 14, 2001.

8. Kaiser Family Foundation, telephone poll of 1,514 adults, July 30, 1996.

9. Massachusetts Mutual Life Insurance Company, telephone poll of 1,000 adults, October 1995.

10. Al Martinez, "When the Audience is Scarier than the Movie," *Los Angeles Times,* November 11, 2002, E9.

11. Martinez, "When the Audience is Scarier."

12. Editorial, "Son, We Need to Talk," *Los Angeles Times,* January 13, 2002, M4.

13. Quoted in Kenneth T. Walsh, "Kinderpolitics '96," *U.S. News and World Report,* September 16, 1996, 51–57.

14. "Cheating Is Widespread among Teens," *Los Angeles Times,* April 30, 2004, A13.

15. "Youth in U.S. Back Religious Conservatism," *Los Angeles Times,* September 28, 2002, B21.

16. Barna Research Group, telephone poll of 620 teenagers thirteen to eighteen years old, February 5, 1998.

17. Athima Chansanchai, "Today's Preteens Put Their Faith in Folks They Know Best," *Los Angeles Times,* March 31, 2002, E4.

18. *Newsweek*, telephone poll of 406 parents of children under three, August 15, 2000.

19. Jamie Talan, "Lazy Teens May Have an Excuse, Scientists Say," *Los Angeles Times*, March 1, 2004, F5.

20. Dana Calvo, "Amnesty's New Cause," *Los Angeles Times*, January 6, 2002, F4.

21. Letters, *Los Angeles Times*, January 20, 2002, Calendar Magazine, 111.

22. Leslie Earnest, "For Teens, Lavish Spending on Clothes Is So Last Week," *Los Angeles Times*, October 18, 2002, C1.

23. Gallup Poll of 1,000 parents, December 8, 1995.

24. "Where in the World? Students Don't Know," *Los Angeles Times*, June 22, 2002, A12.

25. 2003 Statistical Abstract, Table 227, "Educational Attainment by Race and Hispanic Origin: 1960–2002" (includes people twenty-five and older).

26. Monitoring the Future Study, "Long-Term Trends in Lifetime Prevalence of Use of Various Drugs for Twelfth Graders" (Survey Research Center, University of Michigan, Ann Arbor, 2004).

27. Public Agenda Foundation, "Proprietary Association Kids."

28. Public Agenda Foundation, "Proprietary Association Kids."

29. David C. Berliner and Bruce J. Biddle, *The Manufactured Crisis: Myths, Fraud, and the Attack on America's Public Schools* (New York: Addison-Wesley, 1995), chap. 2.

30. Advertisement, *Los Angeles Times*, September 18, 2002, A19.

31. Federal Bureau of Investigation, *Uniform Crime Reports for the United States, 1960–2002* (Washington, D.C.: U.S. Department of Justice, 2003).

32. Quoted in Foon Rhee, "Politicians Stepping in Where Parents Once Ruled," *Times–Picayune*, August 24, 1997, A31.

33. Laura Sessions Stepp, "Baby Steps Made in Well-Being of Children, Data Show," *Washington Post*, March 25, 2004, A1.

34. Donovan, *Wild Kids*, 147.

35. CBS News/*New York Times*, telephone poll of 1,207 adults, May 4, 1999.

36. Donovan, *Wild Kids*, 148.

37. Berliner and Biddle, *The Manufactured Crisis*, 145.

38. Donovan, *Wild Kids*, 192.

39. Donovan, *Wild Kids*, 195.

40. Donovan, *Wild Kids*, 205.

41. Donovan, *Wild Kids*, 205.

42. Donovan, *Wild Kids*, 221.

43. Donovan, *Wild Kids*, 222.

44. Berliner and Biddle, *The Manufactured Crisis*, 142.

45. Anne-Marie O'Connor, "Many Boomers Keep Tight Rein on Teenagers," *Los Angeles Times*, February 19, 2002.

46. Statistics found in Michael J. Weiss, "The New Summer Break," *American Demographics* (August 2001).

47. Quoted in Richard Leiby, "The Reliable Source," *Washington Post*, May 19, 2004, C3.

48. Robert D. Manning, *Credit Card Nation: The Consequences of America's Addiction to Credit* (New York: Basic Books, 2000), 166.

1

Kidnapped!

Childhood Stolen

On February 1, 2002, a seven-year-old girl was taken from her bedroom in an affluent San Diego community. Within days, a video of spunky and cherubic Danielle Van Dam was broadcast nationwide, as were the pleas of her panicked parents. Danielle became America's child for a few weeks, drawing us in with her broad smile, shiny blonde hair, and signature rope necklace. Shots of her upscale Sabre Springs home also became ubiquitous on the news coverage. The neighborhood seemed to represent the American dream, on the surface at least. A jury later found a middle-aged neighbor in this suburban Shangri-la guilty of Danielle's abduction and murder.

Months later on June 5, a fourteen-year-old girl was taken from her upscale home in the Salt Lake City area. Elizabeth Smart was also blonde, also angelic-looking in the home-video footage that aired across the stunned country. As time passed we heard about more little girls taken, and about attempts to take other children against their will. Parents were warned that this could happen to any child at any time. From the heightened coverage it seemed as though a rash of kidnappings was taking place across the country, and that the world was no longer a safe place for children.

So why have we come to believe that the outside world has become increasingly dangerous for children? The fear was fueled in 2002 because the kidnappings of a few photogenic kids dominated the news. Timothy W. Maier wrote in *Insight on the News* that we lacked a "juicy summer sex scandal" in 2002, and kidnappings invoke a preexisting sense "of childhood lost."[1] While there was no real kidnapping epidemic, what *had* exploded in 2002 was news coverage of kidnapping. Newspaper coverage of child abductions was 60 percent higher in 2002 than in 2001 and 31 percent higher than in 2003.[2] News of high-profile abductions and attempted abductions seemed to confirm what we had already suspected, that the world had become a very dangerous place, and that even children tucked away in upscale bedrooms were in danger. In this chapter, I examine how and why news coverage of child abductions both creates and reaffirms our fears that children, and childhood itself, are in danger from the outside world.

HAS CHILDHOOD BEEN STOLEN?

The 2002 kidnapping panic was about much more than the handful of tragedies that happened that year. It represented our mistrust of one another, our feeling that paradise had been lost, and our sense that it had been stolen from children. Kidnapping challenges our perception that the experience of childhood is primarily carefree. According to historian Paula S. Fass, our obsessive fear about child abduction began in the mid- to late-nineteenth century.[3] Certainly kidnappings occurred before, but during the Victorian era the image of childhood shifted from that of an economic one, when their labor was necessary for family survival, to a sentimental and emotional one. No longer valued mostly for their labor on family farms or later in factories, children became emotionally prized, and childhood itself became viewed as a time symbolizing innocence.

Fass describes how before this, young people were traditionally taken from their families for economic reasons, to work off family debts or when a family could no longer afford to feed a child. African-American slave children were routinely sold off as the property of slaveholders. In the twentieth century our economy became less dependent on children's labor, however, and communities also became less interdependent. Goods and services were no longer traded only within small rural communities as city populations grew; thus families gradually became more independent of one another. By century's end, the outside world was largely viewed as a threat to families and the children within them.

The shift toward individualism, and away from a more collective orientation to social life, can be seen in our recent treatment of children overall. We are very afraid of what might happen to our own children, but mostly indifferent to the plight of other people's. This societal indifference is reflected in our reluctance to fund social programs for families in poverty or to provide sufficient funding for schools that serve the poorest children. We maintain the illusion of collective concern when a child, one that could be ours, goes missing, however. As Fass notes, a search for a missing child is often a way to renew and strengthen community bonds.[4] The abduction of middle-class and affluent children hits a nerve that the victimization of other children does not. We are able to project our anxieties for children in general onto these missing kids in a way that we don't when hearing about abused or poor children. We reinforce the idea of childhood innocence by selectively focusing on those children who best represent this image, as we all but ignore those who do not.

In a broader sense, we often fear that something more than individual children will be taken away, that childhood itself is gone. Books like Neil Postman's *The Disappearance of Childhood* and David Elkind's *All Grown Up and No Place to Go* decry the apparent loss of childhood as we once knew it. Children symbolize our past and our future, what we were and what we might become. The loss of that idyllic stage of childhood is something we mourn not only for our children's sake, but for our own.

Childhood is a loaded concept. Idealizing it allows us to reminisce about what our lives were like and bemoan changes that we have experienced. During the last century, we have witnessed drastic changes economically, socially, politically, and technologically, so in some ways the past bears little resemblance to the present. Perhaps more relevant, with many two-parent families working in the labor force, child care has been increasingly relegated to outsiders, whom we may not completely trust. Our concern that the world is no longer safe for children emerges when we take a look around and aren't sure how we got here, and wonder if things weren't better in the past. The fear that our children will be taken away from us is symbolic of the anxiety that childhood itself has been taken away.

The truth is, it hasn't. The experience of childhood has changed in many notable ways, and children in some instances may be less isolated from the adult world than perhaps some of us would prefer. What hasn't changed, as we saw in the introduction, is the concern that children themselves are somehow uniformly different from those who came before them. Kidnapping fears recast all kids as potential victims. Whereas most concerns about kids today consider adults as challenged by the failures of youth, our kidnapping fear is unique in that it casts all unknown adults as potential thieves of childhood innocence.

Of course, this is not to deny that even a statistical rarity can be a major tragedy to a family and community. But our fear that children are at heightened risk of being victims of the world's evil tells us as much about our disconnection from each other and our rapidly changing society as the tragedies that made news in 2002. When we are confronted with frightening accounts of incidents in neighborhoods nearby and across the country, it is only natural that we would then believe that the problem is getting worse. Journalists and news producers are subject to the same social currents as the rest of us in the United States; they sense when we are anxious, and they know that when we are scared we crave more information, which in turn boosts their ratings. News producers bank on our fear to draw us in when we could easily change the channel. Kidnapping scares don't just happen; they are created, and are more likely to be created at some times than others.

ANATOMY OF A KIDNAPPING SCARE

The 2002 kidnapping scare began early, when Danielle Van Dam was taken from her home in February. By the summer, the fear of kidnapping had spread across the country, leading many people to believe that children were being taken and killed more than ever. In the expanded news coverage about kidnapping, we heard about cases we normally wouldn't otherwise; abduction attempts, flashers near schools, and custody disputes that turned ugly became top news stories.

The way these stories were told also heightened our fears and seemed to support the idea that kidnapping was a looming threat to all children. To assess the heightened nature of kidnapping coverage during that year, I examined newspaper reports from around the country from February to the end of September 2002, when Danielle Van Dam's kidnapper was tried and convicted. News tends to be concentrated in cycles, and this case heightened awareness during the spring and summer, which then declined in the fall. Thus, my analysis focuses on the time period when child abductions were at the center of public attention. Although television images are arguably the most powerful in communicating emotion, they are ephemeral and more difficult to analyze on a national scope because of their ubiquity.

I conducted a Lexis-Nexis newspaper search on the terms *child* and *kidnap*, which yielded 608 hits during this time frame, compared with just 391 in 2001, 437 in 2000, and 323 in 1999.[5] Note that these are not reports of 608 kidnappings, but instead 608 articles discussing the subject. In fact, in all 608 stories, only five children were taken and not returned soon after.[6] During these months of heightened attention, stories of child abductions increased by 63 percent compared with the average number of similar news reports during the same time frame over the past three years.

KIDNAPPING EPIDEMIC?

While national statistics on child abductions are murky due to different reporting practices, there was no evidence that child abductions were on the rise in 2002. If anything, FBI data suggested that stranger abductions had slightly declined in the preceding years. Kidnapping is very rare when placed in a context of violent acts against children. Abduction represents less than 2 percent of all crimes against juveniles reported to the police.[7] A 2002 U.S. Department of Justice report, "National Estimates of Missing Children," concluded that 84 percent of all minors reported missing were either runaways or the subject of a report based on miscommunication or a misunderstanding between the child and guardian.[8] Department of Justice estimates suggest that each year about one hundred children are abducted by strangers and are in serious danger because the abductor detains the child overnight, transports the child at least fifty miles, holds the child for ransom, or intends to keep or kill the child.[9] According to the 2002 report, more than half of these kids are returned alive, as Elizabeth Smart eventually was, but a small proportion are never found, and about 40 percent of those abducted under these rare circumstances are killed, as was Danielle Van Dam.

In spite of the fear that these cases inspired, Department of Justice data indicate that a minor's odds of being kidnapped by a stranger and of being in serious danger is less than two in a million.[10] The chance of any American child being killed in this scenario is less than seven in ten million.[11] Children under fifteen are seven and one-half times more likely to die from flu or pneumonia, forty-three times more likely to die of cancer, and sixty-five times more likely to die in a motor vehicle accident than die in a stranger abduction.[12]

Additionally, for the last ten years crime rates have generally fallen, especially violent crime rates.[13] But despite a 42 percent decline in homicides nationally during the 1990s, the public tends to believe that crime has only gotten worse with time.[14] Children under fifteen have been and continue to be the group least likely to be victims of homicides of any type; young adults eighteen to thirty-four are the group most likely to be murdered.[15] Of all minors reported missing, teens make up the majority—74 percent of all cases and 58 percent of the most serious described earlier. But stories of young children's abductions elicit the greatest sense of anxiety.

In spite of the fact that the actual number of children kidnapped by strangers apparently declined in 2002, news reports intimated otherwise. We heard television news anchors dourly state that "there's been yet another kidnapping," and newspapers across the country also told us that things were getting worse than ever. The press did this in several ways: by providing more prominent coverage for both abductions and attempted abductions than in the past; by linking a local kidnapping or kidnapping attempt to a national, high-profile case; and most centrally, by stating that we were in the midst of a new epidemic. Of the 608 news hits mentioned above, I analyzed 88 that were about specific kidnappings or kidnapping attempts and found that fully 40 percent of those stories implied that child abductions were rising at an alarming rate. For example:

> After a summer rocked by a string of child abductions and homicides across the country, three attempted kidnappings have been reported in Cobb County since school began. (*Atlanta Journal–Constitution*)[16]
>
> The attempted child abduction is the latest in a spate across the Bay State. (*Boston Herald*)[17]

A *Boston Globe* headline warned that "Crimes against Children [Are] Common," leading readers to believe that we had indeed entered into a scary, new phase.[18] Other stories used words or phrases like "a string" (*Daily News* [New York]), "latest victim" (*Plain Dealer* [Cleveland]), and "a rash of kidnappings" (*Denver Post*).[19] The *Washington Post* described "a recent wave" of abductions, and the *Daily News* claimed that an attempted abduction they reported on was the "latest in a series of little girls who have been kidnapped in recent weeks."[20]

Stories quoted nervous parents in city after city who seemed to concur that they couldn't let their kids out of their sight, even in their own backyards. Letter writers to the *San Diego Union–Tribune*, Danielle Van Dam's hometown paper, wrote that "this year, children have been kidnapped at an alarming rate . . . even our homes might not be as safe as they were ten years ago," and that neighborhoods, even affluent ones, were unsafe for children, unlike "when we were young."[21] "Places aren't as safe as they used to be," a woman told Minneapolis's *Star Tribune*.[22]

In addition to quotes from scared parents and alarming language, mentions of custodial cases made the headlines in greater numbers. Family members are responsible for the vast majority of child abductions, but these abductions generate very few dramatic news stories. Hearing that a noncustodial parent ran away with a child is certainly not as scary for the general public as when a stranger takes a child. Still, stranger kidnapping attempts and abduction stories during the period I surveyed greatly outnumbered the more common form of noncustodial kidnapping by a margin of about six to one, making it appear that strangers are a bigger threat to a child than the adults the child knows. The *Tampa Tribune* wrote of "lowlifes stealing our children," thus framing the problem as one caused by outsiders entering and violating the sacred space of the family.[23] The fear of kidnapping seemed worse than ever, and the danger seemed to compel parents to restrict children from playing outside their own homes.

In short, it felt like kidnappings were on the rise in 2002 because news reports throughout the country told us that they were. Of course they also told us the truth from time to time, that stranger abductions are rare and are responsible for a tiny proportion of all missing children cases. But we were understandably drawn to the alarming and heart-wrenching stories that told us what we had long suspected, that the world is not safe for children anymore.

THE DANGER OF STRANGER DANGER

With all the attention on *stranger danger*, we run the risk of overlooking the more mundane but even more serious risks children face within their own families. Amid our collective sense of shock and outrage at predators that have taken kids from their families, the much larger problem of family and acquaintance danger gets pushed into the background.

Statistically speaking, the biggest threat children will ever face comes from inside their own homes. U.S. Department of Justice records indicate that when children are kidnapped, it is a parent or other family member that usually takes them.[24] Even when children are murdered, the culprit is still most likely one of the parents. Children are far more likely to be physically or sexually abused by family or family friends than a stranger. According to the U.S. Department of Health and Human Services, of all reported child-abuse cases in 2002, 87 percent of the perpetrators were the parents or other relatives of the child.[25] Family members or acquaintances were also responsible for about three-quarters of all reported cases of sexual abuse.

The younger the child, the more likely he or she is to be killed by his or her parents than by strangers. In 2002, 1,400 minors died as the result of abuse or neglect, and in 80 percent of the cases, the perpetrator was one or both of the parents.[26] Children under four years old accounted for 76 percent of the victims, and 88 percent were under eight. Based on these reports, one might expect about forty kids to die at the hands of strangers in the United States each year (out of over 70 million minors under eighteen), and over 1,100 kids—twenty-seven times as many—to die at the hands of a parent.

But when strangers do hurt children, we are far more likely to hear about it. On some level, we still see children as the property of their parents, so the rare yet highly publicized stranger abduction is perceived as a crime against both the child and the rights and responsibilities of the parent. According to the Department of Justice, of children abducted, nearly half (49 percent) were taken by a family member and nearly a third (27 percent) were taken by an acquaintance.[27] Less than a quarter (24 percent) were taken by strangers.

Children aren't always as safe at home as they ought to be. Nor is media attention typically focused on the consistent danger that many children face at home. Nearly a third of news accounts that I analyzed focused on stranger danger, including specific instructions and safety tips on how to avoid strangers. Kids do need to learn to protect themselves; there is no doubt about that. But focusing attention *only* on strangers as children's central threat presents a skewed version of reality and does nothing to help young people who are victimized by adults they already know.

"Make sure the kids know to stay away from strangers . . . " a *Boston Herald* article began.[28] "Strangers abduct 5,000 children every year in the United States," noted the *Houston Chronicle*, without reference to the fact that the vast majority of these kids are returned unharmed within twenty-four hours, and that nonstrangers are most likely to be the abductors.[29] A mother told the *San Diego Union–Tribune* that her daughter "doesn't have to be polite to strangers," while a *San Francisco Chronicle* article offered the age-old advice, "Don't talk to strangers."[30] The *Atlanta Journal–Constitution* warned parents to "teach your child about strangers," and a *Denver Post* story suggested that children should yell "fire if a stranger tries to talk to you."[31]

Yell fire? Do we really want a society where we grow up universally distrusting each other and are encouraged to be afraid of people we don't know? Not only will this make us more disconnected (and even more likely to be fearful of one another), it may not keep kids safe from the strangers who really are a threat. Gavin de Becker, security expert and author of *The Gift of Fear*, cautions that remaining in a constant state of fear blocks out real messages of danger that our intuition sends us. If every stranger contact is scary, then we never know when we are truly in danger. In fact, strangers often intervene when an actual threat arises, and children need to learn to sense when someone can come to their aid if they are lost or in trouble. "Don't talk to strangers" is a cliché that often does more harm than good.

Aside from the fact that strangers only represent a small threat to children's safety overall, it's not realistic to expect that children won't interact with strangers. As adults, we do so on a daily basis and model these interactions for children. But news accounts continually tell us that strangers are dangerous, and so we close ranks and shut each other out, often to our own peril. By discouraging kids from trusting, we close down a possible safety net for kids victimized by those closest to them.

We are encouraged to teach kids how to fight off a stranger's attack, but not how to cope when the danger comes from inside the family. The fear of child abduction impacts children in other ways too: parents are afraid to let kids out of their sight and are hesitant to allow them to play in their neighborhoods. Ironically, the fear of outsiders may keep some kids in their places of abuse and away from potential sources of aid.

Fear of the outside world encourages us to retreat from our neighbors and communities, to stay home and watch more scary news on television. In a classic study, communications scholar George Gerbner found that the most fearful individuals also watched more television, perhaps creating a vicious cycle of fear. Gerbner called this phenomena the "mean world syndrome," which we could rephrase to the "mean world for children syndrome," one that encourages us to believe that the only really safe place for children is in their own homes, under their parents' watchful eyes.

The problem with the mean world for children syndrome is that it encourages us to ignore the most common threats to children in favor of the most dramatic but least common ones. By focusing on stranger danger, parents are encouraged to control children's environments even more, and to trust outsiders less. In worst-case scenarios, children are therefore placed in greater danger, and are further isolated from other adults that could help in situations of abuse. Whereas in households free of family violence, the danger consists of leaving young people ill-prepared to safely negotiate their interactions with strangers.

Rather than being discouraged from making community contact, kids need to be encouraged to know a variety of adults that they can trust in their lives and that they can turn to if necessary. Children and parents should not bear the entire burden of safety. We also have a long way to go to identify and treat people who victimize children, and that doesn't just mean the creepy pedophile lurking in the dark. This cliché, by narrowly portraying child victimizers, lets the abusive parent or family friend off the hook. By perpetuating the fallacy that sexual abusers are mostly strangers, we miss the most common abusers before our eyes: the outwardly wonderful parent, the upstanding citizen, or even the clergy member. Our discourse of kidnapping tells too narrow a tale about the potential dangers that children face. Those who suffer from more common forms of abuse don't see themselves in these narratives, and thus may be unable to even identify that they are being abused.

The truth is, parents can never fully protect or control their children. By insisting that they can and should, we deprive kids of an important opportunity for learning to navigate the outside world and learning to make appropriate decisions. We also create a burden of shame and guilt for parents whose children have been victimized by strangers. Most perilously, increased parental control in some instances means increasing the power of abusers.

REALITY CHECK?

While two in five news stories in 2002 implied that child kidnappings were a growing trend, about a quarter of the stories I analyzed reminded readers that the threat of stranger kidnappings is quite rare. Interestingly, reality checks often followed sentences that implied an epidemic by using descriptors such as *spate, trend,* or *spurt.* Reality checks promoted the appearance of balance, while still maintaining the drama of fear. But fear often prevails; dry statistics, regardless of how impressive an expert's credentials, tend to make less of an impact than the emotional accounts of parents or community members. These parents appear to feel as many of us do, so we connect with their words much more than with the experts'.

In spite of providing the voice of reason, these caveats tended to be canceled out by the overwhelming influence of dramatic quotes or anecdotes elsewhere in the story. So even though we were occasionally told that there really was no new kidnapping epidemic, we were encouraged to *feel* as though one existed. Emotion is often more powerful than logic when we are dealing with our fears about children's safety.

The *Seattle Times* provides a good example of juxtaposing emotion with reality. A September 10 article noted that parents' fear was "out of proportion to reality," yet for every dose of reality, the story presented the fears of parents, which were much more vivid when compared to the more staid voices of experts.[32] The article contrasted information about the statistical rarity of kidnapping and the greater likelihood of car accidents and drowning. But quotes like "They can tell me as many times as they want that it's not going to happen," from the scared mother of a five-year-old, resonate with a frightened public not interested in probability but instead in protecting their kids at any cost.[33]

A *Tampa Tribune* story acknowledged that stranger abductions are uncommon, but then devoted a large portion of its discussion to suggesting how children avoid strangers, with no information given about how children might cope with threats from adults whom they know.[34] The *Boston Herald* noted that stranger kidnappings represent less than 1 percent of all abductions, but immediately backtracked, stating that "however rare . . . the scenario . . . is a danger that parents should take seriously."[35] The story went on to offer safety tips focused exclusively on guarding against strangers, with no mention of how the other 99 percent of kids might safeguard themselves against threats from people they know. An *Atlanta Journal–Constitution* story titled "Reported Kidnap Tries Leave Parents Fearful" paused after seven paragraphs to remind readers that the number of reported missing children was on the decline, but immediately returned in the next paragraph to discuss "the latest Cobb [County] incidents."[36] The story then encouraged parents "to be on heightened alert" and offered safety tips for kids about how to avoid strangers.

An *Omaha World–Herald* editorial used a "yes-but" approach to the reality issue by stating that stranger abductions are rare, "but Samantha [Runnion]'s story was just days old when a Philadelphia girl was snatched . . . [and] a little girl was grabbed and killed in Missouri. Then, the double California abduction."[37] The list of headline grabbers offset the reality check by invoking an emotional response simply by mentioning the name or locale of a tragedy. A *Washington Post* story used a similar tactic, contrasting a reality check with tearful quotes. A mother interviewed for the article described trying to calm her frightened daughter, who feared being taken from her bedroom as Danielle Van Dam and Elizabeth Smart had been.[38] Neither the mother nor the article offered answers to allay these fears. In a sense we feel we have no answers in the face of extreme fear. Even statistical realities provide little comfort when we hear over and over of the shocking stories of brutalized children.

THE FORGOTTEN CHILDREN

Our media-fed obsession with stranger danger may frighten us so much that we ignore the more common perils that children face in the United States. Compared to other industrialized nations, the United States isn't taking such great care of its children. In our country, an estimated 16 percent of children live in poverty, 896,000 are victims of abuse or neglect, and approximately 14 percent have no healthcare coverage.[39]

While high-profile child abductions can yield massive round-the-clock coverage and public concern, across the country more than 500,000 children's lives are seriously disrupted each year when they are placed in foster care.[40] More than 91,000, or almost 1 in 5, stay in the system for five years or more. These kids are likely to grow up in a series of homes, some caring, and some not so caring. In fact, according to the most recent data, 528 kids died while in foster care in 2001.[41] Sometimes their stories make headlines, but rarely does the wave of fear rival that of stranger abduction cases.

Why is it that we are so attached to the lives of a few but pay little attention to the thousands of young people whose lives are far from an idealized, carefree state of childhood? For one, we tend to focus on and fear the rare event more than the common event. The thousands who grow up without families are so numerous that they are rarely deemed newsworthy unless brutally killed. Awareness of this problem calls for complex institutional solutions, rather than prosecution and punishment of individual offenders. According to a 2004 U.S. Department of Health and Human Services report, all fifty states' child-welfare programs were found to be seriously deficient.[42] Sixteen states, including California, which bears the country's largest caseload, met none of the federal government's basic standards for safety and well-being.

In fact, states have occasionally lost kids in their custody. According to the *Washington Times*, at one point Iowa lost track of about five hundred kids.[43] Florida also received a great deal of criticism for at one time losing track of 393 of its wards.[44] If these young people can fall off the radar of the agencies that are supposed to protect them, it's not surprising that the rest of us don't know about them either.

Perhaps the biggest reason that these kids don't get much attention is the fact that they're not "poster" children—they don't represent the fantasy of childhood innocence as well as girls like Danielle Van Dam and Elizabeth Smart. Many likely live in poverty. Most of these kids, 73 percent, are not white. The blonde, affluent child certainly does not describe the majority of American children, but she represents the height of our fantasy of childhood innocence. The abduction and injury of children like this tend to strike a nerve in a way that the thousands of children in the foster-care system, or other kidnapping victims, do not. For instance, within two months of Danielle Van Dam's kidnapping, a two-year-old African-American boy named Jahi Turner disappeared from a San Diego park. In the first thirty days after Danielle disappeared, her name was mentioned in 183 news stories, while Jahi Turner's disappearance yielded 55 mentions in the first thirty days, less than a third of the attention Danielle's abduction received.[45] As of this writing, Jahi has not been found.

A similar disparity was evident in Cleveland during the fall of 2003. An eleven-year-old African-American girl, Shakira Johnson, disappeared after leaving a block party. No Amber Alert (immediate notification of the public) was issued. Two weeks later, a fourteen-year-old white teen, Amanda Mullikin-White, disappeared from suburban Cleveland Heights, and an Amber Alert was quickly issued. A few hours later, she was seen walking down a street in the community—Amanda had apparently stayed out too late and was afraid of coming home and getting in trouble.[46] Shakira's body was found about a month after she disappeared.

The Cleveland Police Department was soon criticized for not issuing an Amber Alert for Shakira. The department responded that an Amber Alert would have been inappropriate, since there was no concrete evidence that Shakira was abducted, nor was there a suspect or vehicle description.[47] A review board later concluded that neither case qualified for Amber Alert designation because there was no evidence of abduction in either case, but the two cases sparked controversy and concern that children of color are dealt with differently when they disappear.

BEHIND THE 2002 KIDNAPPING PANIC

Kidnapping serves as a powerful metaphor for our time, as we frequently mourn the loss of what appears to be a simpler, safer past. Children, particularly white, fair-haired girls, are held up as symbols of purity, and their violation triggers major concerns about public safety. But if stranger kidnappings are exceedingly rare, are no match for the threat posed by parents, and were on the decline in 2002, where did the panic come from?

Danielle Van Dam's kidnapping took place when we were still reeling from the September 11 attacks less than five months earlier. For many of us, we had never before felt so vulnerable at home, where we had once felt relatively safe from attack. Just as two oceans no longer protected us from foreign attack, the affluent suburbs appeared to provide little protection for these girls. The crimes committed against them seemed to be crimes against innocence: the innocence of sleeping children, and the innocence that should protect us all from the world's evil. As blonde, affluent girls, they became unwitting symbols of innocence violated, much as we felt that America's innocence had been violated on September 11. Just as Wall Street brokers are supposed to return safely to their families in the suburbs after a day at the office, children in these suburbs should be safe at home. Both of these beliefs were tested.

It is not just the act of kidnapping that instills fear, it is what kidnapping represents: our inability to shield children from the dangers of the outside world. Kidnapped children force us to question our beliefs about childhood—if childhood really isn't always a time of carefree innocence, then what is it? More importantly, stranger abductions represent a breakdown in the assumption that parents have an absolute ability to protect their children or to exert complete control over their lives.

But rather than realistically recognize these beliefs as faulty, we try to cling to them even tighter. Books are sold, fingerprint fairs are held, and pundits talk of implanting microchips in kids to track them should they disappear. Safety and awareness are good things, but they can provide the illusion that if we just try harder we can cordon kids off from the world. Public attention should also focus on identifying and preventing people from preying on children. Abductions and homicides of children by strangers allow us to overlook a high prevalence of family violence and to provide a rationale for even greater parental control and monitoring in a world that feels out of control and unsafe for our children.

We have to realize that no matter how hard we try, we can't and shouldn't wall children off from the outside world. Trying to preserve our children's sense of innocence (or ignorance) about the realities of the world may feel comforting to us, but it does nothing to prepare young people to make successful choices and decisions, particularly pertaining to their safety. The innocence that we like to believe used to exist in the world is revisionist history: children have always faced both natural and human danger, and they have always needed to learn how to cope with both. Attempts to shield children from information will not protect them in the end.

Just as pre–September 11 America wasn't quite innocent when it came to experiencing the trauma of violence—millions of Americans in central cities have dealt with our own brand of urban terror for decades—children have never been quite as safe in their homes as we often believe. That is, if children have homes at all. In our despair over the lives of a few, we tend to ignore the despair of many children who are never afforded anything that comes close to our fantasy of innocence.

But while we often fear that childhood has been taken away by the dangers of the contemporary world, we also blame kids themselves for overindulging in the excesses of American society. The next chapter examines our belief that young people today are lazy, greedy gluttons.

NOTES

1. Timothy W. Maier, "Data Missing on Missing Children," *Insight on the News,* September 23, 2002.

2. Based on a Lexis-Nexis search of articles with *child* and *kidnap* in the headline or lead paragraph. The average number of stories was 95 in 2001, 116 in 2003, and 152 in 2002.

3. Paula S. Fass, *Kidnapped: Child Abduction in America* (New York: Oxford University Press, 1997), 6.

4. Fass, *Kidnapped*, 250.

5. A Lexis-Nexis search was conducted in February 2003 for the period February 1–September 30 for all years noted.

6. These were the hits for the search string "child AND kidnap." A search for "child AND abduct" yielded a smaller number, several of which also appeared in the 608.

7. David Finkelhor and Richard Ormrod, "Kidnaping of Juveniles: Patterns from NIBRS," *Juvenile Justice Bulletin*, Office of Juvenile Justice and Delinquency Prevention, June 2000.

8. Andrea J. Sedlak, David Finkelhor, Heather Hammer, and Dana J. Schultz, "National Estimates of Missing Children: An Overview," *National Incidence Studies of Missing, Abducted, Runaway, and Throwaway Children*, Office of Juvenile Justice and Delinquency Prevention, October 2002, 9.

9. David Finkelhor, Heather Hammer, and Andrea J. Sedlak, "Nonfamily Abducted Children: National Estimates and Characteristics," *National Incidence Studies of Missing, Abducted, Runaway, and Throwaway Children*, Office of Juvenile Justice and Delinquency Prevention, October 2002, 2.

10. Finkelhor, Hammer, and Sedlak, "Nonfamily Abducted Children." Calculations based on data from table 7. Total U.S. child population from table 2.

11. Based on an estimated 46 deaths within a population of 70,172,700.

12. Data from Centers for Disease Control and Prevention, National Center for Health Statistics, National Vital Statistics Program, "Child Mortality: Death Rates for Children Ages 5 to 14 by Gender, Race, Hispanic Origin, and Cause of Death, Selected Years 1980–2000," and "Adolescent Mortality: Death Rates Among Adolescents Ages 15 to 19 by Race, Hispanic Origin, and Cause of Death, Selected Years 1980–2000," http://childstats.gov (last accessed January 5, 2006). Note that data on adolescents does not include death by flu or pneumonia.

13. Federal Bureau of Investigation, *Uniform Crime Reports for the United States, 1983–2002* (Washington, D.C.: U.S. Department of Justice, 2003).

14. Richard Rosenfeld, "Crime Decline in Context," *Contexts* 1 (2002): 25–34.

15. Federal Bureau of Investigation, *Uniform Crime Reports for the United States*.

16. Don Plummer, "Reported Kidnap Tries Leave Parents Fearful," *Atlanta Journal–Constitution*, September 26, 2002, 1JF.

17. Franci Richardson, "Defiant Auburn Girl, 4, Foils Abduction Attempt," *Boston Herald*, September 26, 2002, 10.

18. Brenda J. Buote, "Crimes against Children Common," *Boston Globe*, September 22, 2002, 7.

19. Tracy Connor, "Two Safe at Home," *Daily News* (New York), August 15, 2002, 6; Eddy Ramirez, "A Close Call Close to Home," *Plain Dealer*, August 9, 2002, B1; Kieran Nicholson, "Denver Girl Foils Kidnap Attempt," *Denver Post*, August 8, 2002, A1.

20. "Washington in Brief," *Washington Post*, September 11, 2002, A5; Leo Standora, "Drifter Held in Kidnap-Slay," *Daily News* (New York), July 27, 2002, 3.

21. "Difficult Days for Those Who Love Children," *San Diego Union–Tribune*, July 24, 2002, B9.

22. Terry Collins, "Witness Helps Police Nab Abduction Suspect," *Star Tribune* (Minneapolis), March 30, 2002, 6B.

23. Keith Morelli, "Child Abductors Just a Threat Here—So Far," *Tampa Tribune*, July 24, 2002, 2.

24. Sedlak et al., "National Estimates of Missing Children," table 3.

25. U.S. Department of Health and Human Services, *Child Maltreatment 2002* (Washington, D.C.: GPO, 2003).

26. U.S. Department of Health and Human Services, *Child Maltreatment 2002*.

27. Finkelhor and Ormrod, "Kidnaping of Juveniles."

28. Ed Hayward, "Southboro 4th-Grader Eludes Abductor," *Boston Herald*, September 21, 2002, 4.

29. "Stafford Event to Include Bike Rodeo, Child-Safety Tips," *Houston Chronicle*, August 1, 2002, 9.

30. Deborah Ensor, "Body That of Missing Orange County Girl," *San Diego Union–Tribune*, July 18, 2002, A1; Valerie Alvord and Chuck Squatriglia, "Dragnet for Kid Killer," *San Francisco Chronicle*, July 18, 2002, A1.

31. Plummer, "Reported Kidnap Tries Leave Parents Fearful." Nicholson, "Denver Girl Foils Kidnap Attempt."

32. Stephanie Dunnewind, "Parent Panic," *Seattle Times*, September 10, 2002, E1.

33. Dunnewind, "Parent Panic."

34. Morelli, "Child Abductors Just a Threat Here."

35. Azell Murphy Cavaan, "Prevent Every Parent's Nightmare," *Boston Herald*, June 30, 2002, 63.

36. Plummer, "Reported Kidnap Tries Leave Parents Fearful."

37. Editorial, "All-Out Effort on Child Snatchers," *Omaha World–Herald*, August 3, 2002, 10b.

38. Patricia Davis, "Guarding Their Precious Ones," *Washington Post*, July 14, 2002, C1.

39. Children's Defense Fund, "2002 Facts on Child Poverty in America," Washington, D.C., November 2003; Children's Defense Fund, "Children's Health Coverage in 2001," Washington, D.C., February 2003; U.S. Department of Health and Human Services, *Child Maltreatment 2002*.

40. U.S. Department of Health and Human Services, Adoption and Foster Care Analysis and Reporting System, *The AFCARS Report* (Washington, D.C.: GPO, March 2003).

41. Includes medical reasons, accidents, and homicide.

42. Robert Pear, "U.S. Finds Fault in All 50 States' Child Welfare Programs," *New York Times*, April 26, 2004.

43. Cheryl Wetzstein, "Lost in Foster Care?" *Washington Times*, April 29, 2001, A1.

44. Associated Press, "Florida Finds One of Its Missing Kids," *Los Angeles Times*, February 9, 2003, A26.

45. Based on a full-text Lexis-Nexis search on May 5, 2004, of each child's name the month following the date they disappeared.

46. Lila J. Mills and Sarah Hollander, "Missing Girl's Mom Gets Polygraph Test," *Plain Dealer*, September 29, 2003, B1.

47. Donna Iacoboni and Thomas J. Quinn, "Police Search for Girl Missing Since Saturday," *Plain Dealer*, September 16, 2003, B5.

2

Greedy Gluttons

Childhood Indulged

I went on my first diet when I was nine. I had "ballooned" to over seventy pounds and didn't like how chubby my cheeks looked in my fourth-grade class picture. My parents supported my efforts to cut back on sweets and to learn how many calories different foods contained. I also tried to get more exercise, a challenge at times during wintry weather. My favorite activities included reading, playing board games, and watching television; not exactly big calorie burners. But I was allowed to jump rope in the basement, and my dad taught me how to do push-ups, and over the course of a few months I lost about ten pounds. I still remember how good it felt to have relatives compliment me on how nice I looked.

No, this is not my anorexia story. In fact, a year later I was a chubby ten-year-old, having given up the discipline of exercise and abstinence from cookies once I reached my target weight. For the first time in my life, I was picked on in school by a group of boys who called me "porky," and I endured their insults until they moved on to torment someone else.

This humiliation made me very self-conscious as a teen, and I was pretty obsessed with calories and my weight. But I never got too heavy or too thin, never did anything more extreme than try the diets of the month in fashion magazines, which rarely did anything but temporarily make me too weak to get out of bed. In spite of some bouts with being overweight as a kid, I have grown up to maintain a healthy weight so far throughout adulthood. This isn't always the case for kids with weight problems, however. Fully 70 percent of kids who are overweight go on to be overweight adults, and that number rises to 80 percent when they have at least one overweight parent.[1]

Obesity is at once a simple and a complex problem. Consuming more calories than one expends is a simple enough concept. But why we do so is the big question. Self-esteem problems? Fast food? Genes? Trans fat? Carbs? There is no doubt that Americans of all ages have been gaining weight over the last thirty years, children included, which has created a public-health concern.

THE SOCIOLOGY OF FAT

The U.S. Surgeon General suggests that obesity is both an individual and a public-health problem, creating an estimated 117 billion dollars in healthcare costs.[2] While many would agree that gaining weight brings a whole host of health problems, critics like Paul Campos, author of *The Obesity Myth: Why America's Obsession with Weight Is Hazardous to Your Health*, argue that the relationship between poor health and obesity isn't so clear-cut. Campos contends that we conflate weight with health, and that even though people are classified as overweight, they may not be unhealthy or at risk for illness or premature death. Even our definition of obesity fluctuates; it now includes adults with a body mass index of over 30, and children whose weight puts them in the 95th percentile. The body mass index is itself controversial because it compares weight to height and does not take into account muscle mass, using a one-size-fits-all approach to defining healthy weight.

Although the definition of obesity may be debatable, weight is something we constantly hear about. By the current medical definition, kids—and adults—are heavier than ever. Rates of overweight children, teens, and adults remained essentially stable until the 1980s. What happened to make us start to gain weight two decades ago?

For one, we are paying for the unprecedented level of automation in our society. Physical labor has largely been mechanized, and now we can buy appliances and build machines to do much of the hard work in households and in commerce that our predecessors may have done by hand. Our information-based economy, predicated on ideas rather than manufacturing, requires that many of our bodies remain stationary in front of computer terminals for much of the workday.

Obesity may be the result of individual behavior, but social forces also influence our weight. For instance, fear contributes to childhood obesity. As I discussed in the last chapter, we are often so afraid of letting children out of our sight that we are unwilling to let them roam their neighborhoods or walk to school. Many working parents' time and money constraints lead them to buy fast food on a regular basis. And given our current obsession with high-stakes testing, physical education and recess, which can't be measured by standardized tests, are sometimes reduced or eliminated to accommodate budget cuts or overcrowding.

Childhood obesity is about more than diet and exercise. Kids' weight has gone up due to a collection of changes. Meals are eaten quickly, and food choices are now often based more on convenience rather than nutrition. School policies also allow unhealthy foods to flood school cafeterias; what students eat for lunch doesn't appear on a standardized test either, so in the current educational climate, school food may not be a big priority. Detecting the causes of obesity is the domain of medical and public-health officials, but sociological changes have contributed to and continue to set the stage for our collective weight problem.

Additionally, the way we think and talk about weight is a social process. In this chapter, I explore how and why our national weight gain has been framed as a problem of childhood. In contrast to our fears about kidnapping, where the danger lurks outside, our concerns about child obesity cast children as self-destructive dangers to themselves. To assess how the press covers this issue, and thus shapes the way many of us think about children and obesity, I collected a year's worth of stories from major American newspapers that focused on children's weight problems to see how the stories explained child obesity. I found 102 stories published in 2003 (others were excluded if child obesity was just mentioned briefly and wasn't the major focus of the story).[3]

Nearly every story I examined touched on at least one of four themes as a central explanation of why children are heavier than ever. First, the majority of the articles about children and obesity typically focused on schools that sell candy, fast food, and other fattening food in their cafeterias. Additionally, news coverage frequently addressed the lack of physical education in many of our nation's schools. Second, young people's use of popular culture was widely blamed as a cause of the rise in obesity. Television, video games, and time spent on computers instead of playing outside were frequently mentioned as central explanations. Third, parents were condemned for allowing kids to indulge in sedentary activities and for an overreliance on fast and processed foods for family meals. Finally, many stories characterized young people as gluttonous and lazy, thus framing obesity as a problem unique to today's youth. Details about a rising trend of child and teen weight gains seldom mentioned a parallel adult rise in obesity. Certainly there is no shortage of coverage on adult weight problems, and most diet books, fitness programs, and weight-loss products are marketed to adults. Yet by focusing so much collective attention on making children's behavior a unique problem and separate from adults' behavior, we often end up blaming children for behavior that is widespread and now part of the social reality of American life today. Childhood obesity exists in a social context and cannot be isolated from American obesity.

KIDS ONLY?

According to the National Health and Nutrition Examination Survey (NHANES), a nationally representative long-term study of child, adolescent, and adult weight in the United States, three times more twelve- to nineteen-year-olds and twice as many two- to five-year-olds are overweight now compared with the late 1970s,[4] while six- to eleven-year-olds are nearly twice as likely to be overweight as well. In 1980, 6.5 percent of six- to eleven-year-olds were overweight compared with 15.3 percent in 2000. Additionally, 11 percent of teens are now classified as obese.[5]

Of the 102 newspaper articles I examined, 53 percent provided statistics on the growing trend of children and teens becoming more overweight, without including any statistics on adults' even greater weight gains. Readers were thus geared to focus only on children and teens, without considering the very important fact that we're *all* more likely to be overweight than before.

Of the articles that presented NHANES statistics, fully 31 percent of the stories reported them incorrectly. Some, including the *New York Times* and *Washington Post*, confused obesity with being overweight, supplying statistics on overweight kids but calling them obese.[6] Twenty-two percent of these articles added the term *obese* while reporting on statistics of kids classified as overweight. Another exaggeration tactic involved combining statistics for overweight and obese children, thereby inviting the reader to focus on a more serious and dramatic problem. True, someone who is obese is also overweight, but only a small proportion of those who are overweight are obese.

Perhaps the most curious of statistics were those mentioned in three *USA Today* stories and a *Baltimore Sun* editorial, which note that "twenty to thirty percent of children are overweight *or at risk for becoming* overweight" (emphasis mine).[7] What exactly does it mean to be at risk for becoming overweight? Living too close to a Krispy Kreme franchise? In fact, it means being close to the designation of *overweight*; but by combining this undefined group with those classified as overweight, the reports create an inflated sense of alarm, one that Paul Campos, author of *The Obesity Myth*, argues is unrelated to an individual's actual health. Since the threshold for being overweight ignores individual differences in bone structure and muscle mass, the "at risk" category is even more specious.

Several of these stories simply inflated the already troubling trend by stating that rates of overweight preadolescents tripled when they doubled,[8] and that the rate of overweight teens quadrupled rather than tripled.[9] A *St. Petersburg Times* story misleadingly added the adjective *severely* when describing the 15 percent of six- to nineteen-year-olds who are overweight.[10] Stories in the *Boston Globe* and the *Pittsburgh Post–Gazette* respectively claimed that "more than a quarter of all children are overweight" and that "one in five American children are overweight," when it's actually 1 in 7 six- to nineteen-year-olds who are overweight.[11] A letter to the *Denver Post* mistakenly stated that "two out of three children are overweight," when in fact it is two out of three *adults* who are considered overweight, not kids.[12]

More than half of the articles (54 percent) that focused on youth trends alone offered only vague references to the actual age of the kids the statistics referenced. Speaking about "obese children" (*New York Times, San Diego Union–Tribune, St. Petersburg Times, Boston Globe*) or "overweight children" (*Boston Globe, St. Louis Post–Dispatch, Chicago Sun–Times*) gives the reader little information about whether we are talking about all minors or just young children under twelve.[13] Additionally, using vague terms furthers the perception that the problem is uniform among young people, and unique to kids. Typically, reported statistics focused on children six to eleven and adolescents twelve to nineteen. Other stories referred to "American children" or "American kids" (*St. Louis Post–Dispatch, Times–Picayune* [New Orleans], *Milwaukee Journal Sentinel, USA Today, Pittsburgh Post–Gazette, Baltimore Sun*) or simply to "all children," "children," "kids," or "young people."[14] Thus, obesity becomes identified as a childhood problem, rather than simply an American problem.

Eleven of the articles mentioned that the link between adult and child obesity is that "fat children become fat adults," or words to a similar effect.[15] While no one would dispute that a heavy child is more likely than a thin child to grow into a heavy adult, these eleven articles avoided discussing the role that overweight parents play in creating overweight kids. Instead, the adult obesity problem was blamed on obese kids who grow up to be obese adults, subtracting adult responsibility from the child obesity equation. Thus, children are portrayed as the creators of the adult obesity problem instead of vice versa. Certainly parents are very important in understanding why children may be overweight.

ALL MOM AND DAD'S FAULT?

I grew up during a time when awareness of anorexia and bulimia was on the rise. Some people felt uncomfortable with my parents' decision to allow me to go on a diet, fearing that it could set me on the path to a lifetime of eating disorders. But I think my parents also knew I would be on the path to a lifetime of obesity if I didn't make a change. Parents walk a fine line between promoting a healthy body image and healthy bodies.

Parents have also been criticized for not setting limits or teaching kids about healthy eating habits. Of course, parents may have trouble teaching about healthy eating because according to the NHANES studies, adults are gaining weight even faster than kids are. About 15 percent of adults were considered obese in 1980 compared with 30.9 percent in 2000, and 64.5 percent of all Americans age twenty or older were classified as overweight in 2000.[16] Of men over sixty, obesity rates have more than quadrupled since 1960. In 2000, 74.1 percent of men over sixty were classified as overweight, and nearly 68 percent of women in that age range were overweight as well.[17] For young women twenty to thirty-four, obesity rates have tripled since 1960, and men in the same age group are now more than twice as likely to be classified as obese as their 1960s counterparts—so much for the "fitness revolution." So it's too simple to blame school food, gym class, video games, and other youthful habits alone since adults are also heavier than ever, and far heavier, proportionally, than kids are today.

Forty-two percent of the newspaper articles published in 2003 that I analyzed referenced the role that parents play in children's weight problems. Although there certainly may be a genetic component inherited from parents, these stories mainly focused on environmental factors, presumably created by parents.

About half (47 percent) of these stories either noted parental responsibility or flat-out blamed the parents for their children's weight problems. One mother interviewed for a *Daily News* (New York) story claimed that "it's mostly the parent's fault."[18] A letter to *USA Today* agreed: "If you are going to blame somebody, start with the parents."[19] Several stories reminded parents to be good role models and to better control what their family eats. Twenty-one percent of the articles offered specific suggestions to parents about food and exercise for their children.

Almost a third (28 percent) of the stories took a very critical approach to parents, charging that they are in denial about their children's weight problems, or worse yet, enabling them. A *USA Today* article criticized parents for "giving in to convenience foods" and "feeding them French fries cooked in lard," as well as for using food to reward good behavior.[20] A *Boston Globe* story charged that "parental apathy" is responsible for kids' weight gain, and other stories, such as one in the *Atlanta Journal–Constitution*, complained that "parents have long let their kids overindulge."[21] Others bemoaned parents who "do not want to say 'no,'" and who "provide a steady diet of fast food and junk food."[22]

Just eight of the articles noted that many of these parents likely have overweight kids because the parents themselves are overweight. This is more than a footnote in the story of why some young people are heavy. Not only is the family environment important, but parents face the very same obstacles as kids do to making behavioral changes in their lives. Rarely was this reality, or the need for many parents to work long hours, discussed in context with why parents buy convenience foods, which are sometimes the only foods affordable for low-income families. Pediatrics professor Keith Ayoob told *USA Today* that he "never see[s] kids who have better diets than their parents."[23]

Overweight parents might not be clueless or apathetic but rather mired in their own struggles with food, which they subsequently pass on to their kids. If that were easy to change, the weight-loss industry would be out of business.

POPULAR CULTURE CREATED PIG-OUTS?

Parents are sometimes blamed for allowing their children to watch too much television, play too many video games, or spend too much time on the Internet. Forty-one percent of the articles in my analysis focused on popular culture as a major cause of child obesity—as though it is only children who indulge in these pastimes. Of these news stories, 38 percent suggested that parents do more to limit the time that their kids spend watching television and enjoying other forms of electronic media. Of course, balancing one's daily activities is an important skill for parents to teach children, and it is true that time spent sitting will not burn as many calories as more active recreation does.

But some of the suggestions listed repeatedly were unrealistic. First, several articles suggested that parents put a two-hour limit on television viewing. That may be practical for very young children, but the viewing behavior of older kids and teens is much harder to regulate. It's also important to realistically consider *adult* viewing habits here too. If a parent watches three or four hours of television in an evening, it is very difficult for them to instill different behavior in their kids. Further, television, video games, and other forms of entertainment media in the context of an active lifestyle will likely have a minimal impact on an individual's overall weight. So it's not the presence of popular culture in kids' lives as much as the *absence* of other activities that is likely lead to overweight and obese young people (and adults).

Yet many news stories asserted that popular culture is the primary cause of sedentary behavior. Nineteen percent of the articles I examined viewed popular culture not as an attractive alternative to being physically active, but as the core reason for obesity. A *Washington Post* story called television "Public Enemy Number One" and the "primary cause of sedentary behavior."[24] A *St. Petersburg Times* article claimed that research has found a "causal relationship" between television viewing and overweight kids, but the study the story described actually found that the problem is really about heavy eating while watching television, not just turning on the TV.[25] Others complained that ads for snack foods make kids more likely to form unhealthy eating habits. However, a Federal Trade Commission study found that kids today actually see *fewer* food ads per day compared with kids in the 1970s, before weights started to climb.[26] Only a couple of stories noted a related factor: that for some kids it is "safer to watch television or play a computer game" than to play outside.[27]

Nonetheless, a large portion of the popular-culture stories (38 percent) implied that kids today are uniquely lazy and thus drawn to being entertained by media instead of following more active pursuits, and that their parents are irresponsible for allowing them so much media access. A teacher quoted in the *St. Louis Post–Dispatch* complained that all kids do after school is watch TV (although I'm not sure how *teachers* know what their students do at home).[28] Descriptions of "kids *vegetating* in front of the TV" and statements that "kids *overindulge*" (emphasis mine) in video games convey that young people's leisure activities are the equivalent of laziness. Former Georgia Senator Zell Miller told the *Atlanta Journal–Constitution* that child obesity is caused by kids who "sit around on their duffs watching Eminem on MTV and playing video games."[29] This statement and others like it imply that kids are not just people who need to include more physical activity in their lives, but that they are shiftless pleasure-seekers (unlike adults, who apparently all work hard and exercise regularly). No, kids are identified as part of an "electronics-focused generation" by the *Rocky Mountain News*, and as "GameBoy-happy" by the *Daily News* (New York).[30] The only adult role in children's obesity problem apparently lies in overindulgent parents chastised for "using TV as a babysitter."[31]

While popular culture has become a big part of children's daily lives, it is also a major part of American adult life, as is the sedentary lifestyle that critics blame on TV. Interestingly, other sedentary activities, like reading, spending hours on homework, and sitting talking with friends and family are left out of the complaints. Nor is it mentioned that a great deal of time spent on the computer involves doing homework. It has become a cliché to say that all kids do today is sit around, eat, watch TV, and play video games, and that this is what has made kids gain more weight than their predecessors ever did.

But what about the surge in adult obesity? Are adults lounging around the TV with their kids? It's likely in many families that the answer is yes, but popular culture is typically only criticized as a problem for the young.

MEAN KIDS AND GREEDY GLUTTONS

A *Pittsburgh Post–Gazette* story detailed the life of a severely overweight boy and described how he withdrew into video games; in this case and certainly many others like it, spending hours playing video games is just as much an *effect* of being obese as it is the cause.[32] For kids who don't feel accepted by their peers, popular culture offers an escape. Ten percent of the articles noted that kids can be mean to their overweight peers. A teen told the *St.*

Louis Post–Dispatch that his classmates "treated [him] like crap," and "ridiculed [him] every day."[33] Another told the *Seattle Times* of how he "would hide in the library at lunch time to avoid the piggy noises kids made."[34] Certainly, kids can be cruel. But so can adults.

Consider how the press talks about overweight young people. Some newspaper headlines are as cruel to kids as the playground bullies. "Growing Up Too Fat" and "American Kids Fatter Than Ever" appeared in the *San Francisco Chronicle*, a city otherwise known for tolerance and embracing diversity.[35] Overseas it's even worse. Australian headlines complain of a "Lazy Generation: Children Just Want to Watch Television," and claim that "Lounge Lizard Parents [Are] Breeding Lazy Children."[36] Others malign "The Modern Teen: Fat, Lazy, and Apathetic" and claim that "Our Kids [Are]: Fat, Lazy, Sex-Mad" as though these were only young people's vices.[37] Nearly a quarter (24 percent) of American news reports on child obesity in 2003 were directly insulting, describing kids as mindless gluttons.

Several stories described kids as insatiable eaters. "Put kids in front of fast food and they'll likely gorge like pigs. And the fatter they are, the more they're likely to stuff into their mouths," reported the *Boston Herald* in a story on research into children and portion control.[38] A *Baltimore Sun* article on a study about the benefits of eating cereal with milk for breakfast described "the frequent eaters" as "chowing down more than eight bowls in two weeks."[39] Although described as gluttonous, eating eight bowls of cereal in fourteen days is hardly excessive. In fact, the article reported that this group had "a lower Body Mass Index than the others."[40] So even though eating more is a good thing, "chowing down" casts a negative light on healthy eating.

School cafeteria food was also a central focus in these articles. Several included quotes from students blithely describing how they really don't care if the food they eat is unhealthy. "I eat it because it tastes good," a ninth grader told the *San Francisco Chronicle*.[41] The *Chronicle* went on to describe a cafeteria scene in the Bay Area where throngs of students "pressed toward the Burger King window."[42] A school official from Toledo, Ohio, claimed that "if we took the pizza out, there'd be a riot."[43] Apparently when food is involved, kids aren't so lazy after all.

Still others blamed parental indulgence for kids' gluttony. "Try prying your kids' fingers off the remote control," a letter writer told *USA Today*.[44] Another *USA Today* story encouraged parents to "offer children wholesome rewards for not being couch potatoes."[45] The subtitle of a *Chicago Sun–Times* column chided parents for "regularly letting their kids indulge."[46] Kids are characterized as a generation of lazies who, unlike their parents, seem to prefer lounging to hard work. Or, as a *Houston Chronicle* story put it, "nearly half of all Americans ages twelve to nineteen won't break a sweat this week."[47] No mention of their elders, who are probably even less likely to break a sweat than their kids are. So why do kids get called fat and lazy when adults are often as bad or worse? We adults tell children to go out and play while we stay inside. We tell them to walk to school while we almost never walk to work, and to eat fruits and vegetables (at school) without necessarily eating them ourselves. Blaming kids takes the focus off us, whose even larger weight gain is framed as individual and private, and is not used to unilaterally condemn a generation.

Apart from characterizing kids as lazy pigs, several articles resorted to name calling. The *Daily News* (New York) led the way, noting in a January article that the mayor is "out to save fat kids."[48] A September headline called for "A Shape Up for Fat Kids."[49] A July story's subtitle chided that "forty-three percent [of kids] are roly-poly."[50] The article starts off rather brusquely: "Attention kids: Skip the fries, don't supersize, and get some exercise." Sounds more like a schoolyard taunt than a news story.

Other papers also called kids fat—the *Houston Chronicle* and the *Tampa Tribune* respectively warned that kids are "increasingly fat" and "have become fatter."[51] The *Boston Globe* referred to young people as "Generation XL" in two separate stories.[52]

Perhaps one of the most persistent stereotypes about overweight people is that they are lazy and without self-control. For a society with roots in a Puritan ethic of hard work and self-denial, laziness and lack of self-control constitute character flaws that we often find hard to forgive. It is strange then, when an estimated 64.5 percent of American adults are considered overweight, that we continue to stigmatize those who are obese.[53] It could be that many of us know that we are a few hundred calories a day shy of becoming obese ourselves.

The obesity issue is often laid squarely at the feet of young people, presented as the outcome of a lazy, overfed, pleasure-seeking crop of youth, and ignoring a culmination of environmental and social factors. Adult obesity is left out of the picture.

BABY FAT: FEARING INDULGED CHILDREN

The idea that young people are greedy gluttons stems from long-standing beliefs about kids. Sigmund Freud's conceptualization of the id characterizes our earliest childhood experiences as exclusively pleasure seeking, which we learn to control as we mature. In Freudian theory the *polymorphous perverse*, or pleasure without boundaries, begins to end with toilet training, when kids are supposed to find pleasure in self-control.

But we believe that young people today are particularly lazy and self-centered. A 1998 survey of teens found that 84 percent think that adults consider them lazy.[54] The kids are close—a 1999 poll found that 58 percent of parents of teens would describe young people negatively, including laziness as a key character trait.[55] In a 1995 Gallup Poll, 17 percent of parents admitted to calling their kids lazy or dumb.[56]

The image of the hedonist who wants everything without delay is projected onto children and teens. We talk about young people as if they are the only ones who can't say no to pleasure, but a look at adult obesity rates (and consumer debt loads) suggests that many adults know no limits either.[57]

Childhood is idealized as a carefree period—no responsibilities, no worries about calories. Kids are considered naturally playful, and we presume they will burn what they consume in their daily activities. We also believe that kids don't have the burdens of adulthood, and we think that childhood should be a time of leisure and play. Of course this idealized conception of childhood is often more fantasy than reality. So when rates of childhood obesity rise, the concern extends beyond the issue of health. Child obesity seems to belie the "natural" state of childhood. Freedom from obesity is seen as a fundamental right of youth; we ourselves often look back at younger days and think of thinner, less weight-conscious versions of ourselves.

For middle-class and affluent youth, childhood and adolescence increasingly became a time of leisure following World War II, with the automation of both the labor force and household chores. Accusations that young people are lazy have likely been the result of jealousy of an older generation that might not have experienced the same freedom from work late into their teens as the postwar generation did. Today adults may envy children their freedom from adult responsibilities of paying bills and spending long hours at work. This is the paradox of childhood: we want children to be carefree, to have few responsibilities and few demands made on them, yet we are also quick to assert that they are lazy for not having the same responsibilities we do. We often want kids to have what we never had growing up, to have material advantages, and to be happy, but we also find them greedy when they indulge in what we ourselves want them to have and in turn want even more. We can't have it both ways. Calling kids fat and lazy reflects our uneasiness with the way we define childhood as fun; on some level we also want them to exert self-control. Balance is part of the struggle parents are then faced with.

Childhood obesity threatens more than the health of young people. It challenges our fantasy of a carefree childhood that should somehow be untainted by the adult world. Child obesity activates our perennial fear that there is something wrong with the next generation, that they are lazy and obsessed with self-gratification, something we often refuse to see in ourselves.

CAFETERIA CRISIS: CHANGES IN AMERICA'S SCHOOLS

We also fear that kids can now be gluttons in schools by snacking on candy or eating fast food straight from the school cafeteria. School-related issues were the number one topic of the child obesity stories in my analysis: 56 percent of the coverage addressed the role that schools play in contributing to the problem. While a handful of articles addressed the National School Lunch Program and recent cutbacks in its funding, most stories failed to explore why schools have become so dependent on the revenue generated by fattening foods. A few mentioned a pilot program to provide free produce to students in one hundred schools, but most of the articles were simply critiques of the schools for selling unhealthy food. Only one noted that a local district, which had signed a $50 million Pepsi contract, had also recently sustained $32 million in budget cuts.[58]

While the presence of high-calorie, low-nutrient foods in schools is certainly troubling, the news reports usually omitted the broader context of why so many schools are struggling financially and must now depend on students buying junk food to keep operating—free enterprise at its worst. It's one thing to demand that fast food and fattening snacks be removed from schools, but the reasons they got there in the first place remain largely hidden in the bulk of these stories.

School lunch programs started as a way to feed starving children during the Depression and as a way to prevent farm surpluses from further depressing the price of agricultural products by taking them off the market and diverting them into schools.[59] Cafeteria workers were funded by the New Deal–era Works Progress Administration (WPA), so the federal government financed the price of both the food and the labor needed to prepare and serve meals until the program ended in 1943. Kids got to eat, the unemployed got to work, and farmers saw prices stabilize.

Initially, Congress renewed this program on an annual basis, but schools were often reluctant to install costly cooking facilities permanently without some sort of financial guarantee. Thus, the 1946 National School Lunch Program legislated subsidized meals into permanent existence, while the cost burden gradually shifted to the states. Today, about twenty-seven million children benefit from this program, its operating budget is about $6.5 billion, and an estimated $800 million a year goes to the farm industry.[60] However, the maximum reimbursement schools get is about $2.26 per meal.[61]

The program allows the U.S. Department of Agriculture (USDA) to buy surplus meat and dairy products, often at costs negotiated by industry lobbyists. Seen as a win-win situation for both industry and schools, this program provides products high in saturated fat and often fails to meet the health standards set by the government itself. In 2001, the USDA spent more than twice as much money on meat and cheese as on fruits and vegetables.[62] Schools thus have a great deal of cheap, subsidized, high-fat food to cook in times of budget shortfalls.

That is, assuming school cafeterias actually prepare the food themselves. Schools sometimes contract with fast-food companies to raise revenue and outsource food preparation.[63] Kitchen facilities built years ago are often too small to cook for an ever-increasing number of students housed in under-sized schools.[64] Overcrowding has also led some schools to create staggered lunch schedules, where students may only have twenty minutes for lunch, thus driving them to vending machines and other sources of quick, easy-to-eat foods.

Students may be running from the lunchroom to the classroom, but not to gym class. Nearly one-third (32 percent) of the school-related articles dis-cussed the reduction of physical education in American schools. Thanks to budget shortfalls, fewer high-school students participate in gym class now compared to students a decade earlier. In 1999, the Centers for Disease Con-trol and Prevention estimated that 44 percent of American students were not enrolled in a physical education course, and of those that were enrolled, nearly a quarter (23.7 percent) did not exercise more than twenty minutes per class on average. Further, only 29.1 percent of high-school students at-tended gym classes daily, down from 42 percent in 1991.[65] Others may be in gym classes with seventy or more students.[66] Some schools don't have the money or the facilities; a *Daily News* article described how many New York City schools have neither a gymnasium nor a playground, and 94 percent have no athletic field.[67]

Budget problems have also meant cuts in related electives like dance and extracurricular sports. With the push toward standardized testing, fitness has fallen in priority—it doesn't show up on student scores, nor does physical education impress college admission officers as much as advanced place-ment courses do. The skills we want young people to acquire in school, skills that involve problem solving, computer competency, and communica-tion expertise, are obviously mental rather than physical, and our perceived need to create a generation of physically fit youth (during the cold-war threat of conflict) has vanished. For more affluent families, private sports leagues and dance and martial arts classes may fill in the gap. But low-income kids often have little or no access to these activities, and they are less likely to have safe places to play outside informally.

Several stories offered possible solutions: reintroduce home economics to teach healthy cooking skills; provide parents with health report cards to no-tify parents of the health risks overweight children may face; include health-ier options like bottled water and juice in vending machines; and finally, cre-ate opportunities for students to grow their own vegetables at school and learn how to prepare them—a return to our agrarian roots.

Raising awareness about unhealthy food and the lack of physical education is a good start, and I commend the press for covering these problems. But to understand why we have been giving children in public schools the short shrift, readers need to also see the connection between what their kids do and eat at school and the economic and policy decisions that affect their kids.

Schools certainly bear some responsibility for the American weight gain, but the above trends in public education cannot explain why older people are gaining weight even faster than young people. Still, when schools intervene, as a Pennsylvania district did by sending letters to parents of children at risk for obesity-related health problems, they are criticized by many parents for overstepping their bounds.[68]

Soft drinks, fast food, and candy in vending machines doubtlessly contribute to the problem of obesity in young people. But what about the rest of us, who haven't seen the inside of a school cafeteria in decades? We may have taken gym classes with just twenty or thirty kids, never eaten any branded fast food at school, and had a nutrition class, but we are still growing heavier. According to physiologist James O. Hill, obesity "is a normal response to the American environment."[69] If we want to find out the major culprit of obesity in kids, we can't overlook the sedentary nature of our convenience-based culture. In that regard, it's too simple to blame schools, parents, genetics, or any one single factor without keeping the broader context in mind.

FAT, ECONOMICS, AND RACE

Two of the contexts most important in understanding child obesity are socioeconomic and racial-ethnic status. Perhaps most disappointing is the fact that only 12 percent of the 102 stories I analyzed addressed the relationship of race or socioeconomic status and obesity. Surgeon General David Satcher noted in the report "Call to Action to Prevent and Decrease Overweight and Obesity" (2001) that "overweight and obesity are particularly common among minority groups and those with lower income." These two important factors also produce disparities in rates among children and teens. The absence of such information helps the public overlook some of the most important correlates to obesity and instead focus on the mythical lazy child and selfish teen in explaining obesity, at the same time ignoring the many social and environmental factors that get in the way of many young people's health and well-being.

Only three of these articles offered any explanation of the connection between low socioeconomic status and obesity, noting also that poverty prevents purchasing healthier—and costlier—food.[70] A USDA report noted that many low-income residents have access only to smaller stores and supermarkets, which often have higher prices.[71]

Adam Drewnowski of the University of Washington's Center for Public Health notes that "the economics of food choice may help explain why low-income families have the highest rates of overweight," adding that healthier foods also tend to cost more.[72] For families on a tight budget and seeking low-priced food, the "super-sizing" trend is particularly appealing, allowing them to pay a little more money for a lot more food and calories.[73] But of course, there is a cost. According to Greg Critser, author of *Fat Land: How Americans Became the Fattest People in the World*, a serving of McDonald's fries has ballooned from 200 calories in 1960 to 610 calories today, mostly because of super-sizing.[74]

Critser also notes that the rise in American obesity corresponds with the inclusion of cheap additives like high-fructose corn syrup and palm oil in many foods, which were developed to keep food prices low during the inflation crisis of the 1970s.[75] These additives, commonly found in prepared, low-cost foods, have long shelf lives and are used as preservatives. Critser argues that these additives are fat builders, more difficult for the body to break down and use as energy and thus more likely to be stored as fat. Although low in financial costs, these additives have made cheap foods high in health costs.

A 2002 report from the Centers for Disease Control and Prevention noted that 26 percent of adults below the poverty level were obese, compared with only 15.8 percent of those with incomes at least four times greater than poverty level.[76] An *International Journal of Obesity* study noted similar results, and also found that those who did not finish high school, a good predictor of lower socioeconomic status, were also more likely to be obese than those who did (23 percent compared with 16.5 percent).[77] Likewise, a study reported in the *Journal of the American Medical Association* found that obesity rates were lower in adults who had attained more education; 24.1 percent of high-school dropouts were obese compared with 13.1 percent of college graduates.[78]

But the relationship between obesity and economics is far from simple. Although in the United States and other industrialized nations the lower one's income the greater one's likelihood of being obese, in countries such as Russia and China and other transitional or developing countries, this is not the case.[79] Also, the effects of poverty seem to be stronger for women. The Surgeon General reported that "women of lower socioeconomic status (income ≤ 130 percent of the poverty threshold) are approximately 50 percent more likely to be obese than those with higher socioeconomic status," but that there is no difference for men.[80]

For children, the relationship is complex as well. A study published by the *International Journal of Epidemiology* found that socioeconomic status appears to make a difference in American children by age ten.[81] The author notes that "the SES [socioeconomic status] differences across ethnic groups are likely the main explanation for the difference in obesity prevalence across ethnic groups."[82] But there is a marked difference for girls, even when controlling for family income. A study from the *Annals of Epidemiology* compared nine- and ten-year-old white and African-American girls, and found that "the prevalence of obesity was significantly lower at higher household income levels for white girls but not for black girls."[83] The study found the same to be true for parental education levels, indicating that there may be "a greater social tolerance for obesity among African Americans."[84]

So in the complex American context of race, gender, and socioeconomic status, we know that it is often difficult to neatly separate these three categories, and impossible to understand obesity by only examining them separately. Historically, African Americans and Latinos have had higher poverty rates and have experienced more social isolation through residential segregation, and therefore may also have separate cultural practices that could promote obesity.[85] Paul Campos, author of *The Obesity Myth*, suggests that our obsession with weight is a thinly veiled way to control and condemn the poor and the nonwhite.

Additionally, data from the NHANES study show clear racial-ethnic differences for children. While the prevalence of being overweight or obese has risen for all groups, in African-American and Mexican-American young people the rates are significantly higher. White children over five and adults were less likely to be overweight than the African Americans or Mexican Americans[86] counterparts.

As we can see in table 2.1, racial differences in weight are most pronounced in young people age six to nineteen, when African Americans and Mexican Americans are nearly twice as likely to be overweight compared to white kids. When we break down the ethnic categories by gender, white six- to eleven-year-old boys are heavier than white girls (21 percent vs. 12 percent), but in adolescence they reach parity. African-American girls are consistently more likely to be overweight than their male counterparts, while the reverse is true for Mexican Americans. The differences narrow in adulthood, as whites catch up in gaining weight. But why such a big difference between racial-ethnic groups in childhood and adolescence?

The timing of weight gain here is significant. Although white adults are somewhat less likely to be overweight than African Americans and Mexican Americans, white children and teens are much less likely to be overweight

Table 2.1. Percent Overweight by Age and Ethnicity 1999–2000

Age	All	White	African American	Mexican American
2–5 years	10.4%	10.1%	8.4%	11.1%
6–11	15.3	11.8	19.5	23.7
12–19	15.5	12.7	23.6	23.4
20 and older	64.5	62.3	69.9	73.4

Source: National Health and Nutrition Examination Survey (NHNES). Data published in Cynthia L. Ogden et al., "Prevalence and Trends in Overweight among U.S. Children and Adolescents, 1999–2000," *Journal of the American Medical Association* 288 (2002): 1728–32, table 4; and in Katherine M. Flegal et al., "Prevalence and Trends in Obesity among U.S. Adults, 1999–2000," *Journal of the American Medical Association* 288 (2002): 1723–27.

than their counterparts. If we consider youth to be a factor that reduces the likelihood of being overweight, being a white child reduces it even further. While culture and genetics are certainly important, white children are less likely to live in areas of high poverty concentration and will perhaps have more safe places to play outdoors.[87] They are less likely to attend severely overcrowded schools that may not offer recess or physical education (see discussion of this issue in chapter 3). And perhaps most importantly, they are less likely to live in poverty. About 14 percent of white kids under eighteen lived in poverty in 2002, compared with 32 and 29 percent of African-American and Latino kids, respectively.[88]

Only one newspaper article in the 2003 sample addressed this racial disparity, noting a study that found Latina mothers were less likely than other mothers to perceive their children as too heavy.[89] A study of predominantly African-American mothers receiving WIC (Special Supplemental Nutrition Program for Women, Infants, and Children) funding in the Cincinnati area found similar results.[90] An analysis of WIC recipients in New York also noted that Latino parents were least likely to recognize that their children are overweight.[91] Focus groups with WIC counselors suggest that these mothers often use food as a parenting tool and see it as an affordable gift when they can provide so little else materially.[92]

Another study about food availability addressed other possible racial disparities. A team of researchers compared the food selection at grocery stores in predominantly African-American sections of Los Angeles with a predominantly white area and found that there were fewer grocery store chains in areas with higher percentages of African Americans.[93] They also compared the healthiness and quality of the food: only 38 percent of the stores in predominantly black communities sold skim milk compared with 80 percent of those in mostly white neighborhoods. Only 70 percent of the stores in African-American neighborhoods sold fresh fruits and vegetables, compared with 94 percent of stores in white neighborhoods; the quality and selection of the produce in African-American communities was also found to be poorer.

So while race and socioeconomic status were not a big part of the press coverage, they are both very important issues in understanding obesity. Clearly, the rates of overweight children are higher in groups most likely to be economically disadvantaged. But race and economics are complex contributors to the problem, neither easily understood nor explained in a thousand-word news report. In our age of cheap food, the biggest threat poverty might present is, ironically, obesity.

THE BIG BUSINESS OF FAT: WHY INDUSTRY LOVES GLUTTONY

So what's to be done about the expanding waistlines of Americans? The food industry itself has recently been under fire for increasing portion sizes. Some critics have gone so far as to claim that fat is the "next tobacco" and have filed lawsuits against fast-food chains, claiming that it's their fault kids have gained weight because they sell "addictive" food.[94] Of course, the food industry benefits from our propensity to eat too much—after all, if we eat more, they and their shareholders make more money.

New York attorney Sam Hirsch filed two class-action suits against McDonald's, Burger King, KFC, and Wendy's on behalf of the obese.[95] He later withdrew the lawsuits and decided it would be more dramatic to file another suit on behalf of obese children. Media attention focused on a four-hundred-pound fifteen-year-old who claimed to have "eaten at McDonald's nearly every day" since he was six.[96] It's difficult to rally public support for obese adults, but obese children are much more likely to get public sympathy. Even so, the lawsuit was thrown out in early 2003.[97]

Lawsuits against the fast-food industry have irked the personal responsibility camp. Denver's *Rocky Mountain News* asked rhetorically, "Is there any problem the legal system hasn't claimed as its own?"[98] At the time of this writing, Congress is drafting legislation protecting restaurants from such lawsuits. And yes, *everyone* should know that eating Big Macs nearly every day is probably not part of a healthy balanced diet. But there's another industry that helps blur this seemingly obvious reality: the diet industry.

Consumers are provided with mounds of conflicting advice from so-called experts in white lab coats. "Eat less fat." "Don't worry about fat, eat fewer carbohydrates." "Eat based on your blood type." "Eat this special powder." "Eat whatever you want and take this pill before bedtime." The diet industry, by promoting its books, supplements, gym memberships, clinics, and spas benefits from our confusion and our desire for a quick fix. This industry also caters to young people with programs developed specifically for children, such as weight-loss "camps." While the basic principles of consuming and expending calories shouldn't be a big mystery, the weight-loss industry often obfuscates the issue in an attempt to sell us their solution.

While many in the food industry scoffed at the initial lawsuits, the focus on children raised more serious concerns. McDonald's and other fast-food chains are now advertising healthier options. Coke came out with a smaller can in addition to its standard twelve-ounce can. Perhaps "slim sizing" is the next super-sizing; we'll pay either way, in dollars or pounds.

Blaming the food industry is a tough legal battle in the American climate of personal responsibility. Although we value the pleasure of eating and the sense of getting a bargain, we are still a society that expects a certain degree of self-control and sacrifice. Perhaps that's why the stigma of being overweight continues: it represents our ambivalence about consumption and control, and of the dangers of losing control. The food industry and consumer culture in general encourages us to indulge, and obesity is the physical incarnation of what can happen when we do. But if we can consume to our heart's desire—within limits (like having credit-card debt, but not so much that we have to file for bankruptcy)—and if we can eat whatever we want without becoming too heavy, we are thought to be treating ourselves to a little measured indulgence.

Yet the medical community reminds us of the risks of obesity. The Surgeon General now claims that 300,000 Americans die each year from obesity-related illnesses, a number that is creeping closer to those lost from tobacco use. While personal responsibility is certainly necessary, it is also important to recognize that the social context we live in presents serious challenges to shifting this public-health dilemma.

First, we have become a sedentary society through technological changes that render physical labor less necessary, so we often burn fewer calories in our daily activities than generations past did. Second, as I explored in chapter 1, we are often fearful of allowing children to play outside, or to walk to school. Sometimes this is for good reason, at other times it serves to allay adult anxieties, and either way it contributes to many kids' weight gain. Third, our schools are dependent on students buying fast food or unhealthy snacks to stay solvent or maintain extracurricular activities. Schools need to move beyond only preparing students to take standardized tests and to refocus on creating well-rounded individuals, by recognizing the importance of physical education and related courses.

Parents also face obstacles in providing healthy food to their children, whether it be due to time limits, economic constraints, or both. Poverty is the biggest threat to children's health. The threat of the early onset of type 2 diabetes, hypertension, and other serious illnesses is particularly frightening when we consider that the kids who may be most susceptible are also the ones least likely to have health insurance or access to quality health care. Obesity threatens more than the waistlines of Americans young and old: it threatens to upend our already precarious healthcare system.

Even so, while fattening school lunches occasionally make the news, incidents of school violence grab even bigger headlines. In the next chapter, I examine our fear that schools are no longer the safe havens we believe they once were. And once again, kids themselves are blamed for destroying this sacred ground of childhood.

NOTES

1. U.S. Department of Health and Human Services, *The Surgeon General's Call to Action to Prevent and Decrease Overweight and Obesity* (Rockville, Md.: U.S. Department of Health and Human Services, Public Health Service, Office of the Surgeon General, 2001).

2. Roger Parloff, "Is Fat the Next Tobacco?" *Fortune*, February 3, 2003, 51–54.

3. To find the stories, I searched using the terms *child obesity, obese children, obese kids,* and *fat children* on Lexis-Nexis. I did not use *childhood obesity* or *fat kids* in my final search because both terms are now often overused and even clichés. These terms appeared in a large number of articles not focused on children's weight problems or duplicated many hits from the first four searches.

4. Cynthia L. Ogden et al., "Prevalence and Trends in Overweight among U.S. Children and Adolescents, 1999–2000," *Journal of the American Medical Association* 288 (2002): 1728–32, table 4.

5. Ogden et al., "Prevalence and Trends in Overweight." For children, overweight is defined as being above the 95th percentile of body mass index (BMI, or an individual's weight in kilograms divided by the square of the individual's height in meters). Obesity is defined for adults and adolescents as having a BMI of 30 or higher.

6. Elizabeth Becker and Marian Burros, "Eat Your Vegetables?" *New York Times,* January 13, 2003, A1; Sally Squires, "Kids Produce in School," *Washington Post,* February 18, 2003, F1; Editorial, "Obesity Prevention Program," *St. Petersburg Times,* July 8, 2003, 8A; John Fauber, "Obesity Hurts Kids' Lifestyles Like Cancer," *Milwaukee Journal Sentinel,* April 9, 2003, 1A; Bella English, "The Big Battle," *Boston Globe,* August 13, 2003, D1.

7. Nanci Hellmich, "It's Tough Being an Obese Kid," *USA Today,* April 9, 2003, 8D; Marilyn Elias, "New Study Confirms Parents Must Lead the Way in Kids' Weight Loss," *USA Today,* August 12, 2003, 9D; Nanci Hellmich, "Study Suggests Child Obesity May Play Role in Breast Cancer," *USA Today,* October 13, 2003, 6D; Editorial, "Going with the Grain," *Baltimore Sun,* December 5, 2003, 24A.

8. Jim Ritter, "Kids on Front Lines of Obesity War," *Chicago Sun–Times,* July 1, 2003, 8; Cleora Hughes, "Exercise Is Child's Play," *St. Louis Post–Dispatch,* August 11, 2003, 1.

9. Mark Johnson and John Fauber, "Lessons of Poor Eating Learned Early," *Milwaukee Journal Sentinel,* July 7, 2003, 1A.

10. Susan Aschoff, "Healthline," *St. Petersburg Times,* April 15, 2003, 3F.

11. English, "The Big Battle"; Cristina Rouvalis, "More Than Meets the Eye," *Pittsburgh Post–Gazette,* October 12, 2003, G1.

12. "Open Forum," *Denver Post,* September 25, 2003, B6.

13. Becker and Burros, "Eat Your Vegetables?"; Mariko Thompson, "The Weight is Over," *San Diego Union–Tribune,* September 20, 2003, E1; Susan Aschoff, "Thinking Out of the Box," *St. Petersburg Times,* October 14, 2003, 3D; Caroline Louise Cole, "Schools Weigh Unhealthy Snack Ban," *Boston Globe,* October 2, 2003, 5; Alison Arnett, "Fighting for a Fitter Child," *Boston Globe,* January 29, 2003, E1; Patricia Corrigan, "Only 50 Percent of Students Take PE Classes," *St. Louis Post–Dispatch,* March 10, 2003, D3; Hughes, "Exercise Is Child's Play"; Editorial, "Schools Must Pull Their Weight in Helping Kids Battle Obesity," *Chicago Sun–Times,* September 16, 2003, 29.

14. Roberta L. Duyff, "Helping Children Toward a Healthy Weight May Require Lifestyle Changes," *St. Louis Post–Dispatch,* April 23, 2003, 5; Maria Montoya, "The Super-Sized Generation," *Times–Picayune,* April 6, 2003, 1; Fauber, "Obesity Hurts Kids' Lifestyles Like Cancer"; Elias, "New Study Confirms Parents Must Lead"; Hughes, "Exercise Is Child's Play"; Rouvalis, "More Than Meets the Eye"; Hellmich, "Study Suggests Child Obesity May Play Role in Breast Cancer"; Editorial, "Going with the Grain."

15. Editorial, "Schools Must Pull Their Weight in Helping Kids."

16. Katherine M. Flegal et al., "Prevalence and Trends in Obesity among U.S. Adults, 1999–2000," *Journal of the American Medical Association* 288 (2002): 1723–27.

17. Flegal et al., "Prevalence and Trends in Obesity among U.S. Adults," table 4.

18. Nicole Bode, "Parents' Burden," *Daily News*, July 10, 2003, 1.

19. *USA Today*, "Blame Ads for Child Obesity," August 26, 2003, 10A.

20. *USA Today*, "Blame Ads for Child Obesity."

21. English, "The Big Battle"; Elizabeth Lee, "School Lunches: Good Choices?" *Atlanta Journal–Constitution*, May 4, 2003, 1A.

22. Betsy Hart, "Obesity Is Our Fault, Not Kraft's," *Chicago Sun–Times*, July 6, 2003, 28; Lee, "School Lunches: Good Choices?"

23. Nanci Hellmich, "Brakes on the Scale," *USA Today*, August 20, 2003, 1D.

24. Cecilia Capuzzi Simon, "Move it, Kid," *Washington Post*, February 25, 2003, F1.

25. Collette Bancroft, "The United States of Obesity," *St. Petersburg Times*, February 11, 2003, 1D.

26. Caroline E. Mayer, "Fewer Food Ads in Kids' TV Diet, New Study Finds," *Los Angeles Times*, July 16, 2005, E15.

27. Sherri Williams, "Obese Children," *Columbus Dispatch*, November 13, 2003, 1C.

28. Carolyn Bower, "Students Watch Their Steps with Coke's Help," *St. Louis Post–Dispatch*, October 15, 2003, A1.

29. Lee, "School Lunches: Good Choices?"

30. Debra Melani, "'Baby' Fat of the Land," *Rocky Mountain News*, August 26, 2003, 3D; Joe Williams, "A Shape-Up for Fat Kids," *Daily News*, September 24, 2003, 10.

31. Ritter, "Kids on Front Lines of Obesity War."

32. Rouvalis, "More Than Meets the Eye."

33. Cleora Hughes, "A Positive First Step," *St. Louis Post–Dispatch*, August 11, 2003, 4.

34. Julia Sommerfeld, "Teen Weight-Loss Surgery," *Seattle Times*, July 7, 2003, A1.

35. Kim Severenson and Meredith May, "Growing Up Too Fat," *San Francisco Chronicle*, May 12, 2002, A1.

36. Noula Tsavdaridis, "Lazy Generation," *Daily Telegraph* (Sydney), January 19, 2001, 11; Editorial, "Lounge-Lizard Parents Breeding Lazy Children," *The Age* (Melbourne), August 2, 2000, 8.

37. Caroline Milburn, "The Modern Teen," *The Age* (Melbourne), May 12, 2001, 15; Rachael Templeton, "Our Kids," *Sunday Mail*, December 28, 1998, 41.

38. Michael Lasalandra, "Fast Food Plus Fat Kids May Equal Supersized Problems," *Boston Herald*, 2.

39. Editorial, "Going with the Grain."

40. Editorial, "Going with the Grain."

41. Editorial, "Battle of the Bulge," *San Francisco Chronicle*, June 29, 2003, D4.

42. Editorial, "Battle of the Bulge."

43. Karen MacPherson, "Congress Under Pressure to Improve What Kids Eat," *Pittsburgh Post–Gazette*, May 18, 2003, A17.

44. Letter, "Personal Responsibility Weighs into Obesity Debate," *USA Today*, July 3, 2003, 20A.

45. Elias, "New Study Confirms Parents Must Lead."

46. Hart, "Obesity Is Our Fault."

47. Glenn Sattell, "Y Effort Helping to Keep Kids Healthy," *Houston Chronicle*, July 17, 2003, 13.

48. Lisa L. Colangelo, "Mike Weighs in on Child Obesity," *Daily News* (New York), January 10, 2003, 18.

49. J. Williams, "A Shape-Up for Fat Kids."

50. Lisa L. Colangelo, "Little Kids Just Too Big," *Daily News* (New York), July 9, 2003, 5.

51. Editorial, "School Junk Food Contracts Not Worth Kids' Poor Health," *Houston Chronicle*, April 15, 2003, 22; Susan H. Thompson, "Weighty Issues," *Tampa Tribune*, June 1, 2003, 6.

52. Editorial, "Generation XL," *Boston Globe*, May 27, 2003, A14; English, "The Big Battle."

53. Flegal et al., "Prevalence and Trends in Obesity among U.S. Adults," 1723–27.

54. Barna Research Group, telephone poll of 620 American teens age thirteen to eighteen, February 5, 1998.

55. Based on a 1999 Public Agenda telephone poll of 1,005 American adults including 384 parents of children under eighteen.

56. Gallup Poll, telephone poll of 1,000 American parents, December 8, 1995.

57. See Robert D. Manning, *Credit Card Nation: The Consequences of America's Addiction to Credit* (New York: Basic Books, 2000).

58. Logan Mabe, "Pepsi High," *St. Petersburg Times*, August 31, 2003, 1D.

59. Gordon W. Gunderson, *The National School Lunch Program: Background and Development* (United States Department of Agriculture, Washington, D.C.: GPO, 1971), 13.

60. Keecha Harris, "The USDA School Lunch Program," *The Clearing House* (July-August 2002): 310–12, figures from 2001; Barry Yeoman, "Unhappy Meals," *Mother Jones* 28 (January-February 2003): 40–45.

61. Harris, "The USDA School Lunch Program."

62. Yeoman, "Unhappy Meals," 40.

63. Greg Critser, *Fat Land: How Americans Became the Fattest People in the World* (New York: Houghton Mifflin, 2003), 48.

64. Critser, *Fat Land*, 44.

65. Centers for Disease Control and Prevention, Youth Risk Behavior Surveillance, U.S. Department of Health and Human Services, 1999.

66. Cara Mia DiMassa, "Campus Crowding Can Make PE a Challenge," *Los Angeles Times*, November 19, 2003, B2.

67. J. Williams, "A Shape-Up for Fat Kids."

68. Kelley R. Taylor, "Food Fights: Schools, Students, and the Law," *Principal Leadership* (February 2003): 63–66.

69. Quoted in Critser, *Fat Land*, 3.

70. Albor Ruiz, "Meal Programs in Schools Help Reduce Fat of the Land," *Daily News* (New York), January 21, 2003, 3; Leef Smith, "Pounds Pose Real Problems," *Washington Post*, August 21, 2003, T1; Editorial, "A Time of Need Is upon Us," *New York Times*, November 2, 2003, 10.

71. Phil R. Kaufman and Steven M. Lutz, "Competing Food Prices Affect Food Prices for Low-Income Households," *Food Prices* (May-August 1997): 8–12.

72. Adam Drewnowski, "Fat and Sugar: An Economic Analysis," *Journal of Nutrition* 133 (2003): S838–S840.

73. Critser, *Fat Land*, 27.

74. Critser, *Fat Land*, 28.

75. Critser, *Fat Land*, see chap. 1.

76. Charlotte A. Schoenborn, Patricia F. Adams, and Patricia M. Barnes, "Body Weight Status of Adults: United States, 1997–98," *Advance Data From Vital and Health Statistics*, vol. 330 (Hyattsville, Md.: Department of Health and Human Services, 2002).

77. S. Paeratakul et al., "The Relation of Gender, Race, and Socioeconomic Status to Obesity and Obesity Comorbidities in a Sample of U.S. Adults," *International Journal of Obesity* 26 (2002): 1205–10.

78. Ali H. Mokdad et al., "The Spread of the Obesity Epidemic in the United States, 1991–1998," *Journal of the American Medical Association* 282 (1999): 1519.

79. Youfa Wang, "Cross-National Comparison of Childhood Obesity: The Epidemic and the Relationship between Obesity and Socioeconomic Status," *International Journal of Epidemiology* 30 (2001): 1129–36.

80. U.S. Department of Health and Human Services, *The Surgeon General's Call to Action*.

81. Wang, "Cross-National Comparison of Childhood Obesity."

82. Wang, "Cross-National Comparison of Childhood Obesity."

83. Sue Y. S. Kimm et al., "Race, Socioeconomic Status, and Obesity in 9- to 10-Year-Old Girls: The NHLBI Growth and Health Study," *Annals of Epidemiology* 6 (1996): 266–75.

84. Kimm et al., "Race, Socioeconomic Status, and Obesity."

85. Robert Sampson and William Wilson, "Toward a Theory of Race, Crime, and Urban Inequality," in *Crime and Inequality*, ed. John Hagan and Ruth Peterson (Stanford, Calif.: Stanford University Press, 1995), 37–54.

86. NHANES uses these three racial-ethnic categorizations because their sample of members of other racial-ethnic groups was too small to draw significant conclusions.

87. Sampson and Wilson, "Toward a Theory of Race, Crime, and Urban Inequality."

88. U.S. Census Bureau, *Current Population Survey, 2003 Annual Social and Economic Supplement, Age and Sex of All People, Family Members and Unrelated Individuals Iterated by Income-to-Poverty Ratio and Race: 2002, below 100% of Poverty—White, African American and Hispanic Origin* (Washington, D.C.: GPO, 2003).

89. Smith, "Pounds Pose Real Problems."

90. Anjali Jain et al., "Why Don't Low-Income Mothers Worry about Their Preschoolers Being Overweight?" *Pediatrics* 107 (2001): 1138.

91. Miriam E. Tucker, "Obese Children often Seen as Normal by Low-Income Parents," *Family Practice News* 30 (September 1, 2000): 42.

92. Leigh A. Chamberlin et al., "The Challenge of Preventing and Treating Obesity in Low-Income, Preschool Children: Perceptions of WIC Health Care Professionals," *Archives of Pediatrics and Adolescent Medicine* 156 (2002): 662–68.

93. David C. Sloane et al., "Improving the Nutritional Resource Environment for Healthy Living through Community-Based Participatory Research," *Journal of General Internal Medicine* 18 (2003): 568–75.

94. Parloff, "Is Fat the Next Tobacco?"
95. Parloff, "Is Fat the Next Tobacco?" 53.
96. Parloff, "Is Fat the Next Tobacco?"
97. "Daily Briefing," *Atlanta Journal–Constitution*, January 23, 2003, 2E.
98. Editorial, "On Point," *Rocky Mountain News*, August 8, 2003, 36A.

3

School House Shock

Zero Tolerance and the Scary-School Myth

In September 2003, two students were shot and killed by a classmate at school in Cold Spring, Minnesota. "Why—after years of zero tolerance policies, metal detectors inside schools, and efforts to intervene with troubled students—does school violence persist?" a *Boston Globe* story covering the incident asked.[1] The January 2004 *Globe* article reported that "school-related deaths . . . have already exceeded the total from all of last year," warning that perhaps after years of declines in school violence, the coming year could be different.

The high-profile school shootings of the 1990s created nationwide concern that schools were no longer safe places. We feared that the idyllic school experiences of the past had been replaced by threats of violence and mayhem that could happen anytime, anywhere. Our fear that school violence had reached new heights led to more get-tough policies that emphasized harsher punishment for lesser and lesser offenses. But although schools may seem more dangerous today than in the past, U.S. Department of Education statistics indicate that school violence steadily *declined* during the 1990s. So why the panic?

In part, we fear schools and the young people in them because we are continually told by the press that we should. In this chapter, I address this fear created largely by the news media, the realities about school safety, the reactions of school administrators, and the reasons for the hype about schools as scary places. The *scary-school myth* draws on our preexisting fears about the next generation and provides a rationale for imposing stricter controls on young people.

Ideally, schools and their surrounding neighborhoods should be violence-free oases—and usually they are. In most cases of school-related violence, the reported incidents happen *near* schools, often between adults, and in neighborhoods already struggling with a crime problem. Grouping these crimes together with violence between students in schools heightens our fears about school violence, even when violence is in decline or involves no children. School-violence fears draw upon the same fear as kidnapping does, our fear that the world is no longer a safe place for children. But in this case, it is kids themselves that allegedly pose the biggest threat.

PORTENDING DANGER IN THE PRESS

"School Violence Hits Lower Grades," claimed a January 2003 *USA Today* article, warning of "an alarming rise in assaults and threats," and that "safety experts say they're seeing more violence and aggression than ever among their youngest students."[2] Citing unruly kindergartners beating up teachers, the story warns of an onslaught of out-of-control menaces to society, before noting that only a small proportion of elementary school teachers have reported being attacked.

What has changed is our perception of children's behavior and the threat it poses. Kindergarten is where you start to learn that you shouldn't bite if you don't get your way or wet yourself if you don't feel like getting up to go to the bathroom. Early school experiences have always been about learning appropriate behavior. Frankly, I would be surprised if kindergartners *didn't* hit a teacher every once and a while, but now we think of them as sociopaths-in-training rather than as youngsters still learning basic social skills.

The fear of what's to come extends beyond elementary schools. In October 2003, *USA Today* ran a story warning that "a string of fatal shootings, stabbings, and other attacks threatens to make [this school year] one of the deadliest in years."[3] The article, titled "Troubling Days at U.S. Schools," lamented that "young people are dying at the hands of classmates, strangers, and even parents . . . in and around high schools and middle schools." The story cited eighteen incidents in the new school year, all of which, the author claimed, "point to a rough year ahead."

But of the eighteen incidents, a so-called string of events between mid-August and October 1, only two incidents happened between students at school. Three of the incidents were between adults *near* schools, and one involved a fourteen-year-old killed by his father at school.

In the tenth paragraph, the article conceded that "young people are still much safer in school than practically anywhere else." The slaying by the fourteen-year-old's father reflects the reality that parents pose a much greater danger to young people's safety than their peers. The author also noted that violent crime in schools had been on the decline, but by that time the alarm had already been sounded. Violence "is usually worst in spring," the story noted, so fall violence could be a harbinger of danger to come. In spite of dire predictions, according to the 2004 *Indicators of School Crime and Safety*, an annual publication compiled by the National Center for Education Statistics (NCES), serious violent crime rates in schools fell between 2001 and 2003 from four victims per thousand students to two victims per thousand.[4]

NEW YORK CITY PUBLIC SCHOOLS: VILLAGE OF THE DAMNED?

In his December 12, 2003, radio address, New York City Mayor Michael Bloomberg announced that he would be cracking down on violence in the New York public schools.[5] The local papers recounted several violent incidents that "underscore the sorry conditions," as the *Daily News* described the city's schools.[6] A fifteen-year-old ninth grader was stabbed in Brooklyn;[7] a middle-school teacher's arm was twisted while breaking up a fight;[8] kids were allegedly pulling fire alarms "every period";[9] garbage cans were set ablaze;[10] an eighth grader "beat up" a teacher, "punching him in the jaw, chest, and groin";[11] *Newsday* reported that a "flurry of students . . . sent four security guards to the hospital";[12] kids were said to "curse out teachers"; and an assistant principal was "hurled down" an escalator.[13] "It could happen to any one of us any time," a teacher told reporters.[14]

The fear-based stories continued. A *Daily News* article bemoaned "yet another arrest in a week of school violence."[15] The *New York Times* noted that new police officers will "impose order," and a *Newsday* story told of seminars given to "prevent school attacks."[16] Sounds pretty scary, and seems to give credence to every New York stereotype suggesting that the city is nothing but a haven for mayhem and violence, with its public schools on the forefront. But a closer look at our nation's largest school district, with over 1 million students, reveals that things aren't as dire as they may seem.

For one, New York Police Department statistics indicate that school crime rates hadn't actually increased. John M. Beam, executive director of the National Center for Schools and Communities at Fordham University, called the intense media attention to school violence a "synthetic story."[17] Beam noted that New York City Police Department (NYPD) data indicated that the rate of major crimes in New York's public schools was 78 per 100,000, while New York City's major crime rate was 1,691 per 100,000.[18] According to the NYPD School Safety Division, during the 2002–2003 school year, there was an average of 1.1 major crimes, 3.9 nonviolent crimes, and 8.4 noncriminal incidents per 1,000 students.[19] Further, New York had recently been named the country's "safest big city," and the mayor noted that "we brought crime down in the city . . . There's no reason why we can't bring crime down in schools."[20] What the mayor didn't say was that the crime rate outside of school was about fifteen times *higher* than inside schools, and that apparently was cause for celebration.

Nonetheless, a member of city council held a news conference to dispute the idea that school crime was not getting worse. "There is a growing problem. No matter what the Department of Education says, there's a growing problem with school violence."[21] A few weeks later, the mayor supported the idea that schools were blackboard jungles: "We've slowly found ourselves sinking further and further into a pit where anything is tolerated, where teachers don't have a safe environment."[22]

Rather than from increasing crime, the core of the problem stemmed from the district's handling of violent incidents.[23] Suspension hearings had been delayed for weeks, so that kids who were a threat to safety often found themselves right back in school the day after a violent incident. Part of Mayor Bloomberg's plan involved doubling the number of officers hired to hear such complaints, as well as opening new suspension centers for troubled students.

Mayor Bloomberg also dispatched 150 more police officers to twelve schools singled out by the district, which the *Daily News* named the "Dangerous Dozen."[24] Scant media attention addressed possible causes for the higher crime rates in these schools, which on average had two and one-half times as many serious incidents and four times as many noncriminal infractions as the city school average.[25] The *New York Times* described these schools as "severely overcrowded"; and the average student poverty rate for these twelve schools (ten high schools and two middle schools) was a staggering 63 percent; in six of the schools, student poverty rates were over 75 percent.[26]

Instead of addressing the causes of violence, most coverage focused only on student conduct in these troubled schools. "Can't Stop the Violence," complained *Newsday*'s headline the day after the crackdown.[27] The *New York Times* followed with "Six Students Arrested in City Crackdown on Violent Schools."[28] Both stories described how violence continued even with the increased security.

A closer look into the arrests made on the first day of the crackdown reveals that the reported conflicts were between the students and the new security force, not between students and other students. Violations that in other schools might have led to detention or a visit to the principal's office turned into arrests in the new get-tough environment. One student had a "tussle with security guards" after forgetting his student ID.[29] Two students were charged with disorderly conduct for "refusing to leave a hallway."[30] Two brothers were charged with assault after bumping into a security guard who tried to prevent one of them from entering school while wearing a hat.[31]

Parents feared that their kids were being singled out, suspended, or arrested to set an example.[32] A student told the *Daily News* that the increased security caused an hour-long lineup and made her late for class.[33] "I feel like I'm in an airport," another told the *New York Times*.[34] A senior from a Queens high school complained that "they're trying to treat us like criminals," while a Brooklyn teen told *Newsday*, "I believe they treat us like prisoners. They stereotype us because of where we live and our race."[35]

Jill Chaifetz, executive director of Advocates for Children, told the *New York Times* that 97 percent of the students removed from school and assigned to special programs were African American or Latino, and that their new schools tended to focus on behavior and control rather than academics.[36] Fordham's John M. Beam charged that the crackdowns "fail to address the real problems," which he argued were the result of inadequate distribution of resources. Within Beam's study of over a thousand public schools, well-qualified teachers with low absentee rates, good libraries, and updated computers were associated with good student attendance and ultimately low suspension rates.[37] As a *New York Times* reader wrote the day after the crackdown began, "We need more teachers, more books . . . not a system that neglects and stigmatizes those most in need of guidance."[38]

Three months after the crackdown began, *Newsday* reported a slight dip in criminal incidents: 3.02 incidents per day compared with 3.3 in the months before.[39] Noncriminal incidents increased, however, from an average of 8.6 per day to 14.8 per day—an indicator that lesser offenses were more likely to receive formal punishment, and a likely outcome of increased scrutiny. But it remains unclear whether the crackdown actually made the schools any safer. Instead, it seemed only to quell adult fear.

READING, WRITING, AND FEAR

Schools are symbolic safe havens for young people. We think of schools as humane alternatives to factories, and cringe upon hearing of children who spend their days working instead of learning. Any danger in these symbolic safety zones is thus met with extreme collective concern and anxiety.

Fear and America's public schools have a long history. Whether it was the fear of Irish immigrants that was taught in nineteenth-century children's texts, the fear of juvenile delinquency when children's labor became less necessary after the Industrial Revolution, or the fear that immigrant children at the start of the twentieth century wouldn't assimilate, compulsory education in America has historically been based on fear as much as on learning. Historian David Nasaw describes American public schools as "social institutions dedicated *not* to meeting the self-perceived needs of their students but [to] preserving social peace and prosperity."[40] Fears of the growing expectations of the working class led to an emphasis on industrial education, and the belief that the poor were inherently immoral led to a values-based curriculum in many nineteenth-century public schools.

This anxiety continued into the twentieth century, as concern that hungry children wouldn't make good soldiers led to the antecedents of the School

Lunch Program and physical education. Fear of the Soviet Union during the cold war inspired not only the space race but also infused funding into the nation's public schools.

Why should today be any different? Fear of racial-ethnic minorities has been behind the exodus of white affluent children from urban public schools into private schools since desegregation was enforced. Fears that Latin-American immigrants won't assimilate have led to legislation to ban bilingual education and attempts to block undocumented immigrants' children from enrolling in California schools.

Our fear of school violence, whether founded or not, provides justification for more control of the kids within those schools, in the name of public safety. We have a tendency to fear other people's children, especially if they speak another language or are dark in complexion, and schools are filled with other people's children. It's not just the news media that creates this fear—the media merely fans preexisting fears and leads us to believe that schools, and the kids within them, are more dangerous than ever.

The scary-school myth encourages us to believe that deadly violence has entered one of the last sacred spaces of childhood, and that it is children themselves who are ruining this hallowed place. Violence in school feels like an attack on the notion of childhood, and makes us question the illusion of childhood innocence. But our fear about school safety is based on contradictory beliefs. Dangerous schools represent a threat to childhood innocence, a violation not only of individual children but of childhood itself. Yet at the same time, schools are sites of worry because they contain children, specifically, children branded as threatening. The evil child is a staple in horror films and represents our darkest fears. Such a child is seen as not only a threat to innocent children, but to adults as well.

IT'S NOT SUPPOSED TO HAPPEN HERE:
SCHOOLS BEYOND NEW YORK

It's not hard to understand how the public became afraid of schools in the 1990s, with graphic news accounts, the emotional reactions of distraught students, and footage of bloodied teens on gurneys or running for their lives away from their schools. It only takes a few shocking incidents to galvanize the public to say, Never again. The events in places like Littleton, Colorado; Jonesboro, Arkansas; and Paducah, Kentucky, were frightening and tragic. This handful of high-profile school shootings in the 1990s led us to believe in the scary-school myth, especially when it appeared that school violence had crossed an undrawn line. No longer was violence only a product of urban schools in low-income communities, but middle-class and rural schools with white kids now seemed to be equally likely to experience violent events.

Students in urban areas are three times more likely to be victims of serious violent crimes outside of school than on school grounds.[41] Suburban kids are twice as likely to be victimized away from school. Rural youth tend to be the safest both in and out of school: violent victimization rates in rural schools are less than one-quarter of the suburban rates and half the suburban rate outside of school. It bears mentioning that school-based serious violence rates are relatively low for all.[42]

So the high-profile incidents were clearly anomalies. They occurred during a time when we were already on a heightened state of alert about scary schools. Did we see this coming in some strange way, and were these shootings then "proof" of our predetermined conclusion that the next generation was lost and in need of control?

Prior to 1994, national crime rates had been rising for both juveniles and adults, but serious violent crime rates in schools remained low and relatively constant.[43] Nonetheless, levels of fear rose, in large part because of ominous-sounding news reports. A March 1992 *Newsweek* article warned that "It's Not Just New York" that has scary schools, and that "more and more guns" are falling into "younger and younger hands . . . Kids, even fourth and fifth graders, and teachers and school officials are running scared."[44] The story went on to say that it's no longer just "bad" kids who carry guns, but any kid may now be "packing." Incidentally, FBI data do not support the conclusion that "younger and younger" kids are more violent now than in the past. The ten- to fourteen-year-old set were more likely to be arrested for homicide in the early 1970s than in any period before or since.[45]

Newsweek was certainly not alone in predicting disaster. An October 1993 *USA Today* article lamented that "guns, violence and crime [are] just part of life for teens today—even good kids in good schools."[46] The conclusion here is that there are no more good kids, and no more good schools. Stories like these promote the idea that both young people and the schools they attend are out of control, not to be trusted, and in need of a major crackdown.

By the end of the 1990s, crime and violence at school registered significant declines.[47] Total crime in school was cut in half; in 1993 just over 150 students per 100,000 nationwide were victims of crime in their schools, compared with about 60 per 100,000 in 2001. Violent crime at school also fell by about 50 percent during the 1990s. Serious violent crimes at school remained extremely low, with only a couple of victims per thousand students. Homicides, the most severe and rarest of school crimes, hovered around thirty per school year for the nation until 1999, when the number fell below twenty. According to a study published in the *Journal of the American Medical Association*, during the 1990s students had less than a 7 in 10 million chance of being killed at school.[48] To put this number in context, the odds of dying of pneumonia or the flu are 4 times higher for children five to fourteen, and the odds of dying in an accident are 122 times greater.[49] Further, kids are 5 times more likely to be killed by an adult than by other juveniles.[50]

In spite of the fact that schools became safer in the 1990s and early 2000s, many parents erroneously believe that schools are now more dangerous and drug-filled than ever. A 2003 AARP study of baby-boom parents thirty-nine to fifty-seven years old compared their experiences in public school with their perception of their children's experiences. The problems that many parents believe are worse today are often the same or better than they were for the classes of 1973–1982.

For instance, 70 percent of those parents surveyed said drugs and alcohol are a big concern today, with 26 percent reporting that the problem is worse now than when they were in high school. Only 25 percent said that drugs and alcohol were big issues in their high schools. According to Monitoring the Future, a University of Michigan–based study that has tracked high-school trends since 1975, over 90 percent of seniors in 1975 reported drinking alcohol at least once.[51] By 2003, that number had declined to less than 77 percent. During peak drinking years, 1978–1984, the rate hovered around 93 percent. Likewise, drug use peaked between 1979–1985, when over 60 percent reported having experimented with an illegal drug. By 2003 that percentage declined to about 51 percent, down from 1975 levels of 55 percent. Use of marijuana, the most frequently used illegal drug, peaked between 1977 and 1983, when over 55 percent of high school seniors reported that they had tried it at least once. By 2003 that number was down to 46 percent, about the same as the 47 percent reporting marijuana use in 1975.

More than half (54 percent) of baby-boom parents reported that violence and safety are big problems today, while just 7 percent said the same was true in their high-school days; 20 percent felt that the problem had gotten worse. Monitoring the Future tracked school violence from 1976 to 1996, and found that the percentage of students injured in school with a weapon was flat for the twenty-year period, remaining under 10 percent, with peaks in 1981 and 1986.[52] The percentage injured without a weapon also remained around 10 percent, peaking in the mideighties as well.

For the class of 1982, the young baby boomers in this survey, their schools were likely more dangerous than the schools of high-school seniors today, and their peers more likely to experiment with drugs and alcohol. For older boomers, it is likely that their school experiences with danger and substance use were similar to what they are for kids today. But repeated warnings about scary schools in the press have led many of us to drastically overestimate the dangers that most kids face at school.

BEYOND THE SCARY-SCHOOL MYTH:
REALITIES OF SCHOOL VIOLENCE

It's likely that many of the parents sampled in the AARP survey and others have heard about school violence so often in the news that they believe it has risen. The scary-school myth draws on parents' understandable concern for their children's safety as well as on the news reports that suggest that today's school violence makes the past's pale in comparison. Gum chewing then versus gun wielding now, talking out of turn yesterday versus making terrorist threats today. The idea that fists were the weapons of a bygone era replaced by guns today has become such a cliché (even though most school violence today consists of fistfights) that we often accept it as a sad fact of life.

During the mid-1990s, when we are often told that schools began their transition from places of learning to houses of carnage, a nationally representative survey of public-school principals and disciplinarians at all grade levels found that the biggest problem in schools was tardiness.[53] The second-biggest problem was not gun possession but absenteeism—hardly the stuff of Armageddon. Only 2 percent of school administrators reported that weapons were their biggest problem. True, guns and illegal drugs have no place in schools. But are they in schools anyway?

The U.S. Department of Education's Safe Schools Report suggests that only a small proportion of students bring any kind of weapon to school (including guns, knives, and "clubs").[54] While nearly one-third of students claim that drugs have been made available to them on school property, a much smaller proportion admit to actually using drugs on school grounds.[55]

At the end of the 1990s, less than 2 percent of all homicides of fifteen- to nineteen-year-olds happened at school.[56] Seventy-two percent of all serious crimes against school-age children were committed away from school— meaning not on school grounds, nor when kids were traveling to and from school. Ninety percent of schools reported no violent crimes at all.[57] Of those that did, the most common was the old-fashioned fistfight.[58]

Certainly, shocking acts of violence have occurred in schools and subsequently received massive media attention, due to both their tragedy and their rarity. Still, compared with the communities around them, schools remain relatively safe havens. Schools have never been the most dangerous places for children; typically when young people are victims of violence, it is in their homes or neighborhoods.

Most importantly, students themselves report feeling safe. Only 5 percent of students surveyed reported feeling fear of being harmed in school some or most of the time.[59] Additionally, just 5 percent of twelve- to eighteen-year-olds reported being bullied.[60] This is a more serious problem among younger students: 10 percent of sixth and seventh graders said they have been bullied, compared with just 2 percent of tenth through twelfth graders. So schools are not the pits of danger we often fear. Statistically speaking, schools are among the safest places for young people to be.

TEACHER DANGER: THREATENED OR THREATENING?

When we focus on school violence, we tend to view young people as the primary threat. The Department of Education tracks crimes and violence by students against other students and teachers, but not crimes against students by teachers and staff. In 2001, the department reported that 4 percent of teachers were physically attacked by students.[61] It has become a commonly held assumption that young people, particularly impoverished young people of color, are a threat to their elders, but we don't even compile statistics to determine what threat adults may pose to kids in schools. When these incidents do occur, they are coded by the FBI's *Uniform Crime Reports* as crimes by "acquaintances," and grouped with peers and family friends.

Most schools are safe, and adults within schools pose a very minor threat to children compared with adults in children's homes and communities. But occasionally it's the adults who are the problem. We know very little about crimes committed by adults in schools other than anecdotal reports.

One reason we don't see violence by teachers in crime statistics is that violence against students in schools is sometimes encouraged as a form of discipline. In 1977, the Supreme Court upheld the constitutional right of schools to use corporal punishment. A few years prior, a Florida eighth grader, James Ingraham, was beaten for moving too slowly while walking to the school auditorium.[62] *Ingraham v. Wright* challenged that the student's Eighth Amendment protection against cruel and unusual punishment was violated. The Court ruled against him.

Belief in corporal punishment is not just a vestige of the past. A 2002 ABC News poll reported that 26 percent of adults surveyed favored the use of corporal punishment in schools.[63] Teachers and administrators in many states are immune from prosecution for acts that could land a child's parent in jail for abuse. At present, twenty-three states allow corporal punishment in schools, with some allowing parents to opt their children out. Temple University Educational Psychologist Irwin A. Hyman found that corporal punishment tends to be used most often on African-American boys in poor rural districts, areas with the highest poverty and illiteracy rates.[64] Hyman also discovered that the older and larger students are, the less likely they are to be physically disciplined; smaller children are the more likely targets.

Ironically, the scary-school premise builds support for harsher disciplinary measures like using violence to control students. Violence is therefore part of the educational process for some, used by both other students and sometimes teachers and administrators to control behavior. It is shortsighted to exclude the physical and psychological abuses of power by adults in schools when talking about school safety.

If student bullying and violence interferes with learning, so too may violence and intimidation by adults. Students who report abuses by their teachers are sometimes discredited as troublemakers. But more common are reports of teachers involved in inappropriate relationships with students, or accusations of molestation. Even these are difficult to quantify, however, especially because of different local law-enforcement recording practices. Additionally, the criminal or questionable behavior often takes place off school property, while increasing attention is being paid to what happens *on* school property. It's hard to legislate student behavior once students leave school grounds, but while they are in school we have tried to apply as much control as possible.

ZERO TOLERANCE FOR YOUTH

In response to the perception that schools were becoming war zones, Congress passed the Safe and Drug-Free School Act in 1994. Both the safety and drug concerns drew upon fears that schools were the next battleground of the war on drugs, despite the fact that drug use among teens in the 1990s was lower than in the late 1970s and 1980s. The 1994 legislation required that schools receiving federal funding expel any student who brought a weapon to school, a reasonable response when the weapon was a handgun or a semiautomatic rifle.

But the definition of *weapon* quickly expanded to include Swiss army knives, metal nail files, and in some cases imaginary weapons like paper cutouts or fingers pointed like guns. And *drugs* didn't just mean cocaine or marijuana, but Midol, aspirin, and Scope.

By 1998, more than three-quarters of American schools had adopted rigid guidelines regarding weapons and drugs, guidelines that have come to be known as *zero-tolerance policies*, indicating that schools will no longer tolerate the presence of weapons or drugs on campus.[65] *Zero tolerance* has become a catchphrase associated with both a get-tough stance and occasionally absurd overreactions in schools. But zero tolerance satisfies many parents and administrators on a deep level, by allowing them to believe that the implementation of predetermined punishments will make schools safer. We the general public can also feel like we are finally cracking down on the out-of-control kids who we think have been getting away with too much, and that getting tough will scare troubled kids straight and set powerful examples to the rest to toe the line.

Stories about school crackdowns have made news around the country. For example, eighth-grade girls in Ohio were suspended for sharing Midol, seventh graders in Chicago were charged with drug possession for having a small plastic bag of grape Kool-Aid, and an eighth-grade student-council member in Chicago was suspended for throwing a potato chip.[66] While it may seem that stories like these made the news because they were outrageous exceptions, a 1997 study published in the journal *Education and Treatment of Children* found that most zero tolerance–related suspensions weren't related to weapons or drugs, but to relatively minor offenses.[67]

Part of the problem stems from a very literal interpretation of rules with little or no examination of context. We have come to a point of so much fear that we often lose our sense of perspective. Some schools have banned cops and robbers games during recess; another school suspended an eleven-year-old boy for bringing a water gun to school, and elsewhere an eight-year-old boy was suspended for making a paper gun and saying, "I'm going to kill you all."[68] The eight-year-old was formally charged with making a terrorist threat, which a superior court judge later dismissed. Other examples of this lack of perspective or context abound:

- A Seattle high-school student was expelled for carrying a miniature Swiss army knife to a football game. His family appealed and the expulsion was overturned, but he then had a "weapons and explosives" violation on his record.[69]
- A Madison, Wisconsin, third grader was suspended for bringing a glittery manicure kit to school because it contained a sharp object.[70]
- A student was suspended in Kansas for drawing a picture of a Confederate flag. As a result, his parents' legally owned gun was confiscated.[71]
- Students were expelled from a Florida school for compiling a list of people they disliked; the list contained no threats against any of those mentioned.[72]

Zero-tolerance policies also ignore the importance of intent. Certainly, bringing a loaded gun to school, regardless of intent, is a serious problem. But most zero-tolerance suspensions haven't actually involved guns; instead they have targeted everyday devices that can be used as weapons, and even mere representations of weapons.

Knives can be dangerous weapons, but they are also part of our daily routines. Zero-tolerance rules don't always allow administrators to determine when a knife is a weapon or just something to cut food with. The case of sixth grader Christian Schmidt of Madison, Wisconsin, highlights this problem and raises serious concerns about rigidly applying a zero-tolerance policy. Christian, an A student who had never been in trouble before, brought a steak knife to school in March 2002 in order to slice an onion for a science-class experiment.[73] As a result, the principal recommended a one-year suspension in spite of the protests of Christian's science teacher. An independent hearing later overturned the initial decision, calling the punishment "overkill."[74] Christian was allowed to return to school after nearly a month-long absence. Following an appeal, the school stood by its original punishment and complained the decision to allow Christian back sent "the wrong message."[75]

Public reaction to this case was mixed, and reveals our ambivalence about how we should treat young people in schools. Several letters to the *Wisconsin State Journal* concurred with the final outcome, and one letter writer compared Christian's punishment to the Salem witch trials.[76] Other readers sided with the school's initial decision: "Don't we want our children to be safe?" a letter writer asked. The author also expressed anger that the school district paid for Christian's tutor so he wouldn't fall behind in school during his suspension.[77] Apparently this kind of perk should have been withheld from Christian as further punishment. Others declared that his status as an A student was irrelevant, that "common sense and fairness tell us that schools have little choice but to have tough policies on weapons in schools," and that "administrators must follow written rules."[78] For kids, the letter of the law must be followed, but imagine if adults lost their jobs for receiving one nonwork-related e-mail or for surfing the Internet during lunch on an office computer.

These letters reveal the complex nature of our feelings toward kids; even A students with no intent to harm must not be trusted, some argue, and any misstep, no matter how trivial or misunderstood, must be severely punished. After all, rules are rules. In a 2001 poll, 59 percent of American respondents said the number-one mission of education should be obedience.[79] This focus on conformity stems from our widespread fear of youth, which now extends beyond troublemakers with violent histories to all kids, as the Christian Schmidt case illustrates. The truth is, in many ways we have zero tolerance for kids, period. Strict punishments may make many adults feel better, but does zero tolerance really make schools any safer?

Education researcher John Holloway concluded that there is "no data to suggest that zero tolerance reduces school violence."[80] An NCES report found that schools *without* zero-tolerance policies tend to be safer than those employing strict automatic punishments.[81] This may be because schools with higher levels of violence are more inclined to feel rigid policies are necessary. But how zero tolerance has been applied is particularly telling. In many cities, expulsion rates have skyrocketed, mainly because minor offenses are now considered expellable violations.[82] A 1997 study reported that about 80 percent of those students disciplined were not considered real threats to school safety.[83]

Casting such a wide net has serious problems. The NCES study found that students with poor academic skills are more likely to receive harsh penalties, which may lead to less commitment to school and a greater likelihood of dropping out. According to the Applied Research Center, African-American and Latino students are suspended more often than their white counterparts.[84] Alienating more kids from school will not create a safer learning environment.

But for many teachers and administrators, zero tolerance "sends a message."[85] A Florida principal feared that "if kids didn't feel there were any consequences for drugs on school property . . . there would be more problems."[86] But there is a big difference between no consequences and rigid, one-size-fits-all reactions. A central problem lies in the definition of *drug* and *weapon*. How low are we going to place the bar? No aspirin? Nail files? Bread knives? Gil Noam, Harvard professor of education, told the *New York Times* that a "cookbook approach" to discipline can lead to a serious distrust of authority and represents a "lost moment to teach."[87] Education consultants Richard L. Curwin and Allen N. Mendler question whether we really want to teach "zero tolerance for others" and wonder if the policies actually send the behave-or-else message many assume they will.[88] Most centrally, an analysis published in the *Harvard Educational Review* noted that the real aim of zero tolerance is to "reassert the power of authority" rather than create an environment more amenable to learning.

And what of learning in this setting? Ironically, we are asking kids to learn about the American values of democracy and equality in highly authoritarian settings offering little or no due process. In other words, we want them to memorize the Bill of Rights for a test but refuse to let them have all of the same rights adults expect, supposedly "for their own good." That's why in February 2002 the American Bar Association opposed these one-size-fits-all policies that fail to take the context of a violation into account when assigning punishment. Attorney David J. Fish argued that "just because an offense is serious does not mean school authorities have a lesser duty to demand sufficient and reliable evidence that it occurred."[89]

Nevertheless, legal precedent has affirmed the right of schools to act in loco parentis (in place of the parent). That sometimes means less privacy and more intrusion. In June 2002, the U.S. Supreme Court ruled that it was constitutional for a school to impose random drug tests on students participating in extracurricular activities, and that it was not a violation of students' Fourth Amendment right to protection from unreasonable search and seizure.[90] Since extracurricular activities are optional, the majority argued, students could simply choose not to join the chess club or the choir if they didn't want to be tested. This decision followed a 1995 ruling, stating that student athletes could be subject to random drug testing because their high status in school culture meant that their drug involvement could have a strong impact on an entire student body. Both decisions ignore the real possibility that occasional drug users may actually become heavier users if they avoid more conventional school-related activities for fear of being tested.

Whether the Safe and Drug-Free Schools and Communties Act has made schools any safer is still unclear. No evaluation process was written into the legislation to see if it made any real impact on anything other than adult sentiments. This shouldn't be a big surprise. In truth, the passage of this bill and the resulting policies only serve adult needs to further restrict a generation characterized as out of control. Zero tolerance provides a clear course of action for administrators who can then wash their hands of difficult decisions and use the "just following orders" response when challenged. And skittish adults can feel that something is being done to both protect and control kids in scary-sounding schools.

More recently, the No Child Left Behind Act of 2001 contains a clause allowing students in "persistently dangerous schools" to transfer to another school. States were left to define "persistently dangerous" according to their own standards. For example, to receive this designation in California, a school needs to have had at least one student caught with a firearm in each of the past three years, and to have had at least 1 percent of its students expelled each year for hate crimes, extortion, sexual battery, or other acts of violence.[91] Florida guidelines are similar but add that the students, parents, and school staff must be surveyed, and a majority must agree that the school is dangerous.

A *USA Today*/Gannett News Service survey found that only 52 schools (out of about 92,000 nationwide) were designated as persistently dangerous in 2003.[92] Politicians decried the low number, which could tell us that schools are not nearly as dangerous as we are told. But it could also indicate that the legislation has now created political pressure to underreport violence when it does occur. A *New York Times* investigation of Houston schools found major discrepancies between school and police records for assault.[93] Held up as the "Texas miracle" and used as the impetus for the No Child Left Behind Act, the Houston district was also under fire for underreporting dropout rates.

When politics and education collide, politics usually wins. Even if some schools are dangerous, can all the nonviolent students really transfer out, and if so, where do we send them? The problem with our current approach to school safety is that it ignores the roots of the institutional problems with school systems, and the climate of violence in communities themselves.

THE REAL SCARY SCHOOLS

Of course some schools are scary. Underfunded and understaffed, these schools tend to be in the poorest communities and suffer from high dropout rates, low achievement, and public disdain. Washington Prep, a Los Angeles–area high school where teachers and administrators have observed drug use and sexual activity on campus, is one such example.[94] Parents of Washington Prep students are afraid for their kids, and for good reason: the school is plagued with gang activity; outsiders routinely jump the fence and enter school property; and the staff admits they often feel helpless to stop it. But this isn't just any school. This is a school in such an economically troubled community that the majority of its students qualify for subsidized meals. The homicide rate in this area is double the city's overall rate and more than five times higher than the national rate.[95] When schools are violent, it is usually because the communities around them are, and focusing only on the school will not solve the larger problem.

What should scare us about American public education is that more than fifty years after the landmark *Brown v. Board of Education* decision, which ruled that separate was not equal, our public schools are still very segregated and very unequal. According to the Children's Defense Fund, the wealthiest school districts in the nation spend 56 percent more per student on average than the poorest.[96] In a report on inequities of school funding, education researchers Bruce J. Biddle and David C. Berliner noted that the most affluent communities might spend as much as $15,000 per pupil while the poorest spends just over $4,000.[97] Teachers in poor communities are likely to have less training in their subject area and are often paid less than their counterparts in wealthier areas, even within the same district.[98]

Poor and minority students are also more likely to attend school in overcrowded, rundown buildings. According to the NCES, 15 percent of schools where minority enrollment is more than 50 percent are severely overcrowded (25 percent over capacity), which is double the national average and four times higher than schools where 95 percent of the students are white.[99] Similarly, in the poorest districts (defined as those where more than 70 percent of the students qualify for subsidized meals), schools are twice as likely to be overcrowded as in the wealthiest areas (where less than 20 percent qualify for subsidized meals).[100] In schools with a more than 50 percent minority enrollment, 59 percent had at least one building deemed in less than adequate condition, meaning it had serious problems with its foundation, floors, heating, ventilation, air conditioning, or electricity.[101] Sixty-three percent of the poorest districts had at least one building in need of significant repair.

Students who live in the poorest, most segregated neighborhoods of American cities are still the ones with the lowest-quality education. A 2001 ruling by the New York State Supreme Court found that the state had failed to meet its obligation to provide an equal education to all of its students, but funding was cut the next year anyway.[102] Budget cuts, mostly the effect of economic downturns, affect the poorest districts the most because it is often difficult for them to raise private funds. Many affluent districts, however, raise private funds in order to continue funding extracurricular activities and sometimes even teachers' salaries. Education critic Jonathan Kozol has argued that per-pupil spending in New York City schools was on par with suburban schools until about 1970, when 40 percent of the city's students were white.[103] More than three decades later that percentage has dropped to 14.5 percent white, and when the white students left the city, Kozol argues, so did the money.

THE PURPOSE OF THE SCARY-SCHOOL MYTH

In spite of the fact that most schools are actually very safe, why do we continually feed on the scary-school theme? When violence does take place in schools, the national news media tell us all about what happened with heightened immediacy, so it is understandable that we should react with shock and want to do whatever it takes to make sure that schools are safe. The thought of another Columbine-like shooting spree lingers in the back of our collective memory, and we react by clamping down and getting tough.

Beyond the school shooting tragedies lies an undercurrent of anxiety that these shootings heightened. If we didn't already feel concerned about sending our children to large institutions—run by adults who are often strangers to us, and filled with kids whose families we barely know—the incidents might not have hit such a nerve. In many ways, our anxiety about schools represents a growing sense of ambivalence about our communities, which we often fail to fully trust. School violence seems like evidence that these fears are not unfounded.

As counterintuitive as it may seem, we crave news that schools—and the kids themselves—are scarier than ever. Of course we don't want to think of our own kids as in danger or as threatening others, nor are we eager to see young people hurt. But the scary-school motif justifies what we think we already know: that the problems youths face are the result of too much leniency, especially by other parents, so schools need to impose stricter rules, tighter controls, and zero-tolerance policies.

Zero tolerance has little to do with actual trends in violence or drug use but instead is about massaging adult fears of young people. Rather than look to declines in public funding in states like California, where a 1978 change in property-tax laws drastically reduced public-schools' revenues, we prefer to think of the problem as the kids themselves, characterized as a lost generation in need of stricter controls and harsher punishment. Zero-tolerance policies serve to lower the bar and criminalize a generation rather than use its missteps to educate it about appropriate behavior.

The danger in overgeneralizing the scary-school problem is in failing to see the economic and organizational problems that create these untenable situations, where a vicious cycle of hopelessness, anger, and fear keeps students on edge and the most qualified teachers away. Some schools are scary, but this is not only the fault of out-of-control kids—many schools are often not equipped with adequate resources to handle the challenges they face. By focusing on schools as scary simply because of problem young people, we fail to assess the underlying causes of the real issues plaguing many schools: overcrowding, outdated materials, broken-down facilities, overwhelmed teachers, and decaying communities.

By refocusing the debate on a handful of troubled kids and by implying that even good kids are trouble now, we see policy makers as justified in short-changing young people as a whole. It's easy to see how a class of forty-five students is more difficult to keep focused than a class of twenty. The scary-school myth allows us to lay the problem at the feet of the students, without our looking at the educational system as a whole, and it encouraes us to focus on the threat of violence. Instead of facing the challenges of public education as an institutional problem, we let behavioral problems take center stage.

In California, the mid-1990s solution to overcrowded, underfunded schools was to throw kids out, either via expulsion or the politically popular (yet later deemed unconstitutional) Proposition 187, which would have made it illegal for children of undocumented immigrants to attend school. In this context, kids themselves are continually portrayed as the problem, be they foreign born, or non–English speaking, or defiant troublemakers who come to class armed, or "good" kids who suddenly turn "bad" so that the pressure is off policy makers to do much more than keep these kids in line. Expenditures for metal detectors and surveillance equipment then seem jus-tified at the expense of educational materials. And for the rest of us, the sense that these kids today are nothing like we were in the good old days is reaffirmed.

Fixing problems in public education is expensive under any circum-stances. In the early 1990s, echoes of a decade of tax cuts and the presence of a recession made funding public schools all the more challenging. The passage of safety-related legislation is far cheaper than bringing schools up-to-date, and it makes parents feel a little better. After all, if schools really are becoming war zones, what parent doesn't want safety to come first? Unfor-tunately, the scary-school myth has led to an environment that encourages more punitive policies and ultimately distracts us from providing equal ac-cess to a quality education for all students.

There is a real danger in framing schools as sites of violence, as threatened by the kids themselves rather than by policies that have failed to provide ad-equate facilities and learning opportunities. The panic during the 1990s about school violence has led to a reaction of zero tolerance, often leading to no result other than to make schools less flexible, and less welcoming to the young people we should be trying the hardest to reach. Our focus on scary schools draws on the existing discourse of a lost generation and trans-fers the blame for problems in public education from policy makers to undeserving, "out-of-control" kids. Ultimately, the scary-school myth exists to justify increased adult authority, control, and sometimes even violence against young people. We have the responsibility to refocus this debate away from the minor yet emotional problem of school violence and on the major challenge of providing a quality education for all young people. Those who do attend dangerous schools are robbed not only of a sense of security, but of an equal opportunity to succeed. And by our branding all schools as violent, those schools that are violent tend to fall by the wayside in public attention, especially if they are not in predominantly white suburbs.

For some kids, though, it is not just their schools but their peers who represent a threat to their emotional well-being. The next chapter explores bullying and hazing, and examines our belief that kids today are meaner than kids were in the past.

NOTES

1. Tatsha Robertson and Anand Vaishnav, "No Easy Answers as School Killings Increase," *Boston Globe*, January 3, 2004, A3.

2. Greg Toppo, "School Violence Hits Lower Grades," *USA Today*, January 13, 2003, 1A.

3. Greg Toppo, "Troubling Days at U.S. Schools," *USA Today*, October 21, 2003, 1D.

4. U.S. Department of Education, Table 3.1, "Percentage of Students Ages 12–18 Who Reported Criminal Victimization at School during the Previous 6 Months, by Type of Victimization and Selected Student Characteristics: Selected Years 1995–2003," in U.S. Department of Education, National Center for Education Statistics (NCES), *Indicators of School Crime and Safety* (Washington, D.C.: GPO, 2004). Serious violent crimes include rape, sexual assault, robbery, and aggravated assault.

5. Joe Williams and David Saltonstall, "Mike's School Mea Culpa," *Daily News* (New York), December 13, 2003, 5.

6. Williams and Saltonstall, "Mike's School Mea Culpa."

7. Williams and Saltonstall, "Mike's School Mea Culpa."

8. Williams and Saltonstall, "Mike's School Mea Culpa."

9. Williams and Saltonstall, "Mike's School Mea Culpa."

10. Joe Williams, "Worst Behavior," *Daily News* (New York), December 13, 2003, 5.

11. Williams, "Worst Behavior."

12. Rocco Parascandola and Bryan Virasami, "Can't Stop the Violence," *Newsday*, January 7, 2004, A6.

13. Nicole Bode and Veronika Belenkaya, "Cops Not the Rx for Violence: Pupils," *Daily News* (New York), January 7, 2004, 1.

14. Bode and Belenkaya, "Cops Not the Rx for Violence."

15. Kerry Burke, Jonathan Lemire, and Celeste Katz, "Asst. Principal Hurled Down Escalator," *Daily News* (New York), January 17, 2004, 3.

16. Elissa Gootman, "Police to Guard 12 City Schools Cited as Violent," *New York Times*, January 6, 2004, A1; Bill Kaufman, "BOCES Offers Help to Prevent School Attacks," *Newsday*, January 11, 2004, G16.

17. John M. Beam, "The Blackboard Jungle: Tamer Than You Think," *New York Times*, January 20, 2004, A19.

18. Major crimes include homicide, robbery, felony assault, burglary, grand larceny, and grand theft auto. Beam's figure adjusts the rate to account for the fact that the school day is shorter than twenty-four hours, upon which the city crime rate is based.

19. New York City Police Department School Safety Division, "School Location Incident Data for 2002–2003," New York City Department of Education, 2004, www.nycenet.edu/ourschools/SchoolSafety.htm (last accessed January 5, 2006).

20. Gootman, "Police to Guard 12 City Schools Cited as Violent."

21. Bryan Virasami, "Getting Tough on School Crime," *Newsday*, December 23, 2003, A15.

22. Gootman, "Police to Guard 12 City Schools Cited as Violent."

23. Williams and Saltonstall, "Mike's School Mea Culpa."

24. Gootman, "Police to Guard 12 City Schools Cited as Violent"; Bode and Belenkaya, "Cops Not the Rx for Violence."

25. New York City Police Department School Safety Division, "School Location Incident Data."

26. Gootman, "Police to Guard 12 City Schools Cited as Violent."

27. Parascandola and Bryan Virasami, "Can't Stop the Violence."

28. Elissa Gootman, "Six Students Arrested in City Crackdown on Violent Schools," *New York Times*, January 7, 2004, B3.

29. Parascandola and Virasami, "Can't Stop the Violence."

30. Parascandola and Virasami, "Can't Stop the Violence."

31. Gootman, "Six Students Arrested in City Crackdown."

32. Scott Shifrel, "City's Picking on My Boys in HS Row: Dad," *Daily News* (New York), January 8, 2004, 4; Elizabeth Hays, "Mom: Teen Ill-Used in Crackdown," *Daily News* (New York), January 16, 2004, 3.

33. Bode and Belenkaya, "Cops Not the Rx for Violence."

34. Gootman, "Six Students Arrested in City Crackdown."

35. Bode and Belenkaya, "Cops Not the Rx for Violence"; Ellen Yan, "Cops in the Corridors," *Newsday*, February 3, 2004, A3.

36. David M. Herszenhorn, "School Safety Plan at Issue," *New York Times*, January 8, 2004, B3.

37. John M. Beam, "The Blackboard Jungle."

38. Letter, "Curbing Violence in City Schools," *New York Times*, January 7, 2004, A20.

39. Wil Cruz and Ellen Yan, "City Violence," *Newsday*, March 25, 2004, A18.

40. David Nasaw, *Schooled to Order: A Social History of Public Schooling in the United States* (New York: Oxford University Press, 1979), 241–42.

41. U.S. Department of Education, National Center for Education Statistics, *Indicators of School Crime and Safety* (2004), 6–7.

42. U.S. Department of Education, National Center for Education Statistics, *Indicators of School Crime and Safety* (2004).

43. U.S. Department of Education, National Center for Education Statistics, *Indicators of School Crime and Safety* (Washington, D.C.: GPO, 1999).

44. Tom Morganthau et al., "It's Not Just New York," *Newsweek*, March 9, 1992, 25.

45. Federal Bureau of Investigation, *Uniform Crime Reports for the United States, 1964–1999* (Washington, D.C.: U.S. Department of Justice, 2000).

46. Dennis Cauchon, "They Learn History and Science and How to Cope with Guns," *USA Today*, October 29, 1993, 6A.

47. U.S. Department of Justice, Bureau of Justice Statistics, "Rate of Nonfatal Crimes against Students Ages 12–18 per 1,000 Students," *National Crime Victimization Survey, 1992–2001* (Washington, D.C.: GPO, 2004).

48. Mark Anderson et al., "School-Associated Violent Deaths in the United States, 1994–1999," *Journal of the American Medical Association* 286 (2001): 2695–2702.

49. Centers for Disease Control and Prevention, National Center for Health Statistics, National Vital Statistics Program, "Child Mortality: Death Rates for Children Ages 5 to 14 by Gender, Race, Hispanic Origin, and Cause of Death, Selected Years 1980–2000," http://childstats.gov (last accessed January 5, 2006). Fifteen and older grouped with young adults.

50. Mike Males, *Kids and Guns* (Monroe, Maine: Common Courage Press, 2004), chap. 3, p. 12.

51. Monitoring the Future Study, "Long-Term Trends in Lifetime Prevalence of Use of Various Drugs for Twelfth Graders" (Survey Research Center, University of Michigan, Ann Arbor, 2004).

52. Monitoring the Future Study, "Percentage of Twelfth Graders Who Reported that Someone Had Injured Them at School in the Last Twelve Months, By Sex: 1976–1996" (Survey Research Center, University of Michigan, Ann Arbor, 2004).

53. Russell J. Skiba and Reece L. Peterson, "The Dark Side of Zero Tolerance: Can Punishment Lead to Safe Schools?" *Phi Delta Kappan* 80 (1999): 373.

54. U.S. Department of Education, National Center for Education Statistics, *Indicators of School Crime and Safety* (Washington, D.C.: GPO, 2001), 27.

55. U.S. Department of Education, National Center for Education Statistics, *Indicators of School Crime and Safety* (2001), 36–40.

56. U.S. Department of Education, National Center for Education Statistics, *Indicators of School Crime and Safety* (2001), 3.

57. U.S. Department of Education, National Center for Education Statistics, *Indicators of School Crime and Safety* (2001), viii, 16.

58. U.S. Department of Education, National Center for Education Statistics, *Indicators of School Crime and Safety* (2001), viii.

59. U.S. Department of Education, National Center for Education Statistics, *Indicators of School Crime and Safety* (2001), ix.

60. U.S. Department of Education, National Center for Education Statistics, *Indicators of School Crime and Safety* (2001), 13.

61. U.S. Department of Education, National Center for Education Statistics, *Indicators of School Crime and Safety* (2001), 23–24.

62. Irwin A. Hyman, *Reading, Writing, and the Hickory Stick: The Appalling Story of Physical and Psychological Abuse in American Schools* (Lexington, Mass.: Lexington Books, 1990), 52.

63. Julie Crandall, "Support for Spanking," *ABC News*, November 8, 2002.

64. Hyman, *Reading, Writing, and the Hickory Stick*, 21.

65. John H. Halloway, "The Dilemma of Zero Tolerance," *Educational Leadership* 59 (2001): 85.

66. "Laws That Bludgeon: Zero Tolerance Doesn't Mean Zero Discretion," *Columbus Dispatch*, March 27, 2002, 14A; Abdon M. Pallasch, "Boy Wins against School's 'Zero Tolerance,'" *Chicago Sun–Times*, June 24, 2002, 16; Associated Press State and Local Wire, "Eighth-Grade Girl Suspended for Throwing Potato Chip," May 16, 2002.

67. Russell J. Skiba, Reece L. Peterson, and Tara Williams, "Office Referrals and Suspension: Disciplinary Intervention in Middle Schools," *Education and Treatment of Children* 20 (1997): 316–35.

68. Tom Kelly, "Teachers Ban Playground Cops-and-Robbers Games," Press Association, March 29, 2002; Rebekah Denn, "Youth's Expulsion over Key Chain Knife Sparks School Battle," *Seattle Post–Intelligencer*, May 18, 2002, A1; Associated Press State and Local Wire, "Irvington Sued over Arrest of Schoolboys Playing with Paper Gun," March 21, 2002.

69. Denn, "Youth's Expulsion over Key Chain Knife."

70. Doug Erickson, "Girl Suspended for Glittery Weapon," *Wisconsin State Journal*, April 19, 2002, B1.

71. John Derbyshire, "The Problem with 'Zero,'" *National Review*, May 28, 2001, 46–48.

72. Mark Schone, "The Way We Live Now: Putting on Kid Gloves," *New York Times*, March 25, 2001, 30.

73. Doug Erickson, "Don't Expel Boy, Examiner Says," *Wisconsin State Journal*, April 9, 2002, A1.

74. Erickson, "Don't Expel Boy, Examiner Says."

75. Erickson, "Don't Expel Boy, Examiner Says."

76. "Schmidt Case a Vivid Example of Why Zero-Tolerance Is Wrong," *Wisconsin State Journal*, April 19, 2002, A8.

77. "Schmidt Case a Vivid Example," *Wisconsin State Journal*.

78. "Schmidt Case a Vivid Example," *Wisconsin State Journal*.

79. Roy Morgan Research, July 10, 2001.

80. Halloway, "The Dilemma of Zero Tolerance."

81. Cited in Skiba and Peterson, "The Dark Side of Zero Tolerance," 372–76.

82. Schone, "The Way We Live Now," 30.

83. Halloway, "The Dilemma of Zero Tolerance."

84. Rebecca Gordon, Libero Della Piana, and Terry Keleher, "Zero Tolerance: A Basic Racial Report Card," in *Zero Tolerance: Resisting the Drive for Punishment in Our Schools*, ed. William Ayers, Bernardine Dohrn, and Rick Ayers (New York: New Press, 2001), 165–75.

85. Michael Samuels, "School Districts Tighten Zero-Tolerance Policies," *Port St. Lucie News*, June 9, 2002, A1.

86. Samuels, "School Districts Tighten Zero-Tolerance Policies."

87. Dirk Johnson, "Schools' New Watchword: Zero Tolerance," *New York Times*, December 1, 1999, A1.

88. Richard L. Curwin and Allen N. Mendler, "Zero Tolerance for Zero Tolerance," *Phi Delta Kappan* 81 (1999): 119–20.

89. David J. Fish, "United States: Zero-Tolerance Discipline in Illinois Public Schools," *Business and Management Practices* (May 17, 2002).

90. See Dahlia Lithwick, "Urine Trouble: Uncle Sam Wants *You* to Pee in a Cup," *Slate* (March 19, 2002).

91. Duke Helfand, "School Danger Narrowly Defined," *Los Angeles Times*, July 8, 2003, B1.

92. Greg Toppo, "States Label Fewer Schools Dangerous," *USA Today*, October 22, 2003, 5A.

93. Sam Dillon, "School Violence Data under a Cloud in Houston," *New York Times*, November 7, 2003, A1.

94. Joe Mathews, Erika Hayasaki, and Duke Helfand, "L.A. School Described as 'Out of Control,'" *Los Angeles Times*, November 21, 2002, A1.

95. Data from the Los Angeles County Sheriff's Department, "Crime and Arrest Statistics, 2002," (www.lasd.org). City statistics obtained through the Los Angeles Police Department's website (www.lapdonline.org). National homicide rates from Federal Bureau of Investigation, *Uniform Crime Reports for the United States, 2002* (Washington, D.C.: U.S. Department of Justice, 2003).

96. Children's Defense Fund, "Key Facts about Education," Washington, D.C., 2003.

97. Bruce J. Biddle and David C. Berliner, "What Research Says about Unequal Funding for Schools in America," *Policy Perspectives* (2003).

98. Children's Defense Fund, "Key Facts about Education." Jonathan Kozol, "Malign Neglect: Children in New York City Schools Are Being Shortchanged—Again," *The Nation*, June 10, 2002.

99. U.S. Department of Education, National Center for Education Statistics, Fast Response Survey System, "Survey of the Conditions of Public School Facilities, 1999."

100. U.S. Department of Education, National Center for Education Statistics, "Survey of the Conditions of Public School Facilities."

101. U.S. Department of Education, National Center for Education Statistics, "Survey of the Conditions of Public School Facilities."

102. Kozol, "Malign Neglect."

103. Kozol, "Malign Neglect."

4

Hazed and Confused

Mean Kids

Young children, we often observe, can be brutally honest at times, and preteens and adolescents are often accused of a more complex dynamic of social exclusion and cruelty. Yes, kids can be mean to each other. In recent years there has been growing attention to bullying and hazing in schools, particularly when it leads to violence or when girls are involved. In a May 2004 Public Agenda poll, 55 percent of teachers and 46 percent of parents agreed that bullying and harassment are very or somewhat serious problems.[1] Teachers in high-poverty schools were most concerned about bullying and harassment, and 65 percent said the problem is very or somewhat serious. Thirty-eight percent of twelve- to seventeen-year-olds polled in 2001 reported that they observe bullying incidents at least once a day.[2]

But what exactly is bullying? A 2001 study conducted by the National Institute of Child Health and Human Development defined bullying as:

> A specific type of aggression in which (1) the behavior is intended to harm or disturb, (2) the behavior occurs repeatedly over time, and (3) there is an imbalance of power, with a more powerful person or group attacking a less powerful one. This asymmetry of power may be physical or psychological, and the aggressive behavior may be verbal (e.g., name-calling, threats), physical (e.g., hitting), or psychological (e.g., rumors, shunning/exclusion).[3]

Notice that this definition is incredibly broad, and can serve as a catchall definition for all sorts of behaviors.[4] Being picked on by people who are bigger, perhaps older, and who have more social power is likely something that we have all experienced at one point, and frankly it's probably something that we have done to others (especially if we have younger siblings). Applying a broad definition such as this gets our attention and might help us think the problem is larger, but it masks a serious ambiguity: it groups the people for whom bullying is an annoyance with those whose physical safety or emotional stability is constantly threatened. Threats to self-esteem are important, but by lumping all mean behaviors together, this definition makes it difficult to assess the seriousness of the issue.

It's also not possible to know for sure if kids are really any meaner to each other now than in the distant past, as information on bullying has not been collected for very long. We do know that there have been long-term declines in youth violence both inside and away from school, but violence is just one outcome of peer rejection. According to the 2004 U.S. Department of Education's *Indicators of Crime and School Safety*, 7 percent of twelve- to eighteen-year-olds reported being "picked on or made to do things they did not want to do" in 2003.[5] Again, note the broad nature of this definition. Yet this number is down slightly from 2001, when 8 percent said that they were harassed in school. In 1999, 5 percent reported that they had been picked on.

Still, the perception remains that there is a problem and it is getting worse. A May 2004 *USA Today* article described the 1999 to 2001 shift from 5 to 8 percent as "a real and growing trend" and also noted "how cruel pre-teen and teenage girls can be."[6] Yet Department of Education statistics indicate that in 2003, girls were slightly *less* likely to report being harassed than boys were (7 percent for girls versus 8 percent for boys).[7] A National Crime Prevention Council survey also found this discrepancy. While 44 percent of boys age twelve to seventeen reported witnessing bullying at least once a day, only 32 percent of girls did.[8]

Hazing, a concept that fits in with the broad definition of bullying mentioned above, has also become a hot topic in the news, especially if someone is injured or files a lawsuit as a result of the hazing. Hazing typically involves rituals that entrants into exclusive groups must endure to become full members. Stories of fraternity and sorority rites gone awry in Louisiana, Missouri, and Texas have made the news in recent years.[9] A *Sports Illustrated for Kids* article claimed that "hazing has become a serious problem in college, high school, and even grade school sports." The grade school claim was based on conversations with six kids.[10] Note that by using the phrase "has become" the article implies that this is a new phenomenon. An April *USA Today* story acknowledged that "no studies exist that measure how widespread hazing was in the '60s and '70s," but then went on to say, "experts agree it *seems* to be on the rise" (emphasis mine).[11]

While we do know that hazing and bullying have existed for generations, there is no solid evidence indicating that they are really any worse today than in the past. Because both are often hidden from outsiders, it is impossible to quantify how much bullying or hazing actually occurs. Author Hank Nuwer points out that hazing in the United States is centuries old: concerns about hazing at Harvard date back to 1657, and in 1874 the president of the University of Michigan sent letters home to parents about the problem.[12] In 1900, a U.S. House Committee investigated reports of serious hazing at West Point.

Nonetheless, the past is often glorified. In his discussion of a highly publicized hazing incident, CNN anchor Bill Hemmer described school days of the past as "the long lost golden days."[13] An article in *Pediatric Nursing*, "Bullying: It Isn't What It Used To Be," implied that today's kids are now crueler to each other than ever.[14] The *Alberta Report*, a Canadian publication, went one step further with an article called "Teasing Can Be Fatal."[15] While the issue is clearly real, ongoing, and worthy of public attention, characterizing *all* kids as mean and uniquely cruel is a problematic conclusion. This is not to say that we should ignore even minor instances of harassment, which parents and some school districts are starting to take more seriously.

What has changed is that kids now have many more public forums in which to speak out about their experiences. Daytime talk shows like *Oprah* provide a platform for victims of bullying and hazing to tell their stories. Technology can sometimes capture the incidents on videotape, and satellites are capable of beaming a video of a hazing or brutal schoolyard beating around the nation or the world almost instantly to any of a number of the many cable-television channels constantly looking for news. This, coupled with the confessional nature of many talk shows, creates greater awareness of what goes on among kids. Bullying is characterized in these reports and in many books as a problem unique to childhood, something that adults need to know about so they can step in to protect their children from the twisted few (or many) children who choose to torment their peers. And we were primed to hear more about these stories following the high-profile school shootings of the 1990s, which were often attributed to bullying or social exclusion. We're listening now because we fear the consequences of not doing so may be fatal.

DO KIDS LIVE IN HIDDEN WORLDS?

Several books about young people's peer cultures describe them as existing within *hidden worlds*. James Garbarino and Ellen deLara describe "the secret school life of adolescents" in *And Words Can Hurt Forever: How to Protect Adolescents from Bullying, Harassment, and Emotional Violence*. Other books, like *The Secret Lives of Girls: What Good Girls Really Do—Sex Play, Aggression, and Their Guilt* by Sharon Lamb, and *Odd Girl Out: The Hidden Culture of Aggression in Girls*, suggest that parents are not a part of these worlds. The implication of the secret-, separate-, hidden-world theme is that parents and other adults have no way of knowing what it's really like to be a kid (unless they buy a book). Even so, several books within this genre

suggest that adults, if they try hard enough, can actually control the social interactions of teens.

But rarely do we explore exactly if or why these worlds are hidden in the
first place. For one, young people begin to pull away from their families and
to develop a sense of autonomy as early as preschool and kindergarten,
when they first have daily experiences away from their families, and this
process is amplified in adolescence. Developing a self in the outside world,
separate from the family, is a normal and healthy part of maturation.

Second, these worlds often involve few adults due to our current economic
structure, where young people are not needed in the labor force and spend
most of their time separated from adults. As I have noted, young people are
highly segregated by age now compared with a century ago. Previously, children attended school for shorter periods of time; until the 1930s, only a minority attended, let alone graduated from high school. The Great Depression
reduced the labor force tremendously; however, as adults took over jobs that
teens previously had held, and teens entered high school in larger and larger
numbers. This economic shift is perhaps most responsible for creating the
hidden world we now take for granted in childhood and adolescence.

As we have seen, in the past young people had far more responsibility for
maintaining the family household or earning wages outside the home. So it
is only relatively recently that children and teens have had so much time
alone with mostly other kids. The ratio of adults to children in daily life has
also gradually dwindled. Before the 1920s, when most Americans lived in rural areas, children likely attended school for only a few months out of the
year and were less segregated by age while in school. Because a great deal
of their lives were likely spent working on the family farm or contributing to
a pre-automation household, young people spent more time intermingling
with adults and children of different ages.

The great wave of immigration during the late nineteenth and early twentieth centuries swelled urban schools' enrollments, and led to the creation of
a more age-based organization of schools. School enrollments climbed
throughout the twentieth century, as an increasingly automated economy
made young people's labor in the workforce nearly obsolete. This change
was cemented by the economic prosperity after World War II. The baby
boom also increased the number of children, leading to the creation of a very
distinct youth culture and youth market. While a separate youth culture also
became evident in the 1920s, by the 1950s more young people than ever
were in school for a longer period of time, and largely sequestered from
adults most of the day.

Today, children vastly outnumber the adults present in most of their social
experiences, even in those experiences ostensibly controlled by adults, like
day care, school, and adult-run leisure activities. Because children exist in
virtual social isolation from adults, their hidden worlds flourish with little

adult awareness or capacity for intervention on a grand scale. The hidden-world genre offers many suggestions for parent or teacher intervention, but the basic fact remains that on a social level, peer culture carries so much weight because of the way American social life is now organized.

Ironically, adults have worked to maintain the exile of kids from the adult world. We are encouraged to keep adult information away from children for as long as possible. Often children's recreation functions to keep kids busy so parents can continue their own activities. As I noted in chapter 3, compulsory education was itself founded in part to keep kids out of adults' way.

But there is a danger in focusing too much on the idea that young people live in a different world, one that we deride as different from the real world. While young people are more socially isolated from adults than ever before, their lives still exist within the same larger economic and political contexts as adults' lives, and their experiences are certainly no less valid or real than adults. Further, if we characterize young people's lives as completely separate, we fail to see how kids are part of the broader social context, as well as how their behavior is related to similar adult behaviors.

Adults are largely responsible for creating these hidden worlds that they are told to fear, invade, and change. For those of us who attended school well after the postwar era, these are worlds with which we ourselves were once intimately familiar, sometimes miss, but are also sometimes glad to have escaped. It's too simple to say that the mean kids in young people's social worlds have always been there and always will. But it's also naive to think that parents' interventions or new school rules will drastically change small group interactions. The hidden world phenomenon is one created by economic and social changes that we need to address directly if we want to understand how young people interact within them.

When we view the younger generation as meaner than kids of the past, our solution tends to be to demonize all kids and the peer groups they belong to, rather than to examine the contexts in which bullying and hazing take place. Erika Karres, author of *Violence Proof Your Kids Now*, claimed in a *USA Today* article that "when kids get together, whatever the most negatively creative thought one of them has, it will be the common denominator."[16]

In large part these age-old issues have grabbed our attention because we are afraid that both perpetrators and victims of bullying or hazing could become a threat to all of us—we fear them as much if not more than we feel sympathy for them. In this chapter, I consider the social context of bullying and hazing, and how economic and social realities of American life lay the groundwork for both to occur. Concerns about bullying and hazing are also rife with assumptions about and contradictions of gender and sexuality, which are seldom addressed in the attention-grabbing news stories. In addition, I explore how bullying and hazing are covered in the press, and how this coverage serves to demonize not just the perpetrators, but all kids.

MEAN GIRLS?

The stereotype of the conniving, cat-fighting, competitive female is revived frequently in the press and popular culture. Rumors of female costars who seethe at another's success are a tabloid staple. The mean girl is a teen movie villain: one-dimensional, beautiful, popular, and all-powerful. She lays waste to all those in her path only to get her much-deserved comeuppance and humiliation at the end. This caricature furthers the idea that girls are uniquely mean, especially if they are beautiful and powerful.

Yes, girls can be both overtly and covertly mean at times. But the mythology of the mean girl who torments her victim relentlessly until she herself is emotionally destroyed encourages us to ignore why a girl may abuse what power she has. This abuse of power is linked to broader systems of gender and inequality, and is not simply created by each new generation. When girls grow up receiving messages that being female is inferior (by hearing, for instance, California Governor Arnold Schwarzenegger's insult that the state legislature is full of "girlie men"), they strike out against each other in the ultimate act of self-loathing.

For example, in 2003 an off-campus "powder puff" football game with Glenbrook North High School students got out of hand in a suburb of Chicago. The game had been a twenty-year-old tradition between female juniors and seniors. Junior girls expected to be smeared with paint and mustard by the senior girls, but not with excrement and pig intestines as they were.[17] They also did not expect to be choked and beaten, or forced to put paint thinner and raw meat in their mouths. The hazing incident was recorded on video and circulated on cable news talk-shows for several weeks. The incident led to stitches, a broken ankle, and the suspension of twenty-eight students; fifteen students were later charged with misdemeanor battery.[18] Perhaps most significantly, this incident put hazing and mean kids in the headlines—when it's caught on tape, hazing makes for dramatic news-magazine footage.

CNN anchor Kyra Phillips described this incident as a "case of girls behaving badly."[19] Both television and press coverage repeatedly highlighted that the primary participants were girls—the words *girls* or *females* were used over and over again in both print and television. This incident also highlighted contradictions in femininity. By referring to the girls' football game as "powder puff," we have an expectation that the game will be gentle and nonviolent, though football, a traditionally male sport, is anything but gentle. And by highlighting that it was girls who committed these brutal acts of violence, the media framed the girls' assaults as not just violations against other students, but as violations against femininity itself. Punishment for participation in this incident involved being barred from graduation ceremonies and from the prom, a highlight of American teen girlhood.

An in-depth *Chicago Sun–Times* story that explored this and other female hazing incidents claimed that this incident was "par for the course" in many organizations with young women.[20] "There are many things college girls will do for attention," the author stated, using the participants in *Girls Gone Wild* videos and the television program MTV Spring Break as prototypes for young women today. "We were just mean," a sorority participant confessed to the author, explaining that degrading ceremonial rituals are part of a long tradition of initiation that everyone involved has to go through. The only mention of fraternities and male organizations came toward the end of the 2,000-plus word article, but only to detail how sorority sisters compete over the best-looking guys from high-status fraternities. Male hazing—arguably far more common—was not mentioned at all, and the implication in this story is that girls are uniquely cruel.

However, juvenile-crime indicators all point in the opposite direction. Girls today are still very unlikely to be involved in fights or to be arrested. Sociologist Mike Males notes that "the claims [of a new female problem] inevitably rely on adult commentators' selected anecdotes, generalizations from troubled girls in treatment, sanitized memories of a tranquil past and omission of contradictory information."[21]

While shocking examples of school shootings have drawn attention to bullying and violence, recent books like *Odd Girl Out: The Hidden Culture of Aggression in Girls*, and *Queen Bees and Wannabes: Helping Your Daughter Survive Cliques, Gossip, Boyfriends, and Other Realities of Adolescence*, have drawn attention to mean girls. Both address how girls may not use violence or any direct means of confrontation, but may instead resort to more covert tactics like exclusion, rumors, and gossip to display anger and aggression. Rachel Simmons, author of *Odd Girl Out*, suggests a cultural link to girls' behavior, which she says "all but refuse[s] girls open acts of conflict," particularly for white, middle-class girls, taught to be nice above all else.[22]

Journalist Leora Tanenbaum, author of *Slut! Growing Up Female with a Bad Reputation*, describes how this phenomenon is about more than just mean kids. She argues that demonizing other girls as "sluts" enables the "non-sluts" to gain status within the boundaries of conventional femininity. Recognizing that being female is still often devalued within American culture, Tanenbaum connects the sexual double standard to broader gender inequality. So rather than simply a pastime of mean kids, the "slut" label carries on an old tradition, practiced by people of all ages, of setting aside some girls and women as tarnished because of their sexual behavior (or rumored behavior) to preserve the myth of female purity. "Teenagers take sexual cues from the adults around them," Tanenbaum notes, observing that when adults are concerned about teens and sex, the focus is almost exclusively placed on girls.[23]

While discussions of the phenomenon of mean girls have drawn a great deal of public attention (especially after the 2004 release of a movie by the

same name), one form of bullying that is frequently overlooked is sexual harassment. A nationally representative survey conducted in 1992 by the American Association of University Women (AAUW) found that 85 percent of
eighth- to eleventh-grade girls in public schools—and 76 percent of boys—
reported that they have experienced sexual harassment.[24] A key difference is
that far more girls than boys (30 percent versus 8 percent) reported feeling
frightened from the harassment, and girls were more likely to experience declines in self-esteem (43 percent versus 14 percent).

While sexual harassment in school is clearly not a new problem, it is a
serious issue that schools are now legally bound to address. In 1999, the
U.S. Supreme Court ruled that schools could be sued for not stopping sexual harassment if they were aware of an ongoing incident and were "de-
liberately indifferent," meaning that once told of a problem the school did
nothing to try to stop it.[25] Just as in the workplace, schools are required to
provide safe learning environments for students under Title IX legislation
of 1972, which prohibits discrimination in schools that get federal funding.
In one of the first cases filed after this ruling, a thirteen-year-old girl who
was repeatedly groped and harassed by a classmate sued her district in the
Seattle area after the school's vice principal said the school could not guarantee her safety and suggested that she transfer to another district.[26] Students in Northern California sued their district after enduring years of
threats and antigay taunts, alleging that the school was not doing enough
to discipline the offending students.[27] Another district settled with students who had been sexually harassed by a teacher, harassment the students claimed the district did nothing to stop.[28] A 2001 AAUW study found
that 7 percent of students reported being sexually harassed by a teacher,
a type of harassment that can be more threatening and intimidating than
harassment by peers, who may focus on name calling and exclusion rather
than sexual advances.[29]

However, rather than exhibit the same concern as in the Glenbrook North
hazing incident, media reports have often made light of sexual harassment
among children and adolescents. Articles with titles like "Kissing and Correctness," "A Kiss Isn't Just a Kiss," and "Sex and Drugs and Nutty Schools"
ask us to question the need for sexual harassment policies in schools by focusing on cases involving extremely young children, cases that were likely
misunderstandings about appropriate behavior rather than serious incidents
of harassment.[30] However, the AAUW study found that 32 percent of the students who reported being harassed said the first incident happened before
the sixth grade, which points to the need for early intervention, although not
necessarily lawsuits. Still, it is telling to note that widespread sexual harassment in school rarely makes headlines the way stories of mean girls have in
recent years.

BOYS WILL BE BOYS?

While girls' experiences of sexual harassment have been getting more attention, it remains an almost unspeakable topic when boys are victims. Boys'
experiences of sexual harassment often differ from those of girls. While girls
sometimes harass boys, frequently it is other boys who use homophobic
slurs to demean one another. Challenging another boy's heterosexuality is a
direct attempt to reduce his status.

During the summer of 2003, just months after the Glenbrook North powder puff incident made news, reports of another shocking hazing incident
grabbed national attention. While at a Pennsylvania football camp, three
Mepham High School students from Long Island, New York, were accused
of sodomizing three freshman teammates with a broomstick, pinecones, and
golf balls.[31] The accusations were widely covered in New York–area newspapers, in *Sports Illustrated* and *People* magazines, and on *The O'Reilly Factor*, CBS and NBC news, MSNBC, and ABC's *20/20*.

Press coverage focused heavily on the responsibility of the coaches and
the school. Apparently, one of the alleged perpetrators had a history of violence, and parents of another student had warned the principal of this alleged perpetrator's threats against their son. The boy in question was also
given a warning before camp, according to reports. Ultimately two of the
coaches, who held tenured teaching jobs, were reassigned to nonteaching
positions, and the football season was canceled. Although the assaults apparently happened in the boys' cabins, where the coaches were barred by
law from sleeping, the implication was that the coaches were partly responsible because "boys will be boys" without adult intervention. But in contrast
to the Glenbrook North stories, which reminded us constantly that girls were
the main participants, the Mepham articles described the boys in gender-
neutral terms as *players, students,* and *teammates.*

The Mepham High School hazing incident, which many papers clearly identified as sexual assault, led to referral for the accused to a Pennsylvania juvenile court. However, the press coverage largely failed to explore how the perpetrators' behavior was more than just a physical violation, but that the young
boys' humiliation was based on sexual emasculation. This is a common experience in male-oriented hazing. For an example, we need look no further than
one of the most storied franchises in all of sports to see how it chose to hu-
miliate its newest members: in 2003, *Sports Illustrated* reported that New York
Yankee rookies were forced to wear women's clothes in public.[32]

Just as femininity is often denigrated in all-male settings, there are homophobic connotations to the hazing incidents that some boys have endured.
When one of the Mepham victims returned to school in the fall, students who
weren't even at football camp derided him as "broomstick boy."[33] *Sports*

Illustrated reported that a junior player had "placed a banana near his crotch and forced one of the players to simulate oral sex with the banana."[34] A *People* magazine story detailed a Pittsburgh Central Catholic High School student who was held down "while another rubbed his genitals in his face."[35]

Other sexual acts of hazing made the news that year as well. A Plattsmouth, Nebraska, high-school football player was charged with sexual assault in an incident that occurred in the locker room after practice. The school's superintendent insisted that this was a bullying incident and "not sexual in nature," although the seventeen-year-old was charged with "sexual penetration without consent."[36] And at the esteemed Groton School in Connecticut, prosecutors charged that "ritual sexual hazing" had been taking place in boys' dorms for years.[37]

One common denominator between the Glenbrook North and Mepham incidents that went almost completely ignored in the press coverage was football itself. While both events were extreme and do not represent what happens in most young people's experiences of participating in athletics, it is not incidental that football is a quintessential American pastime that sanctions a certain degree of brutality. Being tough and playing with pain are both central to football, even at its lowest levels. It should come as no surprise that these values occasionally become distorted and lead to violence off the field.

The two incidents also had another similarity: parents who either enabled the behavior by supplying alcohol or by allowing their kids to maintain a "locker-room code of silence" after the football camp.[38] Guests on both *The O'Reilly Factor* and National Public Radio (NPR) interviews talked about how no one wants to be a "rat."[39] Some parents hampered both investigations by failing to cooperate with law enforcement. Rather than simply cases of out-of-control kids, both incidents reveal a prevalent attitude within middle-class, upwardly mobile communities to protect their own, even from responsibility, if not doing so means jeopardizing their kids' happiness or opportunities. At Glenbrook North, one powder puff participant's family hired an attorney who filed a preemptive lawsuit against the school to try to prevent the district from taking any disciplinary action against the participant. At Mepham, some parents angrily blamed the victims' families for the cancellation of the football season and for "overreacting." One man who spoke out against the brutal incident received death threats.[40] When parents enable such behavior, the problem is clearly bigger than kids today. To understand the roots of both incidents, we need to look beyond the "kids these days" argument that boys will be boys or girls can be mean. Instead, we must realize that young people's behavior takes place in a cultural context of violence and continual negotiation of the boundaries between both gender and sexuality. And parents can be part of the problem rather than the solution.

ADULT BULLYING AND HAZING

There are a number of parenting books for sale that attempt to get adults to help kids navigate these rites of passage, providing tips on what to say and what not to say to their child, their child's teachers, or other parents. How-to parenting books commonly make suggestions to schools about what sort of anti-bullying or anti-hazing policies they ought to employ and enforce. Yet rarely is adult behavior examined to consider why, leaving aside children's immaturity or adults' ignorance and indifference, these power struggles occur.

When we look at bullying and hazing as only a child's problem, we ignore the fact that similar dynamics occur in many adult social settings as well. Just as students do in high school, adults are prone to define their status rather superficially, commonly using their income, the clothes they wear, or the cars they drive. This is not to say that bullying and hazing for young people are completely identical to adult experiences, but we need to look beyond simply blaming mean kids and examine the broader picture to understand other facets of social life where bullying and hazing are common.

For instance, domineering parents may have little power in the outside world but may abuse the power they do have within their family, using verbal and physical force to control and intimidate. And office politics can be equally as petty and vicious as school bullying. While a great deal of research has been conducted in Australia and Europe on workplace bullying, only a few studies have been conducted in the United States on this issue, and it has received next to no press coverage compared to school bullying. The National Institute for Occupational Safety and Health defines workplace bullying as "repeated intimidation, slandering, social isolation, or humiliation by one or more persons against another."[41] The institute's initial study found that nearly 25 percent of companies surveyed had documented cases of bullying and intimidation within the past twelve months. Workers in certain occupations, such as nursing and customer service–related positions, are especially prone to verbal abuse by supervisors and patients or customers. While we fear that childhood bullying could lead to violence, workplace violence is actually far more common than school violence. For example, in the 1999–2000 school year, sixteen students were killed at school. In contrast, in 1999 alone, 651 people were murdered at work.[42]

Both bullying and hazing are about the assertion of power and the creation or reaffirmation of status, particularly in groups that have social hierarchies and social power. Professional athletic organizations, military institutions, law-enforcement agencies, fraternities, and sororities all have been sources of well-documented incidents of hazing newcomers. These types of organizations lend themselves to ritual initiations: they are hierarchical, exclusive, tend to be homogeneous and to encourage conformity, and they offer power and status to members. These organizations are similar to what sociologist Erving Goffman referred to as "total institutions," a term used to describe a setting that encourages a total commitment by its participants. Becoming a member of such an institution means reconstructing one's identity, and within this process members often have limited contact with people outside the institution. They are encouraged, sometimes through force or intimidation, to conform to the norms of the group, and are discouraged from deviation.

There is one key difference between adult experiences of bullying and hazing and children's experiences, however: in many cases, adults have the option to escape situations in which they may face social rejection. They may be able to find a new job, leave a bad marriage, or even move to a new community. Not that these are easy changes to make, but adults have more choices than kids do. In rare instances young people facing the same rejection can transfer to a new school, but only with the support of their parents and other adults.

THE UNIQUE SETTING OF SCHOOLS

In some ways, schools are similar to total institutions. Students spend most of the day there, and may spend much of their free time in school-sponsored activities or may socialize with their classmates when out of school. An emphasis on "school spirit" encourages loyalty and commitment. Students are segregated by age, and often by race and socioeconomic status. Schools are hierarchical and have somewhat regimented environments—students have limited autonomy within their classes and little choice in whether to be part of the institution or not.

School can sometimes seem like the entire universe. I went to a small school and met most of my high-school classmates in elementary school, if not sooner. Social rejection then would have been traumatic because it would have been ongoing, and because I never knew a world without those people. At the time I couldn't imagine that most of them would someday become a distant memory. A small group of people can comprise an entire social world, one where people occasionally come and go but often stay until young adulthood arrives or longer.

So in an environment of limited freedom that emphasizes conformity and obedience, kids struggle for what power they can get from each other. As young people, they have very little social power outside this realm, and thus interpersonal domination becomes one way that some children respond to this condition.

Sociologist Murray Milner Jr., author of *Freaks, Geeks, and Cool Kids: American Teenagers, Schools, and the Culture of Consumption*, notes that teens' social behavior is firmly rooted in their environment and in their position as teens in the larger world. Because they lack the power to make the central decisions that affect their lives, young people in turn create a system where they make the rules. Milner argues that this does not stem from a lack of maturity or values, as is so often thought to be the case, but is instead a reasonable response to their broad-scale disempowerment. He says this phenomenon is not unique to teens, but exists in many instances "where groups are excluded from economic and political power and given little respect," and so "they build a new identity rooted in a new status system."[43] Milner adds that all groups define boundaries and make conformity imperative yet difficult to maintain in order to prop up the importance of the group. Milner provides the example of Nobel Prize winners, a very small super-elite group that maintains its status in part through its exclusivity. Likewise, social prestige is achieved if only a few people can have it.

In some environments, status can be attained through excelling academically, while in others it can lead to social rejection. Athletic ability can create instant status (particularly for boys) in many schools, as can parental wealth or wearing the right clothes or driving an expensive car, markers of status for adults too. But young people have a far more limited audience to impress.

In a relatively closed social setting, hierarchies take on more meaning and can be more difficult to avoid. Popularity won through threat or intimidation is very similar to the power struggles in a dictatorship, where fear predominates and conformity is required. Power is obtained through forming allegiances and making connections with other people who have status. Being known by others, so central in our culture of celebrity, is also a key to power and popularity in school. To understand young people's intergroup relationships, we need to look beyond individuals, or even individual groups or schools, and to understand the broader meaning of being a teen or a preteen in society today.

A controversial prison experiment conducted by Philip Zimbardo at Stanford University in 1971 can offer us insight into the social cruelty that sometimes emerges at school. While schools are not the same as prisons and so the analogy is imperfect, the role that power plays in a closed social environment is applicable in both instances.

In order to study the psychological impact of being a prisoner or a prison guard, Zimbardo recruited Stanford University students to construct a mock prison. The students were assessed to ensure that they were emotionally healthy, and then randomly assigned to a role as prisoner or guard. After six days, Zimbardo decided to end the experiment because the subjects seemed to have totally internalized their roles; guards became arbitrarily cruel, and prisoners turned hopeless and docile.

This famous experiment informs us of how quickly a social setting can affect behavior, and how those with power may abuse it when they perceive that they have the authority to do so. Although prisoners and their guards are in the same environment twenty-four hours a day and students are not, students still spend a great deal of time with their peers in one setting. The abuse of power is not just an outgrowth of mean kids or troubled individuals, but of the social environment as well.

THE BOTTOM LINE ON BULLYING AND HAZING

Our fears of kids' bullying and hazing stem from the fact that bullying and hazing are very widespread, common experiences that most of us can relate to. These experiences of childhood may bring back painful memories, which we relive if we have children who experience the same social discomfort. Since the postwar era, parents often have had the luxury of worrying about their children's emotional well-being, because childhood diseases have largely been eradicated and the physical survival of children is all but assured. Peter N. Stearns, historian and author of *Anxious Parents*, notes that at a time when most parents have relatively little to worry about regarding their children's physical survival, we have become obsessed with children's happiness. Concerns about bullying and hazing are legitimate, especially for parents and teachers; however, we should not mistake growing concern for a growing problem. For all but a miniscule number of young people, bullying and hazing are threats to happiness, and are not a question of life or death.

Both hazing and bullying serve as social levelers; they are attempts to gain or maintain status in an overall context when young people tend to have very little power elsewhere. There is no evidence that either has gotten worse, but only that we are paying more attention now, and there's nothing wrong with that. Because most people are very familiar with one if not both of these experiences, news stories reporting on extreme bullying or hazing touch a nerve and get our attention.

But while neither should be ignored, there is a danger in placing too much attention on bullying and hazing if we ignore other more common and serious threats that young people face. As I discussed in chapter 1, children are far more likely to be verbally and physically abused by their parents than by their peers.

Bullying and hazing fears may also send the message that the biggest emotional and physical threats children face come from each other rather than from adults. Some of us may come to believe that if we put enough energy into teaching kids to be nice and to respect each other, that will solve major social problems and eradicate violence. While respect is an important lesson, it is one adults can only effectively teach by example. Unfortunately, by focusing on mean kids as a central explanation of childhood victimization, we may be discouraging ourselves from looking at our own behavior on both an individual and societal level. And if kids are mean and callous, it seems to give us permission to be mean and callous right back, employing more punitive policies in schools and in the juvenile justice system. Sensitivity awareness programs may be cheap to fund and easy to support, but they will not make up for policy decisions that lead to cutbacks in services like mental health care and education. These decisions and the cutbacks that result, coupled with reduced assistance for families in poverty, appear dangerously less significant if we only focus on trying to make kids be nicer to each other.

Yet while we worry about the kids who don't fit in, we may also be concerned about what kids will do to gain their peers' approval. The next chapter explores our belief that young people are prone to taking dangerous risks with their own safety and well-being.

NOTES

1. Public Agenda Foundation, mail survey of 725 public middle- and high-school teachers, March 12–April 9, 2004; Public Agenda Foundation, telephone survey of 600 parents of public-school students in grades five through twelve, March 11–18, 2004.

2. National Crime Prevention Council, telephone survey of 513 U.S. teens age twelve to seventeen, October 25–28, 2001.

3. Tonja R. Nansel et al., "Bullying Behaviors among U.S. Youth: Prevalence and Association with Psychosocial Adjustment," *JAMA* 285 (2001): 2094–2100.

4. For further discussion, see Joel Best, "Monster Hype: How a Few Isolated Tragedies—and Their Supposed Causes—Were Turned into a National 'Epidemic,'" *Education Next* 2 (2002): 51–55.

5. U.S. Department of Education, National Center for Education Statistics, "Bullying at School," *Indicators of School Crime and Safety* (Washington, D.C.: GPO, 2004).

6. Kimberly Shearer Palmer, "'Mean Girl' Movies Ignore Supportive Role Parents Can Play," *USA Today*, May 17, 2004, 13A.

7. U.S. Department of Education, National Center for Education Statistics, "Bullying at School."

8. National Crime Prevention Council, telephone survey of 513 U.S. teens. Gender differences were noted to be statistically significant.

9. Coleman Warner, "Loyola Students Sue over Hazing Case," *Times–Picayune*, April 21, 2004, 1; Jennifer Leopoldt, "WU Investigates Allegations of Hazing at Sigma Chi Fraternity," *St. Louis Post–Dispatch*, April 6, 2004, B8; Evan Moore, "A&M is Barred from Hazing Punishment," *Houston Chronicle*, February 25, 2004, 19.

10. Erin Egan, "Kids Speak Out," *Sports Illustrated for Kids*, June 2004, 50.

11. Tom Weir, "Hazing Issue Rears Ugly Head across USA," *USA Today*, April 4, 2004, 1C.

12. Hank Nuwer, ed., *The Hazing Reader* (Bloomington: Indiana University Press, 2004), xxv.

13. Bill Hemmer, *Live from the Headlines*, CNN, May 20, 2003.

14. Janice Selekman and Judith A. Vessey, "Bullying: It Isn't What It Used To Be," *Pediatric Nursing* 30 (2004): 246–49.

15. Barrett Pashak, "Teasing Can Be Fatal," *Alberta Report*, Oct 25, 1999, 6.

16. Weir, "Hazing Issue Rears Ugly Head."

17. Bryan Smith, "Girls Expected Game to be Rough, But Not Brutal," *Chicago Sun–Times*, May 7, 2003, 7.

18. Abdon Pallasch and Art Golab, "Judge to Hazing Girl: Suspension Stands," *Chicago Sun–Times*, May 15, 2003, 1; Carlos Sadovi, Janet Rausa Fuller, and Abdon M. Pallasch, "Fifteen Students Expected to be Charged," *Chicago Sun–Times*, May 16, 2003, 3.

19. Kyra Phillips and Jeff Flock, "Live Event/Special," CNN, May 12, 2003.

20. Alexandra Robbins, "'Pledged': From Pricking to Hard-Core Porn," *Chicago Sun–Times*, April 14, 2004, 64.

21. Mike Males, "Dumping on Girls: Now That's Mean," *Los Angeles Times*, May 30, 2004, M3.

22. Rachel Simmons, *Odd Girl Out: The Hidden Culture of Aggression in Girls* (New York: Harcourt, 2002), 11.

23. Leora Tanenbaum, *Slut! Growing Up Female with a Bad Reputation* (New York: Perennial, 2000), 100.

24. Alice McKee, "Hostile Hallways: The AAUW Survey on Sexual Harassment in America's Schools," *WIN News* 19, (1993): 74–75.

25. Harriet Chiang, "Justices Say Schools Liable in Sex Harassment Cases," *San Francisco Chronicle*, May 25, 1999, A1.

26. Nancy Bartley, "Student's Suit Blames School for Harassment," *Seattle Times*, January 19, 2000, B1.

27. Stacy Finz, "Emerging from a Secret," *San Francisco Chronicle*, June 12, 2000, A1.

28. "Students Get Settlement in Harassment Lawsuit," *San Francisco Chronicle*, July 26, 2000, A18.

29. American Association of University Women (AAUW), *Hostile Hallways: Bullying, Teasing, and Sexual Harassment in School* (Washington, D.C.: American Association of University Women Foundation, 2001).

30. Andrew Phillips, "Kissing and Correctness," *Maclean's*, October 14, 1996, 49; "Sex and Drugs and Nutty Schools," *The Economist*, October 12, 1996, 31; "A Kiss Isn't Just a Kiss," *Time*, October 7, 1996, 64.

31. Jose Martinez and Tracy Connor, "Teen Abuse Horror," *Daily News* (New York), September 13, 2003, 4.

32. Grant Wahl and L. Jon Wertheim, "A Rite Gone Terribly Wrong," *Sports Illustrated*, December 22, 2003, 68.

33. Lesley Stahl and Peter Van Sant, "Hell Week," *48 Hours Investigates*, CBS News, April 14, 2004.

34. Wahl and Wertheim, "A Rite Gone Terribly Wrong."

35. Thomas Fields-Meyer et al., "Too Cruel for School," *People*, November 3, 2003, 68.

36. John Ferak, "Student Suspended from School, Team," *Omaha World–Herald*, August 28, 2004, 2B.

37. Marie Szaniszlo, "Groton School Officials Indicted in Hazing Case," *Boston Herald*, June 8, 2004, 2.

38. Selena Roberts, "Sports of the Times," *New York Times*, September 28, 2003, 9.

39. "'Personal Story' Segment Hazing Incident," *The O'Reilly Factor*, Fox News Network, September 25, 2003; Bob Edwards and Brian Mann, "Hazing Investigations in the Nation's High Schools," Morning Edition, National Public Radio (NPR), September 23, 2003.

40. "No Defense: High School Football Players Sexually Assaulted by Teammates," *20/20*, ABC News Transcripts, October 17, 2003.

41. Nancy Grover, "NIOSH Study Sheds Light on Bullying and Workplace Stress," *Risk and Insurance* 15 (2004): 10.

42. U.S. Department of Education, National Center for Education Statistics, "Bullying at School"; Bureau of Justice Statistics (1999–2002), Table 3.135, "Workplace Homicides, by Victim Characteristics, Type of Event, and Selected Occupation and Industry, United States," *Sourcebook of Criminal Justice Statistics* (Washington, D.C.: U.S. Department of Justice).

43. Murray Milner Jr., *Freaks, Geeks, and Cool Kids: American Teenagers, Schools, and the Culture of Consumption* (New York: Routledge, 2004), 30.

5

Jackasses and Copycats

X-treme Behavior

In February of 2001, a new MTV show called *Jackass* began getting a lot of bad press. A thirteen-year-old Connecticut boy and his friends had defied the show's "don't try this at home" warning and lit himself on fire, following an episode in which the host (in a flame-retardant suit) lay down on a grill with some steaks. The boy suffered serious injuries, and calls to ban the show followed, as did complaints that "the antics have apparently inspired a lot of kids to go out and copy their jackass heroes."[1] Dozens of other news stories documented pranks and stunts gone awry. Some of the stunts were similar to those featured on the show; others were allegedly inspired by it or simply considered "*Jackass*-like." In the case of sixteen- and seventeen-year-olds who jumped over a moving car (and videotaped it), the kids vehemently denied that they were imitating *Jackass*, and the MTV show had never aired such a stunt.[2] It was the police who insisted this was a copycat incident.

While it is unclear exactly where the ideas for such acts of daring stupidity may originate from in situation to situation, press accounts support the popular belief that "kids will do a lot of stupid things."[3] An ABC *20/20* broadcast featuring the burned thirteen-year-old described how kids think that they are "immortal," and a *U.S. News and World Report* story argued that "teens tend to think they're invincible and are drawn to risky behavior that looks exciting."[4]

This certainly appeared to be the case in many of the "stupid teen tricks" reported that year: teens pretending to be escaped prisoners, faking a kidnapping, dragging a dead cat, and assaulting homeless people, all captured on the perpetrators' own video cameras. While the word *teen* was often featured prominently in the high-profile *Jackass* headlines, many of those involved were actually adults age eighteen and nineteen, and probably old enough to make their own decisions, however poor, without being under the spell of the MTV show.[5]

Can young people sometimes act stupid, reckless, and violent? Yes. But are these qualities really endemic to the teen years? Certainly most young people do not engage in this type of behavior, particularly if they are female. But even the vast majority of young boys would stop short of setting themselves on fire or jumping over a moving car.

So why do we associate risk-taking and extreme behavior with young people? In this chapter I will explore the perceptions and realities of the risks young people take with alcohol, drugs, sex, and other behaviors. Sure, the extreme cases are there if we look for them, but risk-taking does not define the teen years as much as we might think.

Since we have been primed to believe that kids these days are out of control, it doesn't take much prodding from the news media to support what we think we already know. By associating such dangerous behavior with youth-oriented MTV, we malign both. But MTV is certainly not the only network to celebrate dangerous and risky behavior. NBC's *Fear Factor* features guests eating the otherwise inedible and doing death-defying stunts. ABC's long-running family show *America's Funniest Home Videos* includes lots of cute pets and babies, but also frequently airs footage of people getting hurt either accidentally or while doing stunts, and videos are even accompanied by cartoonish sound effects. During its brief run, *Jackass* did not accept audience submissions and provided warnings not to try the featured stunts at home by starting each broadcast with the message that "Jackass features stunts performed by professionals and/or total idiots. In either case, MTV insists that neither you nor any of your dumb little buddies attempt the dangerous crap in this show."[6] In contrast, the ABC program *America's Funniest Home Videos* airs only submissions and offers prizes for the best video. It is highly likely that this show could have caused injury to viewers staging stunts in hopes of winning some money. Yet it is interesting that this show hasn't received the same sort of vitriol or calls for its cancellation as *Jackass* did from parents and Senator Joseph Lieberman of Connecticut, the home state of the thirteen-year-old who allowed himself to be set on fire.

But even if most kids aren't really "jackasses" and would never invent or reenact a dangerous stunt, a valid question remains: Why would watching *Jackass* and other presentations of extreme risk-taking behavior appeal to so many young viewers, particularly teen and young-adult males? If the next generation isn't made up of "jackasses" or copycats, why might they like to watch those who are, and why would everyone else be so fascinated and disgusted by this propensity?

First, the elusive young-male audience is highly prized and sought after by advertisers, who know that teen and young-adult males don't watch a lot of television. Shows like *Jackass* and other types of entertainment that feature people pushing the limits of acceptable behavior are desperately trying to reach a very fickle audience that has lots of other entertainment choices today.

Second, by flouting conventions of acceptable behavior, *Jackass* appeals to an antiauthoritarian impulse that many young people feel. As Hank Stuever describes it in the *Washington Post*, "They've tapped into something deep and meaningful in all that pointlessness: cultural revolt."[7] He also goes on to describe a scene in the *Jackass* movie, where the pranksters go to a golf course, the ultimate symbol of male social acceptability, and blow air horns just as golfers are about to swing. "The jackasses stick it to the Man," notes Stuever.

The appeal of *Jackass* and other shock-style programs may have less to do with the audience members themselves and more to do with the difficulty of reaching that audience in any other way. And for those who did watch *Jackass* before it went off the air in 2002, there is no evidence that the show itself made them any more likely to become risk-takers. The reported cases where people got hurt were isolated, sad incidents, but we have no way of knowing all of the factors that led to the participants' decision to do something that they clearly should not have.

RISK-TAKERS BY NATURE?

Not that risk-taking is always a bad thing. Our society encourages risk in many forms, be it economic, emotional, or physical. Professional athletes, Olympians, and marathoners are often lauded for pushing themselves, or even for playing while hurt. Capitalism is based on risk; if we weren't willing to take chances with our money, the stock market would collapse and no one would ever create a new business. The most successful entrepreneurs and innovators have to be able to take risks, risks that many others may be too afraid to take. We have a love/hate relationship with risk in many ways, being envious of those whose risks pay off, and often judgmental of those whose don't. Gamblers who win a lot of money are sometimes lionized (as during televised poker tournaments), while those who lose a lot are considered to be suffering from an addiction.

Risk involves change, something younger people may be more comfortable with. Perhaps that's why historically young people have been on the front lines of social movements. Change can be scary; as representatives of change, young people may create anxiety in their elders, who may be fearful of change and of not knowing what will come next.

Recent research and debate have considered whether there is a neurological reason for teens to take risks, focusing on the idea that the part of the brain that promotes inhibition is not fully formed until early adulthood. Presuming this were true, we would expect near universal teen risk-taking, in varying degrees of magnitude. We might even accept it as normal and as a phase that people are meant to pass through in a normal life course.

Actually, the idea that adolescence is a time of biology-based rebellion and risk-taking is over a century old. G. Stanley Hall's work on adolescence introduced the idea that the teen years are a naturally stormy time. He largely based this theory on his own stormy adolescence and struggles for autonomy with his father.[8] Rather than considering the teen years an experience based on a number of contextual factors, Hall pioneered the idea that the teen years were a return to savagery, and that adolescents should not have too much stimulation, at the risk of awakening the temptation that lurked within them. At the end of the nineteenth and beginning of the twentieth century, urbanization was one such stimulation that was thought to bring out the savage in young boys, because adults who were likely raised in rural surroundings felt cities were unnatural places to come of age. Margaret Mead famously challenged the notion of Hall's universal adolescent experience in *Coming of Age in Samoa*, noting that much of what we associate with the biological is in fact social and cultural.

And while it is true that some teens may take personal risks, such as engaging in dangerous stunts, promiscuous behavior, or substance use, so do many adults. And certainly not every young person lacks inhibition. At the same time, lowered inhibition may not always be a bad thing. The adolescent brain, as some claim, may be wired to take chances, but not necessarily with the adolescent's safety. Risky behavior might include pursuing a seemingly impossible dream, running for class president, or attending a university far from home in a strange place. Regardless of biological debates, the social meaning of adolescence in the contemporary Western world means self-discovery, independence, and identity. Adolescence is the time when young people begin to chart a course for their adult lives, a course sometimes far away from their parents. But often, as journalist Barbara Strauch notes in her book *The Primal Teen*, young people have too *few* outlets for healthy risk-taking, and see only one path for themselves—often the one their parents have laid out for them—and are not aware of other choices.[9]

If adolescence is marked by rebellion and conflict, it's likely not just neurological or hormonal. Teens in the United States today straddle the fence between childhood and adulthood, with expectations that they behave more and more like adults while still being regarded as immature and even dangerous. Adolescence is stormy in part because we make it that way.

ARE TEENS NATURALLY CRAZY?

But some of us continue to insist that it is the teens themselves, not their circumstances, who are out of control. For those who wonder why some teens are prone to lighting themselves on fire or jumping over moving cars, modern science purports to have another answer: temporary insanity. This claim has been made based on recent neurological research that indicates that teen brains are still evolving, and that the adolescent years are a time of major neurological change. Yet the brain continues to change throughout the life course, in part as a response to a person's environment. While some scientists have labeled the adolescent brain "primitive," much as G. Stanley Hall insisted, our negative perception of teens is likely coloring the so-called hard science of brain research.

We have the tendency to consider adults finished, somehow complete in their humanness, and to consider children and teens as being in less than the idealized adult state. But we can also see that younger brains are less rigid and more able to adapt, particularly when it comes to language. The neural pathways that the brain carves out to become more efficient also make it difficult to make changes as we get older. A study published in *Nature* notes that aging in the brain appears to actually begin in early adulthood, but we rarely attribute social problems of the middle aged to a decaying brain.[10] In any case, the language that is often used to describe the neurological traits of adolescence is often loaded with the baggage of our viewing teens as a problem. Although infants and toddlers have far less impulse control than teens do, we would be reluctant to label them "insane." But then again, we often define insanity based on fear, and we have a long history of fearing teens.

EXTREME REACTIONS

Maybe it is the anxiety we feel that comes with the growing independence of adolescents that causes many of us to fear teenagers. We think they might have more opportunities to get into danger than infants and toddlers do (though accidents are also the leading cause of death for young children).[11] The fact that teenagers are the subject of derision is less about any biochemical or neurological reality and more about our reluctance to acknowledge that some of the behaviors we fear most may start in adolescence, but are present in many adults too.

In the next sections I will explore several types of behavior that scare many adults: alcohol and drug use, promiscuity, piercing, "extreme" sports, tattooing and cutting, and thrill-seeking in general. In addition to looking at the perception and the reality within each behavior, I will consider what role adults play in these so-called teen behaviors. Rather than take the more common, isolated approach that teens who get into trouble do so because of temporary insanity, or because of the negative influence of popular culture and other teens, I will suggest that parents and the other adults in young people's lives are powerful role models whose behavior is sometimes mirrored by the teens around them. In many cases, young people are actually less likely to engage in dangerous behavior than the adults in their lives.

In addition to maligning the many young people who do not engage in dangerous behavior, conceptualizing adolescents as temporarily insane normalizes behaviors that may actually be cries for help or indicators of not-so-temporary mental illnesses that do not necessarily just fade with time. We have probably all heard or used the phrase that someone is "acting like a teenager." In the next few sections, I will challenge exactly what that means.

DRINKING GAMES

Underage binge drinking, which in some cases can be fatal, is also a common news story, especially in the spring after graduation or in the fall after antsy parents have dropped their kids off at college dorms. A 2002 study conducted by the National Center on Addiction and Substance Abuse, Columbia University, found that 49 percent of adults were "very much concerned" about underage alcohol use, and 31 percent believed underage drinking to be a very big problem in their community.[12] Not surprisingly, alcohol and drugs take the lead as the most commonly feared "jackass" and copycat behaviors.

Tragedies certainly do occur involving alcohol and drugs, and substance-related injuries or deaths should never be minimized. Yet concern tends to focus mainly on young people's misuse of alcohol and drugs, while as we will see, it is older adults who are more likely to use and abuse both, with even more deadly consequences.

But headlines like the *Hartford Courant*'s "Headlong Descent into the Depths of Alcohol: Drinking Was Just Part of College for a Quinnipiac Student and His Friends—Until One Tragic, Late-Night Binge" tell the heartbreaking story of a college student's death after drinking an incredible amount of alcohol.[13] Stories like this and others that make news are in fact tragic and help us think that alcohol is a youth problem, not a societal problem that at times involves young people.

While substance abuse can and does impact people of all ages, we tend to blame young people for creating the problem. True, the abuse often starts in adolescence, but the reasons that people abuse any mind-altering substance go beyond just teen peer pressure. As far as drinking is concerned, we have defined it in the United States as an important marker delineating adult status and maturity. Considered socially appropriate in social gatherings and celebrations, it is a very accepted practice for adults and considered off-limits for children. While teens and young adults under twenty-one are not children, they are not considered mature enough to handle alcohol. Stories about binge drinking seem to support this. Young people aspire to be adults, and want to be seen engaging in behaviors that make them seem more adult-like. Drinking is one threshold that is relatively simple to cross over. If young people are drawn to drinking alcohol, it is in part because they want to seem more like their elders.

But contrary to inflammatory news reports, teen drinking is not universal in the United States, nor is binge drinking. According to Monitoring the Future, the rates of teen drinking have been declining. In 2004, 48 percent of high-school seniors reported that they had consumed alcohol within the past thirty days.[14] Some of this alcohol was likely consumed with peers, but this number also includes those who may have had wine as part of a religious ritual or family event. Thirty-three percent reported being drunk in the past thirty days. While these numbers may seem high, as I discussed in chapter 4, young people today are actually less likely to report drinking or binge drinking than their parents or people my age were. During the 1970s and 1980s, about 90 percent of young people reported having drunk alcohol at least once, while by 2004 the number had declined to about 77 percent.[15]

Yet according to a *Pittsburgh Post–Gazette* story, "everyone seems to agree [that teen alcohol use] is getting worse statewide," a statement that encouraged readers to fear the consequences of this perceived trend. The writer conceded later in the story that this perception may be the result of more news publicity.

Graduation and prom season usually bring a flurry of concern about underage drinking. A May 2005 *Denver Post* story, "Graduation Celebrations often Leave Teens at Risk," noted that "teens too often confuse celebration with intoxication," and that "teens who drink are more likely to commit or be the victim of violence." These statements may be true, but they are certainly not only true for teens. In fact, as I will discuss in the next chapter, adult drunk driving is a far worse problem that teen drunk driving (which has been dropping), as are adult alcohol-related arrests and health consequences. According to the 2003 National Crime Victimization Survey, a nationally representative survey conducted annually, 17 percent of all crime victims believed their assailant was drunk at the time of the crime, with about 6 percent believing that the perpetrator may have been using a combination of drugs and alcohol.[16] Results from the 2003 National Survey of Drug Use and Health (NSDUH) indicate that heavy drinking is highest for twenty-one- to twenty-five-year-olds. For those under eighteen, adults outdo them in heavy drinking until age fifty.[17]

In some cases, our focus on teens has bordered on the absurd. In June 2005, police raided a backyard graduation party in Maryland, asking teens to undergo Breathalyzer tests following a noise complaint. No one tested positive at this highly chaperoned party, which featured a moon bounce and a s'mores pit. Before the police left, they ticketed cars parked on the street for minor infractions. "It's almost like they were angry that they didn't find anything," a parent noted.[18]

Even when teens are not drinking, they are the focus of concern. The *Houston Chronicle* reported on a school district in Fort Bend, Texas, where a survey found that 75 percent of the district's students reported that they do not drink. Yet the district received more than $600,000 from the U.S. Department of Education to reduce alcohol abuse and applied for an extension to continue to receive money.[19]

Why would a district that has so little underage drinking need federal money for a problem that barely exists? True, some students could have lied on the survey, and alcohol consumption rates could actually be higher. But then we would also expect people to lie on other alcohol surveys, and we still find rates of alcohol consumption far higher nationally than at this school. Let's presume for a moment that the survey was more or less accurate. Why would the federal government, currently mired in budget problems, fund a program when a problem is minimal at best?

For one thing, no politician would dare stand up and vote against funding a program to stop teen drinking. That would be political suicide. Alcohol makers are on this bandwagon too, with "We Card" campaigns, thereby letting their real customers think that they are caring corporations. It's more likely the corporations simply don't want teens to give their products any bad publicity. By focusing on teen drinking and the tragedies that sometimes result, we take the focus off the roles that adults play in both teen drinking and alcohol-related social problems.

This is not to say that underage drinking should be ignored or minimized. According to the National Longitudinal Alcohol Epidemiologic Survey, teens who start drinking before the age of fifteen are four times more likely to become alcoholics than those who start at twenty-one.[20] But as any addiction counselor will tell you, substance abuse does not happen in a vacuum, and it's not simply exposure to alcohol that creates problematic behavior.

Those that become addicted are often the children of alcoholics or are attempting to manage emotional problems with the substance. According to the NSDUH, approximately five million adults with children living in their homes are dependent on alcohol—affecting approximately 9 percent of all kids under eighteen.[21] These parents are far more likely to also use illegal drugs than nonalcoholics (36 percent versus 11 percent), and are more likely to abuse prescription drugs (16 percent versus 5 percent of nonalcoholics). Not surprisingly, these parents also report more instability in their homes. Kids with mothers diagnosed with a serious mental illness are also more likely to have used alcohol or drugs during the past month compared with others (27 percent versus 19 percent).

In truth, alcohol abuse by adults is far more of a threat to young people's health and well-being than teen use is a threat to society. Parents involved in domestic violence, driving their kids while drunk, and creating an overall unstable family life are far more destructive than teens who may drink at a graduation party, often without causing problems for themselves or others. But unlike prom season, there is no "destroyed family" time of the year to trigger those horror stories in the press.

ALCOHOL'S EVIL TWIN

Where teens are concerned, alcohol is hardly mentioned without its more menacing-sounding peer, drugs. Typically when drugs are mentioned we think of hard-core illegal drugs, which seem to represent turning away from conventional society. While alcohol use by both teens and adults dwarfs illegal-drug use, the fear of illegal drugs is just as strong. According to Monitoring the Future, 23 percent of young people reported using an illegal drug within the past month, and 11 percent used an illegal drug other than marijuana in 2004.[22]

Drug use creates fears in parents and politicians alike. As with alcohol, many young lives have certainly been ruined by drugs, as have many not-so-young lives. According to the Drug Abuse Warning Network (DAWN), in 2003 thirty-five- to forty-four-year-olds were the age group most likely to visit emergency rooms for cocaine-, heroin-, marijuana-, and stimulant-related problems.[23] DAWN estimated no cocaine-, ecstasy-, LSD-, or PCP-related visits for people under eighteen. In California, drug overdose deaths among young people have declined slightly, while for those over forty, overdose deaths rose 73 percent between 1990 and 2003.[24]

Further, the FBI estimates that about 5 percent of all homicides in the United States are drug related.[25] Of people eighteen and over on parole or supervised release, approximately 24 percent were illegal-drug users, compared with 8 percent of adults not on parole.[26] But as with alcohol, public focus and concern centers on young users and virtually ignores the individual and social problems brought on by adult use. The foster-care system alone spends millions to provide placement and care for thousands of children each year whose parents can't take care of them due to substance abuse.

As with alcohol, even when no problem exists, adults still worry. The *Boston Globe* reported on a statewide survey that indicated cocaine use was "on the rise" in Massachusetts, but officials in the town of Framingham, Massachusetts, had seen little cocaine use there.[27] This is no surprise, since nationally the percentage of high-school seniors who have ever tried cocaine has hovered around 8 percent for many years, and it has been even lower for younger kids (3 percent of eighth graders and 5 percent of tenth graders).[28] But the story cautioned readers not to let go of cocaine fears, quoting an official who said, "its use may remain 'under the radar.'" The article also cited a substance abuse counselor who noted that she "has treated thirteen- and fourteen-year-olds who have used cocaine." A juvenile court judge was also quoted, who observed "an almost casual approach among youths to alcohol and marijuana." Of course, these professionals do not encounter the average teen in their work, but those already in trouble.

In truth, illegal-drug use among teens is lower now than it was in the late 1970s and early 1980s. The percentage of high-school seniors who have ever tried marijuana dropped from 60 percent in 1979 to 46 percent in 2004.[29] Nearly a third of high-school seniors in the late seventies reported having used marijuana within the last month, which was down to about a fifth in 2004.[30] Other illegal drugs are much less significant among high-school students, according to Monitoring the Future. In 2004, 8 percent of high-school students had tried cocaine, down from a peak of 17 percent in 1985, while 1.5 percent of twelfth graders had tried heroin (down from 2.2 percent in 1975), and 5 percent had used LSD (down from 11 percent in 1975). Drugs such as ecstasy and crystal meth have gotten a lot of attention lately, but only 8 and 4 percent of high-school students have ever tried them, respectively. In recent years ecstasy use has declined while crystal meth use has held steady, although its use has declined slightly since the late 1990s.

Even a few young people lost to drugs is too many, but it is erroneous to describe substance use and abuse as primarily a teen problem. Teens do encounter many adult-like experiences that may include drugs and alcohol, but they are entrants into an existing problem, not the central cause of the problems that are often the result of this use.

As I noted with alcohol, if we want to understand why young people sometimes use drugs, we need look no further than the adults around them. Illicit-drug use peaks in early adulthood, but between 8 and 9 percent of adults between thirty and forty-four are estimated to use illegal drugs.[31] Our society also has a deep ambivalence about drugs used for medicinal purposes. We have become a society comfortable with medicating all sorts of problems, from shyness to high cholesterol (which helps us to continue our poor eating habits).

Drugs obviously have many legitimate medical purposes, but illegal use of legal drugs is a major problem, and not just for teens. In 2003, an estimated 31.2 million Americans twelve and older used painkillers for nonmedical purposes.[32] However, this is not a new issue at all. Estimates suggest that the biggest period of drug abuse in the United States was not the 1960s but actually at the end of the nineteenth and beginning of the twentieth century. So-called health tonics of the period contained highly potent substances like morphine, heroin, and marijuana. Of course, Coca-Cola got its name from the cocaine it once contained, and was served as an alternative to alcohol. When the Food and Drug Act was passed in 1906 all ingredients had to be listed, but before then consumers had no idea that they were dosing themselves—and their children—with highly addictive drugs. The largest group of addicts was middle-class white women living outside cities, who purchased the tonics from catalogs or traveling salesmen. And today, the hidden addicts, the ones who get relatively little public attention and few national prevention programs, are also middle-class suburbanites who take pills, sometimes prescribed for them, sometimes not. Just as our predecessors of a century ago, we are still likely to look for a pill to cure what ails us.

But teen drug use gets the most attention, perhaps because it reinforces what we think we know about teens. Our contemporary fear is not unlike what past generations thought they knew about Mexican Americans, who were blamed for the problems brought by their alleged marijuana use in the 1930s, and which cleared the way for a Depression-era repatriation policy enabling Americans of Mexican descent to be deported to Mexico. Later, African Americans in central cities were blamed for their decline due to crack use in the 1980s. Groups with the least social power, such as teens, become the target of blame for problems we would rather not face ourselves. The population currently most feared as out of control is typically the group of focus when it comes to the abuse of mind-altering substances.

GIRLS GONE WILD?

Images of young college students drinking on beaches in barely-there bathing suits, and the ubiquitous late-night cable-TV ads for *Girls Gone Wild* videos, seem to substantiate our belief that young people today are not just drunken drug users, but sexual risk-takers. Sexual behavior by young people is often thought by adults to be the result of peer pressure, and many adults fear that sex has become something that means very little to kids today. Talk shows with sexually adventurous teens and their frustrated parents also seem to confirm a very powerful stereotype about teens, that "everybody's doing it."

But they aren't. According to the Centers for Disease Control and Prevention, between 1991 and 2003, teens were *less* likely to have ever had sex (47 percent versus 54 percent in 1991), and if they had, were much more likely to have used a condom during their last sexual encounter (63 percent versus 46 percent in 1991).[33] But what about the so-called oral-sex epidemic discussed on *Oprah* and *Dr. Phil* episodes, where teens allegedly engage in sexual behavior conveniently not labeled as "sex"? In spite of the sometimes shocking anecdotes that scare parents, there is no systematic evidence that this behavior has increased.[34] We can thank former president Bill Clinton for putting oral sex into public discussion—and for characterizing it as different from actual sex. In our confessional popular culture, disclosing extremely private information, such as by talking about sexual practices, is no longer as taboo as it once was, but has become instead a ticket to the media attention so many people of all ages often court.

The truth is that young people today by all accounts are less promiscuous, and are much better at preventing pregnancy than teens of just a decade ago. Yet according to a 2003 Kaiser Family Foundation survey, 35 percent of adults wrongly believe that the problem has gotten worse.[35] Teen pregnancy rates fell 28 percent between 1990 and 2002, and abortion rates fell 33 percent between 1990 and 2000.[36] In 2003, the rates for pregnancy and giving birth for fifteen- to seventeen-year-olds dropped to their lowest point in American history.[37] As far as sex is concerned, kids today are actually showing more restraint than their parents' generation did, even when they go on spring break. "Most kids are well-behaved," a restaurant owner in San Padre Island, Texas, told the *Houston Chronicle* about the visitors who come to this currently popular spring-break locale.[38]

So why is it that we think teens and young adults are sexually out-of-control when trend data tell another story? As I discuss in my book *It's Not the Media,* because popular culture is laden with sexual imagery, there is an erroneous assumption that teens will imitate what they see. More to the point, news stories about teen promiscuity are more interesting to read than stories about the typical experience of an American teen today. Salacious news gets more attention than chastity. Plus, there is something alluring to older people about the idea of being young and carefree and even irresponsible. It is this image that no doubt attracts students to spring-break resorts, as they are hoping to be part of the action, or at least to be closer to it.

Shaking our heads at young people's fun is an old pastime, and seems to make getting older a little easier if we redefine fun as stupidity. Of course, the fun we associate with youth is often exaggerated. Adolescence and early adulthood are rarely the best years of our lives or a nonstop party. Young people themselves may feel like they are missing out on something when life doesn't match the stereotype of what youth is supposed to be like. Instead, the party in their minds and ours is rather an aspirational lifestyle that marketers peddle and that sells spring-break travel, clothes, and other products that both young and not-so-young people hope will make their lives fun and make up for what they think may be missing.

While promiscuity may seem like a new and urgent problem, with deadly sexually transmitted diseases (STDs) that we never heard of thirty years ago a possibility today, these concerns are not as unique to our times as we may think. Before antibiotics, many now treatable sexually transmitted diseases could be deadly. And teens today are not the first generation to be accused of going too far. "It has struck sex o'clock in America. A wave of sex hysteria and sex discussion seems to have invaded the country," claimed a 1913 article in *Current Opinion.*[39] These fears were based on the growing independence of women in cities who were moving about on the streets without male supervision. Similarly, fears today largely focus on girls, as do the *Girls Gone Wild* videos. In the beginning of the last century, critics were openly concerned that girls of questionable morality would spoil good boys' virtue, not the other way around. Today little has changed, because we rarely address boys' promiscuity, when in fact it is boys who are more likely to be sexually active at earlier ages. According to the Centers for Disease Control and Prevention, boys are two and one-half times more likely to claim that they have had sex before thirteen compared with girls.[40] Assuming this is not an exaggeration, it is unknown whether these sexual experiences are consensual or coerced. For many young people, their first sexual encounter is unwanted sexual abuse.

As the median age of marriage rises and the onset of puberty drops, we are left with a large gap between sexual maturity and marriage. Although attitudes about premarital sex have become more accepting (25 percent of Americans felt in 1998 that it is always wrong, compared with 29 percent in 1982), some people's fears about sex have seemed to grow in proportion to others' acceptance.[41] Currently, abstinence-only programs that provide limited information about birth control and sexual health are national policy. There is nothing wrong with abstinence, but teaching only abstinence may not be very effective. A comprehensive study of sex-education programs found that the ones most successful in preventing teen pregnancy were those that gave clear and accurate information, were interactive, and focused on behavior rather than on trying to impact values or self-esteem.[42] A 2005 study published in the *Journal of Adolescent Health* found that teens who made virginity pledges were less likely to use condoms when they did have sex, and were just as likely to test positive for STDs as non-pledgers.[43] In spite of the fact that a 2003 survey found that 67 percent of Americans supported providing comprehensive sex education, the federal government spent $167 million in 2005 and in 2006 proposed to spend $206 million to fund abstinence-only education.[44]

EXTREME SPORTS

Just as concerns about substance use and sex have grabbed headlines and attention, fears about youth violence also never seem to go away. As I talked about in chapter 3, actual rates of youth violence have been on the decline, especially in schools. So rather than just focusing on actual violence, the news media gives us headlines about the violent games that kids (especially boys) play, again capturing public concern.

In *It's Not the Media*, I devote several chapters to fears about the media and violence, and will not duplicate that discussion here. Video games in particular have come under fire by politicians and activists who fear violent games will create violent kids. While no research conclusively supports this fear—although studies using questionable measures are often used as proof—the fear continues, because it seems rational to us that if kids play violent games, they themselves will adopt violence in their lives.

Parents sometimes point to rough play to validate concerns about media violence. Where else could kids be getting it from, they might ask? As Gerard Jones points out in *Killing Monsters: Why Children Need Fantasy, Super Heroes, and Make-Believe Violence*, boys especially often play fight, without ever intending to hurt anyone. He postulates that because kids, especially young children, are often powerless in the world, this is their way of feeling more powerful. For older kids, this need may be played out through so-called extreme sports, which include skateboarding and in-line skating stunts, snowboarding, and even backyard wrestling and fighting.

In 1995, ESPN started the X-Games, so named for their focus on nontraditional extreme sports like skateboarding and stunt-bike riding. But this is certainly not the first time that risk has been incorporated with leisure. Mountain climbing, surfing, sky diving and bungee jumping all involve an element of danger and are enjoyed by adventurers across the age spectrum. Roller coasters are appealing because they provide us with excitement, generated by a perception of risk, even if the potential for real danger is minimal.

Skateboarding is a sport met with ambivalence by many adults, but its popularity is widespread, thanks in part to the X-Games and celebrity skateboard heroes like Tony Hawk. Of course, skateboarding has been around for decades—it is believed to have been created by surfers in the late 1940s as a way to have fun on land. According to a 2001 online survey, swimming remains the most popular sport in America among teens thirteen to nineteen, but 46 percent of boys (and 19 percent of girls) responded that skateboarding is their sport of choice.[45]

Yet in many cities across the country, skateboarding is illegal on public streets. True, it can be loud—a good number of skateboarders favor careening off obstacles on my street—and stunts can cause injury. Some communities have created skate parks where riders can practice stunts, and in some cases these communities issue tickets if park users are not wearing safety gear like helmets and kneepads.

But some cities are reluctant to allow skateboarding anywhere. As one Florida resident told the *St. Petersburg Times*, skate parks can become "teenage hangouts," which she clearly found objectionable.[46] Skateboarding complaints often have little to do with skateboards at all. In the 1980s, young people were prohibited from playing hackey sack in some public places. For those unfamiliar with the fad, the hackey sack is a small, golf-ball-sized beanbag that players basically juggle with their feet and kick to others. Kicking a small beanbag is a rather quiet and safe activity, but it was the teens gathered in public places that were considered the problem. Restrictions like these not only criminalize popular youth pastimes, but make being a teen in public tantamount to a public nuisance. Skateboarding may be a misdemeanor in some places, but it remains a very common activity and mode of transportation with young people. Some of my university students ride a skateboard to make sure they get across campus in time for class.

Far less common than skateboards are fight clubs and backyard wrestling, where participants stage fights and invite others to watch. Because of their underground nature, there is no way of knowing for sure how common they are, but a July 2005 Google search for the phrase *backyard wrestling* yielded 243,000 hits. Videotapes are widely available for sale online, and video games have been created based on backyard wrestling. While reports of police breaking up fight clubs are sporadic, because these staged events are often recorded by participants to be posted online, they can easily make their way onto cable news talk-shows.

Shots of graphic violence and injury lead many of us to ask why anyone would participate. A British newspaper, *The Independent*, examined one backyard wrestling group in Ventura, California, a community just northwest of Los Angeles.[47] The reporter found that parents were often actively involved, even supportive of their kids' participation. The kids themselves, mostly boys in their mid- to late teens, saw the activity as a form of showmanship they were dedicated to perfecting, as they practiced carefully choreographed moves and accepted the blood and bruises that came with them.

Beyond just viewing the kids as "jackasses," the author notes that these kids had felt unsuccessful in nearly every other aspect of their lives. Academic success or skills in more conventional sports proved to be elusive, and this was the one way that many of the participants could gain the admiration of their peers. Backyard wrestling became a way for the boys to gain a sense of self, ironically through the creation of characters and personas similar to professional wrestling. Some of the boys have posted their characters' "bios" online and have hopes of later becoming professionals. When one boy's injury ended his backyard career, he became a coach to the other boys.

It may seem absurd for kids to engage in such dangerous behavior. Montreal's *Gazette* published a story with the headline "Stupid Human Tricks Include Extreme Backyard Wrestling," and claimed that backyard wrestling "is sweeping America, the latest symptom of a whole generation's craving for thrills."[48] Once again, all young people are implicated, not just those who have obtained a sense of identity through their participation. For some, being in a club or league is something they have given a lot more thought to than critics may realize. As one backyard wrestler in Northern California told the *San Francisco Chronicle*:

> We are given a government that is a lie, no more real than the choreographed endings of wrestling matches where major corporations pull the strings of our puppet governmental figureheads like Vince McMahon pulls the strings of the superstars working for him. Underground backyard wrestling gives me a way to

make the kids of this generation feel again, it gives me a way to act out important lessons of humility and put forth ideals of good and evil in a way that even the desensitized youth of today can take to heart. Extreme underground wrestling allows me to work with the anger inside that has built up as I grow older and become more aware of the lies prepared for us by our fathers for many generations.[49]

Critics of wrestling may claim that young people like the one quoted above are victims of a violent media culture and unaware of the consequences of violence, but the appeal goes beyond movies, television, and video games. Fighting as a sport predates televised wrestling by centuries. Just as the Romans would draw the masses to a slaughter, boxing continues to attract the wealthy to ringside seats and millions to pay-per-view. Fighting draws a crowd. The National Hockey League accepts a certain amount of fighting, and unexpected melees during football and baseball games regularly make the sports highlight reels. Whether or not we like to admit it, fighting is exciting to many people. The difference between backyard wrestling and fighting is that entertainment is the point, rather than settling a score. That's probably what makes many people shake their heads in amazement, but it's what adults have been doing for centuries, continuing a long tradition of human bloodlust.

TATTOO U

Tattooing is also an ancient tradition, now largely associated with young people. When I've brought up the topic of tattooing, piercing, and other types of body modification in my deviant behavior courses, most of my students say that they view these practices as former signs of deviance, but certainly not current markers. I show news clips of kids suspended from school for having pierced tongues, and almost to a student they scoff at older school administrators who just don't get it. Maybe in the past it would have been strange to have multiple piercings or tattoos, they tell me, but not anymore. Students in my classes will often volunteer their own reasons for getting pierced or tattooed, usually something as simple as they liked the way it looked, and will say it is no big deal to them.

But concerns about teen tattooing and piercing remain. For one, without parental consent they are usually illegal before eighteen. And as news reports detail, fears about tattooing and piercing are a rite of passage for anxious parents of teens as much as for some teens themselves.

This anxiety was probably enhanced in 2002 by the publication of two studies in *Pediatrics* that looked at whether there was a relationship between tattoos, piercings, and other dangerous behavior in adolescents. The first study, published in June 2002, received news coverage across the country with headlines like "Body Art May Be Tip of Child's Wildness" and "Marked for Trouble."[50]

Overall, 13.2 percent of the study's sample had at least one tattoo, and more than two-thirds of them got their first tattoo when they were seventeen or older. While the authors claimed that only 3 to 8 percent of the general public have a tattoo, a 2003 online Harris Poll found that 16 percent of adults surveyed had at least one.[51] The *Pediatrics* study found that piercing was more common than tattooing; of those surveyed, 26.9 percent had at least one piercing (defined as anywhere other than the earlobe). The most likely site was on the ear cartilage, 13.6 percent, while 11 percent had belly rings; nipple or genital piercings were the least common at 2 percent.[52]

The study's authors claimed to have found a relationship between having a tattoo or piercing, and substance use, sexual activity, and even suicidal thoughts. The authors also found that those who modified their bodies at earlier ages were more prone to substance use, and that if the tattoo came from a professional artist, they were less prone to be violent than those with a self-created or nonprofessionally created tattoo.

The authors were careful to note that the tattoo or piercing was not the *cause* of any of the behaviors defined as risky. They also pointed out that the mere presence of a tattoo or piercing did not mean that any one individual necessarily engaged in the behaviors they singled out. Other physicians responded to this study with some skepticism, warning that it was important for doctors not to overreact or make assumptions about their younger patients based on their appearance alone.

Additionally, this study had several serious shortcomings. First, it included "adolescents" between the ages of twelve and twenty-two. Forty-three percent of their sample of 484 was over eighteen. Although some people might not like the fact that young adults may have sex, smoke cigarettes, or drink alcohol, it is perfectly legal for many of them to do so. There's a big difference between the behaviors acceptable for twelve- or twenty-two-year-olds, and combining these behaviors in a study dilutes the potential of finding out more about kids and risk. It is quite likely that getting tattooed or pierced and engaging in sex, drinking, smoking, and experimenting with drugs are all associated with a third factor: getting older.

Second, as the authors acknowledged, the study involved only military dependents who received health care at the Naval Medical Center in San Diego, California, which the authors rightly noted is not a group that is representative of the entire population of people their age.

However, a second study about tattooing and adolescent behavior, published in December 2002, was based on a nationally representative sample. The surveys on which this article was based were conducted with 6,072 young people age eleven to twenty-one in 1995 and 1996. The study's first wave found that 4.6 percent of respondents had at least one tattoo. A year later, the second survey found 3 percent had a tattoo. The authors conceded that tattoos might be much more common now and their findings might be different if the surveys were conducted later. Within this group of respondents, tattoos were associated with lower parental income and education and greater likelihood of living in a single-parent household. The tattooed respondents were also more likely to report having friends who use drugs, drink, smoke, have sex, get into fights, and skip school.

The authors noted that their goal as physicians was to alert practitioners to consider tattoos a clinical marker of possible risk-taking behavior in their patients. Of course, kids in low-income families are less likely to have access to regular medical care to begin with. What is interesting here is that tattoos themselves have become the warning signs and risk factors rather than a possible indicator of poverty and its known impact on young people's health and well-being. Tattoos revealing gang affiliation would certainly indicate a serious health risk, but it is the tattoo's meaning, not just its existence, that we need to consider.

These two studies were clearly constructed to find negative behaviors associated with tattoos and piercings, rather than to look at issues like creativity, independence, or academic achievement. Sometimes the questions we *don't* ask are even more important than those we do. The studies were also designed to serve as a warning to adults that antisocial behavior may be predicted by young people's appearance.

We can't completely dismiss tattooing and piercing as inconsequential. In spite of a common perception that these are new practices, historically both have represented rites of passage into adulthood, particularly in tribal cultures. In more recent American history they have come to symbolize antiauthoritarian behavior and group affiliation, be it gang or military. That's why it is so interesting that military kids' tattoos would be studied without including the history and context of the meaning of tattooing in their lives, in a study that instead views their body modification as problematic.

Tattoos and piercings have somewhat contradictory meanings in contemporary American society. They aren't uncommon; as noted earlier, a Harris Poll found 16 percent of all adults reported having at least one tattoo. According to the poll, they are most common among people in their midtwenties and thirties: 36 percent of those age twenty-five to twenty-nine and 28 percent of people age thirty to thirty-nine reported having at least one tattoo.[53] The percentage of young people with tattoos in the two studies discussed above ranged from 3 to 13 percent, which means kids are less likely to have tattoos than people in their forties at 14 percent. Kids are more on par with people age fifty to sixty-four at 10 percent, or even with their grandparents sixty-five and over, of which 7 percent of those who responded to the poll were tattooed.

But the size and placement of tattoos or piercings make a big difference in whether someone is really setting themselves apart from conventional society. A small, hidden tattoo versus a large tattoo or piercings covering the face yields very different reactions and social consequences. The secret tattoo or piercing has little social cost and has become a status symbol, a form of coopting a countercultural style without really taking an outsider stance.

A *Chicago Sun–Times* story asked the question many parents might have asked themselves: "What's with all this body piercing? Head shaving? Tattooing? Purple hair? Weird clothes? Don't you wonder if teens really, truly like that stuff, or are they doing it to shock us?"[54] "The fads of teenagers can run from the ridiculous to the absurd," stated a *Milwaukee Journal Sentinel* article on body piercing.[55]

Adolescence and young adulthood are about exploring identity, about trying to be unique individuals while still fitting in with our peers. Tattoos and piercings are often ways to do that; however, the more body decoration we adopt, the more we may be differentiating ourselves from the mainstream and aligning ourselves with countercultural subgroups. But neither practice is isolated to teens and young adults. As sociologist Clinton R. Sanders discovered in his interviews with people who have tattoos, people of all ages use tattooing as a way to create a sense of self-definition, and tattoos are often an important marker of transition or a central life event rather than a passing teen fad.[56]

What some young people have done is make practices of subcultures more mainstream, adopting the "coolness" of the outsider stance while remaining an insider among like-minded peers. Even those whose appearance some may consider shocking find connections with others so adorned, relating to each other in their rejection of mainstream appearance norms. While the authors of the *Pediatrics* articles discussed above warned that these are kids practitioners should be on the lookout for, viewing their style as possibly indicative of risk-taking behavior, it is important to look beyond appearance and to understand why some of these kids may feel like outsiders to begin with.

MISREADING TEENS

"It's hard to believe there's ever been a time in America when the body parts of teenagers were so ornately decorated or, some would say, mutilated," an article in the *Oregonian* began.[57] Not only is there a real problem in dismissing tattooing and piercing as only a teen fad, but there is a real difference between adornment and mutilation. While one person's idea of style may certainly vary from another's, having a tattoo or nose ring is no more about mutilation for the wearer than getting a face lift or a nose job is for the cosmetic-surgery patient. Both are appearance changing, involve pain, and are attempts to achieve a desired look prized by particular groups. Conflating body modification with self-mutilation masks the very real problem of people who purposely cut themselves—not because it is a fad, but because it is a way for them to manage emotional troubles. If self-destructive behavior is considered par for the teenage course, we miss real danger signs when this behavior happens. We may be tempted to think that these warning signs are a phase that many teens go through, and to brush off truly alarming behavior as garden-variety teen angst. But it's important to distinguish a multiply pierced or tattooed person who enjoys the style from the person who enjoys the pain—a frequent observation of those who have treated people who harm themselves.

Cutting has received a lot of public attention recently, but it is not a new phenomenon. An organization to treat people who self-injure, called Self Abuse Finally Ends (SAFE), was founded in 1985. It is difficult to estimate how many people intentionally hurt themselves without the goal of committing suicide because they often go to great lengths to hide their actions and only self-injure on hidden parts of their bodies. Sociologists Patricia A. Adler and Peter Adler interviewed self-injurers, and found that they tend to be loners who generally see their behavior as shameful and otherwise "subscribe to conventional norms."[58] Often victims of physical, sexual, or emotional abuse, self-injurers use cutting or burning as a coping mechanism, not as a fashion or identity statement like tattooing or piercing. This practice is a good example of the problem of viewing adolescence as a period of temporary insanity. We may minimize the experiences of being a teen, or accuse them of overreacting to the stress in their lives, and in so doing may trivialize their emotional struggles.

Some cutters describe the experience as a reminder that they are alive, in contrast to their feelings of emotional deadness. Young people who are thrill seekers may be experiencing similar emotions, and may feel stimulated by taking chances with danger. Instead of dismissing these emotional difficulties as "raging hormones" or attributing them to simply being a teen, we ought to take the signs more seriously when they do appear. If we view adolescence itself as a time of "normal" mental illness, we might dismiss symptoms of depression as a normal state of adolescence. Depression is very different than having a few bad days and expressing anger that may annoy adults, however, and it is something that should not be overlooked. Behavior that makes adults complain that "teens think they're invincible" may in fact be a cry for help—or just kids testing their own personal limits in their quest for independence. It's hard to know for sure without investigating the circumstances, but we will not know if we stick to well-worn generalizations about kids.

Perhaps the key condition that affects many young people today isn't adolescence as much as it is boredom. While we often hear about the issue of overscheduled children, some communities lack much of anything for older teens to do. Because young people gradually have had less responsibility for bringing home wages to their families, and because household chores have become more automated, young people have a lot more free time on their hands now than did the young of past generations. Instead of just condemning young risk-takers, we need to offer more opportunities for young people to channel their energy in safe and constructive ways.

THE COPYCAT IN THE MIRROR

While fears that young people will imitate shows like *Jackass* or their peers' substance use or body modification circulate between news reports, activist groups, and politicians, it is easy to overlook the biggest influence on young people's lives: their parents. Yes, friends are important, but when it comes to seriously dangerous behavior, chances are good it was a long time coming, and not typically a spur of the moment bad decision. If we are worried about kids emulating other people's behavior, parents should be our first concern, especially if the parents are substance users or living chaotic lives themselves. When young people seek stimulation that may seem reckless, we also must ask what sort of stress many otherwise well-functioning adults may thrive on too. The stress we accept of work, debt, and other aspects of contemporary life may send the message to our children that being an adrenaline junkie is normal.

And in spite of our worries about peer pressure and popular culture, conformity isn't always negative. Knowing how to fit into a variety of groups is a valuable social skill, particularly if we can do it without completely losing our individuality. Most young people deal with educational and religious institutions, which promote high levels of conformity and sometimes discourage them from asking critical questions and making self-guided choices. Parents often encourage, if not demand conformity from their kids. So it's no wonder that young people seek acceptance and may not challenge perceived group norms.

What teens and young adults are doing when they experiment with sex and alcohol in particular is attempting to conform and adapt to adult practices. When given few guidelines as to how to safely engage in these behaviors, they come up with their own rules. Other Western countries don't expend nearly so much energy trying to shield young people from knowledge about sex and the use of alcohol. Instead, particularly with alcohol, young people are slowly introduced to drinking alcohol under supervision, rather than learning to drink in secret, as many Americans do.

In truth, most American young people are *not* acting with reckless abandon. National trend data indicate that if anything, young people are now better behaved and less prone to take risks with drugs, alcohol, and sex. For those who do, the causes are likely more complex than simply being a teenager. While some rebellion is a normal part of becoming independent, kids who take big chances with their health and safety are likely acting out against years of instability in their lives, and even against social conditions that limit young people to an increasingly narrow, one-size-fits-all path. The next chapter explores a teen rite of passage commonly associated with risk: driving.

NOTES

1. "This Show Must Go," *Broadcasting and Cable*, April 30, 2001, 82.
2. "Judge Orders Reading of the Classics for Teens," *International Journal of Humanities and Peace* 17 (2001): 75.
3. "This Show Must Go," *Broadcasting and Cable*.
4. Marc Silver, "You're Looking at a 'Jackass,'" *U.S. News and World Report*, February 12, 2001, 62.
5. Craig Schneider, "Cobb Teenagers Admit Bizarre Prank with Dead Cat," *Atlanta Journal–Constitution*, 3B; Paul Purpura, "'Jackass' Act Draws Catcalls for Teens," *Times–Picayune*, November 14, 2003, 1; Kieran Crowley, Selim Algar, and Dan Mangan, "Five Teens Busted in Turkey 'Prank' That Ko'd Driver," *New York Post*, November 19, 2004, 5.
6. Cited in Paul D. Winston, "Modern Approach to Natural Selection?" *Business Insurance*, February 12, 2001, 21.
7. Hank Stuever, "The Rear End of Civilization as We Know it," *Washington Post*, November 8, 2002, C1.
8. See chapter two in Ann Hulbert, *Raising America: Experts, Parents, and a Century of Advice about Children* (New York: Vintage, 2003).
9. Barbara Strauch, *The Primal Teen: What the New Discoveries about the Teenage Brain Tell Us about Our Kids* (New York: Doubleday, 2003), 106–7.
10. Tao Lu et al., "Gene Regulation and DNA Damage in the Ageing Human Brain," *Nature* 429 (2004): 883–91.
11. Centers for Disease Control and Prevention, National Center for Health Statistics, National Vital Statistics Program. "Child Mortality: Death Rates for Children Ages 5 to 14 by Gender, Race, Hispanic Origin, and Cause of Death, Selected Years 1980–2000," accessed via http://childstats.gov (last accessed January 5, 2006).
12. National Center on Addiction and Substance Abuse, Columbia University, telephone poll of 900 respondents, 2002.
13. Janice D'Arcy, "Headlong Descent into the Depths of Alcohol," *Hartford Courant*, January 2, 2003, A1.
14. Monitoring the Future Study, "Trends in 30-Day Prevalence of Use of Various Drugs for Eighth, Tenth, and Twelfth Graders" (Survey Research Center, University of Michigan, Ann Arbor, 2004).
15. Monitoring the Future Study, "Long-Term Trends in Lifetime Prevalence of Use of Various Drugs for Twelfth Graders" (Survey Research Center, University of Michigan, Ann Arbor, 2004).

16. U.S. Census Bureau, "Victim's Perception of the Use of Alcohol and Drugs by the Violent Offender, 2002," *National Crime Victimization Survey* (March 2003).

17. Substance Abuse and Mental Health Services Administration, *2003 National Survey on Drug Use and Health: National Findings* (Rockville, Md.: Office of Applied Studies, 2004).

18. Nancy Trejos and Daniel de Vise, "Police Ticket Cars in Lieu of Teens," *Washington Post*, June 7, 2005, B4.

19. Robert Stanton, "Underage Drinking Targeted in Schools," *Houston Chronicle*, May 19, 2005, 1.

20. National Institute on Alcohol Abuse and Alcoholism, "Understanding Underage Drinking," National Institutes of Health, U.S. Department of Health and Human Services (September 2004).

21. Substance Abuse and Mental Health Services Administration, "Alcohol Dependence or Abuse among Parents with Children Living in the Home"; and "Children Living with Substance-Abusing or Substance-Dependent Parents," (Rockville, Md.: Office of Applied Studies, 2003).

22. Monitoring the Future Study, "Trends in 30-Day Prevalence."

23. Substance Abuse and Mental Health Services Administration, "Illicit Drugs, by Patient Characteristics," table 7, *Drug Abuse Warning Network, 2003: Interim Estimates of Drug-Related Emergency Department Visits* (Rockville, Md.: Office of Applied Studies, 2004).

24. Cited in Daniel Costello, "Boomers' Overdose Deaths Up Markedly," *Los Angeles Times*, October 10, 2005, A1.

25. U.S. Department of Justice, Bureau of Justice Statistics, "Drug Related Homicides," ONDCP Drug Policy Information Clearinghouse staff from FBI, *Crime in the United States: Uniform Crime Reports*, annual.

26. Substance Abuse and Mental Health Services Administration, *2003 National Survey*.

27. Christopher Rowland, "Few Local Signs of Rising Cocaine Use," *Boston Globe*, November 7, 2002, 1.

28. Monitoring the Future Study, "Long-Term Trends in Lifetime Prevalence"; Monitoring the Future Study, "Trends in 30-Day Prevalence."

29. Monitoring the Future Study, "Long-Term Trends in Lifetime Prevalence."

30. Monitoring the Future Study, "Trends in 30-Day Prevalence."

31. Substance Abuse and Mental Health Services Administration, *2003 National Survey*.

32. Substance Abuse and Mental Health Services Administration, *2003 National Survey*.

33. Centers for Disease Control and Prevention, "Trends in the Prevalence of Sexual Behaviors, 1991–2003," *Youth Risk Behavior Surveillance System* (Washington, D.C.: Department of Health and Human Services, 2003).

34. Lisa Remez, "Oral Sex among Adolescents: Is It Sex or Is It Abstinence?" *Family Planning Perspectives* 32, 2000.

35. National Public Radio (NPR), Kaiser Family Foundation, and Harvard University telephone poll of 1,759 adults, with an oversample of 1,001 parents of children in grades seven through twelve, September and October 2003.

36. U.S. National Center for Health Statistics, "Teenagers' Births and Birth Rates by Race and Age: 1990 to 2002," and "Abortions by Selected Characteristics: 1990 to 2000," *Vital Statistics of the United States,* annual.

37. Federal Interagency Forum on Child and Family Statistics, "Birth Rates for Females Ages 15–17 by Race and Hispanic Origin, 1980–2003," *America's Children: Key National Indicators of Well-Being* (Washington, D.C.: GPO, 2005).

38. Harry Shattuck, "Road Trip," *Houston Chronicle,* March 7, 2004, 1.

39. Cited in David Nasaw, *Children of the City: At Work and At Play* (New York: Anchor, 1985), 140.

40. Centers for Disease Control and Prevention, *Youth Risk Behavior Surveillance Study* (Washington, D.C.: Department of Health and Human Services, 2003).

41. National Opinion Research Council (NORC), *General Social Survey* (Chicago, 1998).

42. Douglas Kirby, *Emerging Answers: Research Findings on Programs to Reduce Teen Pregnancy (Summary)* (Washington, D.C.: National Campaign to Prevent Teen Pregnancy, 2001).

43. Hannah Brückner and Peter Bearman, "After the Promise: The Consequences of Adolescent Virginity Pledges," *Journal of Adolescent Health* 36 (2005): 271–78.

44. National Public Radio (NPR), Kaiser Family Foundation, and Harvard University Kennedy School, telephone poll.

45. Reported in Michael J. Weiss, "The New Summer Break," *American Demographics* (August 2001): 49, based on Element Online Survey of 1,143 thirteen- to nineteen-year-olds, May 14–May 21, 2001.

46. Michael Sandler, "Slew of Letters Grinds Skate Park to Halt," *St. Petersburg Times,* September 15, 2002, 1.

47. Ajay Singh, "Wrestling: In for the Kill," *Independent,* March 31, 2001, 10–16.

48. Marcus Warren, "Stupid Human Tricks Include Extreme Backyard Wrestling," *Gazette* (Montreal), January 6, 2003, A12.

49. Sam McManis, "Backyard Wrestling—All Pain, No Brain," *San Francisco Chronicle,* December 1, 2000, 1.

50. Lisa Prue, "Body Art May Be Tip of Child's Wildness," *Omaha World Herald,* October 8, 2002, 1E; Suz Redfearn, "Marked for Trouble," *Washington Post,* June 11, 2002, F1.

51. Harris Poll of 2,215, conducted online, July 14–20, 2003.

52. Sean T. Carroll et al., "Tattoos and Body Piercings as Indicators of Adolescent Risk-Taking Behaviors," *Pediatrics* 109 (2002): 1021–27.

53. Harris Poll.

54. Barbara Cooke, "When Teen Flair Is Scare; New Look Could Signal Problem," *Chicago Sun–Times,* March 10, 2000, 48.

55. Jane Brody, "Looking at the Hole Picture," *Milwaukee Journal Sentinel,* April 24, 2000, 1G.

56. Clinton R. Sanders, *Customizing the Body: The Art and Culture of Tattooing* (Philadelphia: Temple University Press, 1989).

57. Margie Boule, "No Loopholes in Laws on Body-Part Piercing and Oregon Teens," *Oregonian,* November 9, 2004, E1.

58. Patricia A. Adler and Peter Adler, "Self-Injurers as Loners," in *Constructions of Deviance: Social Power, Context and Interaction,* 5th edition (Belmont, Calif.: Wadsworth, 2006), 337–44.

6

Hell on Wheels

Teen Drivers

Across the country, stories about the perils of teen drivers make news, warning readers of teens' alleged carelessness, their risky behavior behind the wheel, and the threat they pose to the rest of us. "Lax Parents [Are] Giving Teen Drivers a License to Kill," warned the *Los Angeles Times*.[1] The *Denver Post* complained that "Reckless Teen Driving Rattles Adults."[2] "Limit Teens' Driving," demanded a *Hartford Courant* column.[3] In these stories, it is taken for granted that teen drivers are a major menace to public safety. Within this chapter, I will explore the actual threat new drivers pose, comparing them to other drivers to assess who really causes the biggest danger on American roads.

The automobile carries a great deal of symbolic weight in America. It represents our celebration of individualism and freedom, because we in our cars are individual units of transportation, free to go wherever we want, whenever we want. Automobiles have always represented mobility and independence, something we prize for adults but fear for young people. The car today represents the tension between unrestrained freedom and civic responsibility. As gas prices rise to new heights, the automobile causes us to ask questions about our relationship to the environment and oil-producing nations. The car has also historically allowed young people more freedom of movement, which adults struggle with. If adolescence is all about the quest for autonomy, the car is right in the center.

For the teenager growing up in a car culture, getting a driver's license is a huge rite of passage, especially for those living in the suburbs and rural areas who are dependent on cars for everyday transportation. As a teen, I couldn't wait to get my driver's license and be free to go wherever I wanted. Never would I have imagined that years later and living in Los Angeles I would find driving clearly the most stressful aspect of life for me and probably the thousands of others I am stuck in traffic with on a regular basis. Buying a car is also a ceremonial marker within the auto-loving American culture. All the better if the car's a new one, with its own special smell and pristine interior. The day I bought my first car, fresh off the lot, will always stand out in my memory. It also was my first major purchase and my introduction to another American tradition, consumer debt.

The automobile rises and falls with our economic outlook, prompting a General Motors executive in the mid-twentieth century to note that what's good for GM is good for America, and vice versa. Twentieth-century America is intricately tied to the history of the automobile. A combination of prosperity in the 1920s and Ford's assembly line and mass-produced automobile introduced car culture to Americans, including adolescents. Already challenging the mores of their Victorian parents, young people of this era now had another means of evading parental control. Cars brought kids space and separation from adults and were blamed for enabling teens' sexual experimentation.

Later in the postwar economic boom of the 1950s and 1960s, cars took on mythic status within youth culture. A whole genre of popular music paid homage to the car as a source of not just fun but youth itself. Songs like "Little Deuce Coupe" by the Beach Boys were really love songs to cars, celebrating their speed, style, and their ability to attract girls.

Not only have cars been associated with youth in popular culture, but they are also closely tied to conceptions of masculinity. During the 1920s, young women who drove violated conventions of femininity. Until the rise of the suburbs and the advent of the two-car family, driving was seen as the prerogative of the man of the house. Cars were sold primarily to men, using nubile young models to draw attention to a car's various features.[4] Working on an old car became a common male pastime, and cars became pivotal in the American male psyche: fast, sleek, and easy to handle and control. Being in control is central to our perception of what masculinity is all about, and being in control of one's car is key.

As life in the twentieth century sped up, so did cars, which were marketed for their "muscle" in the 1960s and 1970s, and later for their torque, horsepower, and acceleration. If young male drivers worship speed, it's because our culture has also done so since the advent of the assembly line. Much of the bad driving behavior attributed to teens is bound up in the way that we have constructed traditional masculinity. In a society where control over females has diminished, mastery of a car and other forms of technology has replaced more traditional forms of male power. And as we will see, concerns about teen drivers reflect central tensions between youth, freedom, and control.

THE DANGER OF PLEASURE

The automobile also represents fear and denial: our fear of teen drivers, yet denial that auto accidents by drivers of all ages continue to be a major source of injury and death, particularly when alcohol is involved. According to the National Highway Traffic Safety Administration (NHTSA), 42,815 people were killed on the road in 2002—approaching our death toll in Vietnam, and about fourteen times the death toll of the September 11 terrorist attacks.[5] An average of six children under fifteen are killed in auto accidents every day in the United States, dwarfing the danger of kidnapping and school violence.[6]

Yet this source of danger remains relatively absent from many discussions of child safety. Because for many of us driving is such a central part of daily life, confronting its risk is likely to be too overwhelming. If we feared the very real threat of car crashes as we do the unlikely dangers of school shootings or stranger abductions, we would be paralyzed with that fear.

The danger of being in an auto accident is very real, yet we project most of our anxieties onto teen drivers. Yes, the elderly occasionally get our attention after an accident happens, like the 2003 crash that killed ten people at a farmers market in Santa Monica, California. But because we tend to view older people as responsible and well-intentioned, the level of public concern over these types of crashes falls as fast as it rises. The political power of groups like AARP all but ensures that the elderly driver's privileges won't be too restricted.

Drunk drivers are certainly a major source of public concern and outrage. Because we have tended to associate drinking with young people and problem driving with teens, they receive the lion's share of attention when it comes to our fear of drunk drivers. According to NHTSA statistics on drivers involved in fatal crashes, sixteen- and seventeen-year-old drivers are among the *least* likely to have been intoxicated (defined as having a blood alcohol level over .08).[7] The only group less likely to have been drunk are drivers sixty-five and older. And drivers twenty-one to forty-four years old have the highest rates of driving drunk.[8] In 2002, 17 percent of drivers age sixteen to twenty in fatal crashes had a blood alcohol level at .08 or higher compared to 33 percent of twenty-one- to twenty-four-year-olds, 28 percent of twenty-five- to thirty-four-year-olds, and 26 percent of thirty-five- to forty-four-year-olds.[9] Those drivers forty-five to sixty-five years old involved in fatal crashes were equally as likely as young drivers to have been intoxicated; their rate was an identical 17 percent.[10]

When we break down the young drivers by age, we see a big jump between sixteen- and seventeen-year-olds and eighteen-year-olds involved in fatal crashes; for the newest drivers, their intoxication rates were 13 and 14 percent, respectively.[11] But 24 percent of eighteen-year-olds involved in fatal crashes were intoxicated. As young adults, their behavior starts mirroring that of their older counterparts. The fact that they are likely to be away from home and have greater access to alcohol enables them to behave more like adults and less like children, yet their intoxication rates are still lower than most adults under the age of forty-five. So as NHTSA boasts of the numerous lives saved by strict restrictions on teen drinking, the problem remains focused on teen drivers instead of the major drunk-driving culprits: adults. It's not the teen drivers, perennially portrayed as risk-takers, who think they're immortal, it's young and middle-aged adults who think that they are capable and experienced, and who pose the biggest risks on the road when it comes to drinking and driving.

Additionally, auto fatality rates for Americans under the age of thirty-five fell dramatically between 1982 and 2002, particularly for children under age nine.[12] This change (a 38 percent decline) was likely due to the greater use of child-restraint systems and to public-service announcements promoting keeping kids in the back seat. The young-driver age group, sixteen to twenty, experienced a 21 percent decline in auto fatalities, and the twenty-one to twenty-four age group's death rates fell 31 percent. But for older adults, fatality rates increased: by 40 percent for the thirty-five to forty-four group, and by a whopping 69 percent for adults forty-five to fifty-four. While there is no definitive explanation for this disparity, a possible reason is the rise in sport utility vehicle (SUV) purchases by more affluent drivers. NHTSA estimates that during the same twenty-year period, fatalities for occupants of SUVs increased by 386 percent.[13] It's not teen drivers who are in danger so much as SUV drivers and their passengers, because SUVs handle differently than passenger cars do and are more prone to rollovers.

THE ADULT MALE MENACE

Age is not the only factor in understanding auto safety. On the road, the combination of age and gender is much more important than age alone. For instance, rates of speed are a function of both age and gender in all except the oldest drivers. In almost every age group, males are about twice as likely to speed as females. And although speeding steadily declines with age, older male drivers involved in fatalities are more prone to have been speeding than younger female drivers.[14] It's not until men reach the thirty-five to forty-four age group that their speeding rates drop lower than the youngest female drivers.

Alcohol is more likely to be involved in fatal crashes with male drivers than females by a two to one ratio.[15] Although the vast majority of passengers now wear seatbelts, males are less likely to wear seatbelts than females (except for kids under sixteen).[16] As for young drivers (under twenty-one) involved in fatal crashes, they are nearly three times more likely to be male than female.[17] In short, being a male driver poses the greatest risk to public safety, but we would never create public-service campaigns targeting males, nor do we often consider the role that masculinity plays in driving behavior. Speed, power, and not backing down when feeling challenged are all characteristics associated with being a tough guy, and all potentially dangerous traits in a driver. But instead of confronting this fact, we allow our attention to be deflected almost entirely onto young people, which leads us to believe that they pose the greatest risk behind the wheel.

CONSTRUCTING THE TEEN THREAT IN THE PRESS

Part of the reason the mythology of the threatening teen driver continues is because we continually hear about them in the news. While it's no longer acceptable in most social circles to put down women drivers as it was a few generations ago, teen drivers are fair game in the press. Certainly some young drivers deserve to be criticized. Those who blast their car stereos are rude and annoying, and aggressive drivers who speed excessively are a threat at any age. But teens as a group are not the major threat to public safety that press reports so often suggest, reports that subsequently lead us to believe that the teen driver is a major social problem.

A January 2003 article in the *Los Angeles Times* reminded readers that even good teens are a threat once they get behind the wheel.[18] "No matter how responsible and good the kid is, they're still kids," the article noted. A parent complained in a March 2002 story that "when kids get out in these cars themselves, they take on a whole new persona."[19] In December 2002, a columnist for the *Hartford Courant* called teen drivers a "major hazard" and said that "there's no way in hell that sixteen-year-olds should be driving."[20] That same month, a *Houston Chronicle* commentary claimed that teens of the past were more responsible than kids today, and called today's teen drivers an "extreme risk."[21]

This sort of language pervades reporting on teen drivers, generalizing the misdeeds of some as characteristic of the group. Stereotyping seems justified by oft-repeated assumptions that many by now have taken for granted as true. We think it's a fact that teens believe that they're invincible and can't help themselves when it comes to taking risks. Or as the *Los Angeles Times* noted, "many teens are bent on driving dangerously," and teens "frequently engage in high risk behaviors, such as speeding and/or driving after using alcohol and drugs."[22] A California state senator proposed a ban on cell phone use for teen drivers, using the same stereotypes and questionable biological arguments that pepper news reports. In defending her teens-only ban, the senator reasoned that "it's just not the way their brains work. They tend to look at the cell phones. Older people, when talking on the cell phone, for whatever reason, really don't do that."[23] If there's one thing that many teens do well, it's talk on cell phones, but allegedly their brains are programmed to *look* at the phone while talking? There's no evidence to suggest this other than one person's observation that is interpreted to be a fact. Of course distractions of any kind, for drivers of any age, pose threats to public safety, and we should all be warned against doing anything other than concentrating on the road while driving.

Additionally, many stories about teen drivers begin by reporting that auto accidents are the leading cause of death for teens. This is true, but it is also true for everybody age two to thirty-three who is otherwise unlikely to die, period.[24] Adolescents are less vulnerable to illness than young children are and are highly unlikely to be plagued with the diseases that typically kill older adults, such as cancer and cardiovascular disease. Another common tactic in news stories is to compare teen drivers with an ambiguous category of older drivers, as the *San Francisco Chronicle* did in a February 2003 story.[25] Teen drivers are involved in more fatal crashes than drivers fifty-five and older, but are less likely to be involved in fatal crashes than drivers age twenty-five to forty-four.[26] Yet the language of stories like these may lead readers to think that *older* means anyone who is not a teenager, ignoring young and middle-age adults in the process.

Reports also tend to ignore safe teen drivers and those who are well aware of the risks reckless driving can pose. For instance, the *Denver Post* reported on its front page that a seventeen-year-old drove 84 miles per hour in a 40 mph zone during lunchtime to "see what it was like" to drive as fast as some of his classmates had been driving when they were killed three days earlier.[27] Reckless and stupid, without a doubt. But the *Post* went on to make this a teen problem, rather than an individual example of extremely poor judgment. "Kids this age are really impulsive," a local health worker told the *Post*, which noted that teens are "especially prone to disregard traffic laws." Yet later in the story the reporter noted that upset classmates ostracized the speeder when they heard about his reckless behavior. Rather than focus on the anger the other teens felt, in the very next sentence the author returned to the subject of teens' "impulsive nature."

The central reason we think teens are so much more dangerous than other drivers is that statistics on teens are seldom reported in conjunction with statistics on adult drivers. For example, an October 2003 *Los Angeles Times* story called "Teens Not Sold on Use of Seat Belts" reported that while seatbelt use is high, some teens (actually a small minority) still do not use them, and the author wondered why. The writer brought up the old invincibility argument, as well as how some teens might think it is "uncool" to be seen wearing a seatbelt. But as noted earlier, NHTSA data indicates that most teens *do* wear seatbelts, and that young female drivers are *more* likely to wear a seatbelt than men age twenty-five to sixty-nine.[28] The article didn't explore the possible "macho" factor at all, nor did it discuss why adult men are less likely to wear seatbelts than teen girls and adult women.

Teen driver stories also tend to ignore the role that parents play in influencing their kids' driving behavior. As driver's ed gets cut from many school budgets, parents are increasingly given the task of teaching their kids to drive. California, for example, requires fifty hours of parent training over a six-month period before a young driver can be fully licensed. I'm not sure exactly how those fifty hours can be verified, but in any case, parents may not always be the best role models. Many of these state-appointed driving instructors are the middle-aged speeders and even drunk drivers whom we often forget about when focused on teen drivers.

DRINKING, DRIVING, AND DENIAL

The press is also more likely to provide extensive coverage of teen drinking and driving, although non-teen drivers are typically more prone to drive drunk. By hearing more about the teens who drive drunk than about someone their parents' age, we begin to believe that this is a problem especially for adolescents. For instance, an editorial in the *Los Angeles Times* about a nineteen-year-old drunk driver began by saying, "This could be just the story of another teenager making a dumb, tragic mistake."[29] But the young woman described was not just another teenager: she was a repeat drunk driver whose license had been suspended during most of the period that she was eligible to have one. Ultimately, her drunk driving killed a friend riding as her passenger. So she is not just the girl next door, like any teen who makes a thoughtless mistake, but clearly a troubled, irresponsible young woman. To associate her behavior with all teens is rather unfair to the majority of responsible young drivers; we would never claim that a forty-year-old was indicative of his or her age group if that forty-year-old were caught driving drunk.

To assess how stories like this help shape our perception of teens, I analyzed coverage in major U.S. newspapers of drunk-driving fatalities for the first six months of 2004. Looking closely at word choice and imagery, I found that news reports use subtle but significant techniques to tell stories about drunk driving differently for teens compared with non-teens.[30] While teen drivers were responsible for 14.6 percent of all auto fatalities in 2002, 21 percent of the news coverage focused on drivers under twenty.[31] Teen stories also tended to be longer, yielding 30 percent more words than stories not involving teen drivers, even if a victim of the adult driver was a teen or a child.[32]

Several of the teen stories stood out from the group because they focused on the problem of teen drinking in general, while none of the non-teen stories expounded on adult drinking as a major problem. Instead, if it was discussed at all, drinking in non-teen cases was mainly constructed as individual failure and not representative of a larger societal problem.

For example, a February 2004 *Boston Globe* article was more than twice as long as the overall average story length, and included statistics from the Youth Risk Behavior Survey on the prevalence of teen drinking.[33] It failed to note that alcohol use has been declining among teens nationwide, and instead quoted a local basketball coach, who felt that "drug and alcohol use is a problem for schools in all communities, and that abuse has become more common."[34] So instead of using actual statistics on long-term trends, which are readily available, the article painted a picture of a major youth problem that was only getting worse. The basketball coach may work with kids every day, but he was falsely presented as an expert. While he might know a little about a handful of kids, he was not qualified to speak about "schools in all communities." The *Globe* also suggested that "quick attention placed on underage drinking . . . often fades away months after a problem occurs." Thus, young people were portrayed as not appreciating the gravity of drinking and driving. While this may well be the case, it is likely true for many adults too.

Similarly, a March 2004 *New York Times* article focused on the death of a popular student more than two years earlier, noting that "like so many fatal accidents involving teenagers, alcohol played a role. The girl . . . and her friends had started drinking early in the morning on the day of the school's annual pep rally. The death left the student body stunned, and for a while, students said, behavior seemed to change. But not for long."[35] Of course teens are not the only ones with short memories, but the problem is considered unique to adolescence. "Students are no strangers to alcohol," the *Times* reminded us, and quoted a fourteen-year-old who described teens as "so rebellious that they don't care about the facts." A May *Boston Globe* article also suggested that drunk driving is mainly a teen issue by quoting a parent who said that "the reality is that kids are going to drink; they're going to make bad choices."[36] Never mind the adults who drink and make bad choices. The *Globe* also described the accident in the story as but "one in a string of Silver Lake student deaths and injuries stemming from alcohol-related accidents," further bolstering the impression that teens are a unique hazard on the road. "With kids this age, it's really, really hard," a community leader of Students Against Drunk Driving told the *Globe*.

Within the press coverage, teens are almost expected to become drunk drivers, so those who do drive drunk are not described as significantly different from their peers. A March *Boston Globe* story explored why teens may drink and drive, coming to the conclusion that "teenagers in the community have no place to call their own."[37] A local tenth grader added, "There are no movie theaters, malls, or anything else to do for entertainment, so most teens turn to drinking." Yet none of these articles explored the broader question of why older people, who do have places to "call their own," drink and drive.

In two stories covered by the *Rocky Mountain News* and the *Star Tribune* (Minneapolis), employees of a liquor store and others were charged with helping teens get alcohol.[38] These developments suggested that drunk driving is caused by more than just the decision of a few individuals, and is the outcome of a complicit alcohol industry and a culture of bingeing. But when non-teens are involved, the net is not cast as wide, and we overlook the cultural influences on both alcohol consumption and drunk driving.

While teens as a group are implicated in drunk-driving stories, non-teen drunk drivers are depicted as individually irresponsible, victims of their own personal demons, or basically good people who made a mistake. A *San Francisco Chronicle* story about a sixty-nine-year-old attorney who killed a bicyclist while driving drunk described the attorney as possibly suicidal and "a very personable, very humorous and very kind man."[39] A forty-six-year-old drunk driver in the Bay Area killed another bicyclist just days later, but the *Chronicle* initially explained that the area itself might be to blame, describing the accident site as a "stretch of winding road with no shoulder space."[40]

Articles describing fatalities that did not involve a teen driver tended to be rather brief unless the drivers or victims held some kind of status. One of the bicyclists mentioned above was the nephew of a member of the California State Assembly. The story of a New Orleans judge's twenty-six-year-old son, who had an accident and killed a court reporter while driving the reporter home, also received thorough news coverage. The judge's son had been drinking with many New Orleans officials at a holiday party described by the *Times–Picayune* as an annual affair "which draws scores of lawyers and other courthouse regulars . . . for holiday food and drink."[41] The forty-three-year-old court reporter later died of complications from the accident. The driver's attorney described the accident as "just an isolated thing," and attributed the woman's death to poor medical care rather than his client's drinking. The attorney also noted that the man had a troubled past, but he had served in the army and "was apparently doing well."

The *St. Louis Post–Dispatch* paid significant attention as well to Leonard Little, a St. Louis Rams defensive end who had been changed with driving while intoxicated, six years after driving drunk and killing another motorist. A *Post–Dispatch* sports columnist asked the Rams organization to sever ties with Little if Little was convicted of the newest charge, noting that

> It's difficult to comprehend why the Rams would want to continue their relationship with Little. . . . If the Rams were serious about [condemning drunk driving], Leonard Little would have been removed from the roster after pleading guilty to involuntary manslaughter. . . . And he certainly wouldn't have received a $17.5 million contract from the Rams after the 2001 season.[42]

A jury acquitted Little of the charges in April 2005, in spite of the fact that he had failed three field sobriety tests and refused to take a Breathalyzer test.[43]

Two *San Francisco Chronicle* stories focused on a synchronized swimmer who hoped to compete at the 2004 summer Olympics in Athens, Greece. She had been drinking when she lost control of her SUV and hit two trees, killing her boyfriend and his twelve-year-old student who was riding with them. The *Chronicle* described her: "Fighting back tears and failing, eyes rimmed red, synchronized swimmer and prospective Olympian Tammy Crow spoke in a quavering voice of how she would do anything to take back her actions."[44] An Olympic official commented that her status as an Olympian would not be threatened, and that "a misdemeanor does not constitute any violation of that code of conduct. There is nothing that has happened that would preclude Tammy from participating." A U.S. Olympic Committee panel later recommended that she be allowed to compete and serve any jail time after the Olympic games ended. The dead twelve-year-old's parents were outraged, but the mother of the Olympian's late boyfriend said, "It was an accident. Bad decisions where made, but every human being makes bad decisions."[45] Crow went on to win a bronze medal in synchronized swimming and spent seven weeks in jail, but not before visiting the president at the White House with her Olympic team.[46]

Like news stories about the swimmer, several of the stories about non-teen drunk drivers noted that the drivers had received relatively light sentences, such as probation, for previous fatal drunk-driving incidents. Even a Minnesota man who killed a sheriff's deputy received probation, as did a man whose drunk driving resulted in his mother's death.[47] Rams defensive end Little had received a suspended sentence and probation after the 2001 incident.[48]

Of the in-depth, non-teen stories, many noted that the driver had a history of drunk driving. For instance, a nanny who was accused of driving drunk and killing two children before fleeing the scene of the accident had a "history of DUI convictions," according to the *San Francisco Chronicle*.[49] However, her attorney contended that "Ms. Barreto does have a prior DUI history, but it certainly doesn't confirm that she was intoxicated the day of the incident," a claim one could only make after a hit-and-run accident. Another *Chronicle* story detailed a driver whose license had "been suspended six times" and was "able to drive after four drunken-driving arrests because he either made bail or failed to show up in court or for counseling sessions. . . . And in at least two cases, [the driver] pleaded guilty to lesser charges of reckless driving, resulting in fines and probation."[50] This driver's latest drunk-driving arrest had come after a police chase that resulted in the death of a thirty-three-year-old motorist making a turn. Meanwhile, a Missouri man served a four and one-half year sentence in the drunk-driving deaths of his passengers—his girlfriend and a cousin—then was given an eighteen-month sentence for driving drunk shortly after his release from prison.[51] After yet another DUI arrest, he was given thirty months in prison, but was also given the option of boot camp instead. His aunt told the *St. Louis Post–Dispatch* that his "continuing problems with drunken driving showed a lack of remorse for her daughter's death."

These tales of leniency beg the question about whether we are dealing with adult drunk drivers effectively, although none of the stories explored this issue. If driving drunk is a choice, and therefore never really accidental, is probation ever an acceptable sentence when someone's life is lost? These stories failed to ask even basic questions about adult drunk driving in our society, leaving it up to us to do so.

By and large, stories about non-teen drivers occasionally offered accounts of the devastation caused by the drunk driver, but not of that caused by drunk driving as a whole. Unless teens were driving, news coverage tended to overlook our overall culture of excess, our relatively lenient drunk-driving laws, and the many adults in our society who won't stop drinking and driving.

While education about the dangers of drunk driving is important and should start early, it clearly needs to continue beyond high school. Teens may be described as rebellious risk-takers who don't appreciate the value of life, but what about older repeat offenders? We should strive to eliminate teen drinking and driving, but we also need to recognize that teens are just a small part of the larger problem. It is a problem teens don't necessarily create but sometimes unfortunately grow into.

HOT RODS

Drinking and driving isn't the only major risk to public safety. Speeding accounted for 13,713 deaths in 2002, or 31 percent of all fatal crashes.[52] The culprits were typically male, mostly young, but not only teens. Yet news coverage of the quest for speed on the streets continually characterizes this as a teen problem.

On November 27, 2002, the Associated Press reported that "a teen driver speeding down a San Diego, California, street slam[med] into a passing car, killing its driver."[53] At that point San Diego had experienced about fourteen deaths that year attributed to street racing, causing concern and fear among law enforcement and the community, who saw this as a prime example of dangerous teen drivers.[54] Yet estimates suggest that most street racers range in age from eighteen to thirty.[55] Several stories that year focused on the tragic deaths of two teens, nineteen-year-old college sweethearts.[56] But they weren't racing their car, they were driving home when one of two racers, speeding with his lights off, smashed into them in October 2002. The racers, aged twenty-nine and thirty-two, were charged with murder.[57]

In spite of the involvement of young adults, kids became the major focus of concern. "Why are kids still killing each other with their speeding cars?

When will these kids learn?" a reader wrote the *San Diego Union–Tribune.*[58] "I outgrew that stupidity by my early twenties," said another reader.[59] The Associated Press noted that law enforcement was concerned about the Thanksgiving holiday because kids would be out of school and have more time to race. However, the teen driver mentioned in their story was eighteen, and possibly out of school already.[60] A mother whose thirty-year-old son died in a street race responded to reports that a Qualcomm Stadium drag strip would have limited hours due to sporting events. She noted that "the kids are all upset," but the closure "doesn't give a right for kids to go back out on the street."[61] "The kids who build these cars are going to run them," a thirty-eight-year-old racer who built fast cars noted.[62]

While these news stories focused on kids as the source of the street-racing problem, racing is certainly not new, nor was it invented by this generation of teens. "Ever since there were two cars, there was a race," says Jim Wangers, publisher of *Pontiac Enthusiast.*[63] Street racing began in Southern California on dry lake beds and flood channels during the 1920s when enthusiasts began altering Model Ts to increase their speed.[64] The weather and terrain were conducive to year-round racing and tinkering with cars. Fast forward to the twenty-first century, when cars can go much faster and once-deserted rural areas are now built-up suburbs, and street racing can pose a major hazard to public safety.

In context, street racing is a somewhat minor threat nationally. NHTSA estimated that 135 people were killed in racing accidents in 2001, compared with 12,850 for all speeding-related deaths.[65] But the problem was particularly bad in San Diego, where nearly 12 percent of the nation's racing deaths occurred that year, but where less than 1 percent of the nation's population resides. Since the late 1990s, San Diego police have created a special unit to address the problem, and a San Diego State University professor helped found RaceLegal.com, which works to organize legal races off the streets. This program focuses mainly on young adults because racing is not just an activity for "rebellious teenagers," as a Missouri newspaper reported.[66]

Automobile racing is a sport that people of all ages participate in and enjoy. The National Hot Rod Association (NHRA) reports having eighty thousand members nationwide, and the National Association for Stock Car Auto Racing (NASCAR) is a multimillion dollar industry. A *San Diego Union–Tribune* reader wrote to the editor, "I am nearly at the half-century mark. I also love fast cars."[67] Being a teenager is certainly not the only qualification for the need for speed.

Breaking the sound barrier and supersonic travel are both examples of our drive to master the limitations of our existence. Speed provides a thrill in amusement parks, and it's no accident that several illegal drugs are referred to as "speed." Our culture encourages, maybe even requires us to live a sped-up existence to accomplish as much as we can in as little time as possible. The age of mass production, ushered in by the automobile, all but eliminated the art of craftsmanship, and certainly altered our appreciation of the virtue of taking one's time.

With speed comes danger, however, which provides both thrill and fear. There is something about adolescence that we view as dangerous, and much like speed, the danger is both thrilling and frightening. Teens are characterized as reckless and without fear of their own mortality. While we outwardly condemn these qualities, especially when it comes to driving, we celebrate risk-taking too. Living on the edge may be dangerous, but danger lets us know that we're alive. While we vilify teens, we deny many of our own propensities to take risks.

Yet many teenagers are anything but reckless and are even more afraid of taking chances than many of us realize. Holding teens up as bad examples hardly serves to encourage conformity and safety, on the road or otherwise.

CONTROLLING THE TEEN DRIVER

Since teens are depicted in press reports as uniformly prone to drunk driving and speeding, it may appear that all teen drivers should be restricted. A *Houston Chronicle* commentary railed against parents who allow their sixteen-year-olds to get driver's licenses.[68] A "typical sixteen-year-old is on par with a typical Depression-Era twelve-year-old," insisted the author, a psychologist, without explanation. More than half of the states have acted on the premise that teens today are less responsible than their predecessors by restricting the types of driving privileges they can have. Some states limit the number of passengers allowed in a new driver's car or the hours a new driver may be on the road. Others have proposed raising the driving age altogether.

In 2003, the National Safety Council reported on the outcome of such graduated license programs, championing their success.[69] Fatal crash rates were down for sixteen-year-olds in several states with the new restrictions. A 2002 study by the Automobile Club of Southern California also reported that alcohol-related accidents were up for slightly older drivers who were licensed before the new restrictions became law.[70]

This seems like a slam-dunk case supporting more restrictive licensing laws, but there are several problems with attributing these trends to the changes in the law. For one, as noted earlier, alcohol-related crashes traditionally rise for drivers in their late teens and early twenties, so a restrictive law would likely not be responsible for lower rates among young teens. Further, long-term trends indicate that auto fatality rates for young people were *already* on the decline before the licensing changes. Such drops are probably the result of higher seatbelt use in recent years, improved safety features in newer cars, and medical advances that today convert what might have been a fatality a decade ago into a serious yet survivable injury.

There is nothing wrong with providing more supervision and driver training. Good training, however, is costly and involves more than showing a
gory movie of highway accidents and more than assuming that parents can
be adequate teachers. Defensive-driving courses and special training for SUV
drivers would be beneficial to drivers of all ages. Simply limiting experience
will not create safe drivers.

The biggest problem with graduated licenses as our policy solution for
road safety is that this only targets teens and ignores the complexity of the
dangers we face on the roads. In response to the idea that his state's driving
age be raised to seventeen, driving instructor John R. Berger wrote to the
Hartford Courant that "a vast majority of drivers, teenage or otherwise, are
grossly incompetent," and that lack of skills, not age, is the major hazard.[71]
Berger went on to say that in his experience, younger drivers are somewhat
easier to teach because they have had less time to create bad habits.

Competency is a central issue here. In a car-loving culture such as our
own, we all want to think of ourselves as capable drivers, able to handle our
vehicles and any challenge the road throws our way. It's part of the American spirit of rugged individualism. We are rarely able to admit that we are
bad drivers, but are quick to point out that others are, particularly if they are
young. We are reluctant to publicly address or challenge the many experienced drivers of all ages who take their competency for granted. Condemning teen drivers allows us to feel that our driving competency is superior to
someone else's, and of course in some cases it is. The danger lies in overlooking the 85 percent of fatal crashes that *do not* involve teen drivers.
There's nothing wrong with helping new drivers become better drivers, but
there is something wrong when we are unwilling to examine the biggest
safety hazards and instead focus all of our efforts on controlling teens.

Ultimately, news stories about teen drivers aren't just about driving, they
are about young people themselves. The media's presentation of driving
tragedies serves as another outlet for condemning teens while avoiding the
role that older adults play in auto safety. The number of young people killed
by non-teen drivers dwarfs the carnage caused by teens, but this is not a big
theme in the press. The myth of the teen driver as menace serves to justify
further restriction and control of teens and to limit their movement in the
name of public safety.

For parents anxious to regulate their teenager's behavior, new businesses
have sprung up that allow parents, or the motoring public, to spy on teen
drivers. "Black boxes" can be installed in cars to monitor teens (and other
drivers), a technology based on that of flight data recorders.[72] Devices currently on the market record speed and acceleration rates, location, and in
some cases seatbelt use. Parents or users can then download from a website
the information gathered by the system. A more low-tech solution involves
toll-free numbers on bumper stickers in order to "encourage motorists to

snitch on reckless youths."[73] These services cost anywhere from $19 to $55 a year to let parents know if their teen has offended other drivers.

Aside from teen embarrassment and expense to parents, these measures overlook the role that parents play in modeling unsafe driving habits. Instead, manufacturers promote the myth that teen drivers are uniquely aggressive and deluded by the belief that "nothing bad can happen to them," since it is in the manufacturers' financial interest to encourage us to believe that teen drivers are a breed unto themselves.[74] But by relying on these and similar services rather than improving driver training (for drivers of all ages) and law enforcement, we focus only on teen drivers and needlessly demonize many young people, while ignoring the threat that other drivers pose.

Bringing the arguments above and in the preceding chapters together, in the final section of this book I explore how our fears of teen drivers, risk-takers, bullies, school safety, obesity, and kidnapping translate into dollar signs for the businesses that profit from our anxieties about kids today.

NOTES

1. Jeanne Wright, "Lax Parents Giving Teen Drivers a License to Kill," *Los Angeles Times,* January 23, 2003, G1.

2. Ann Schrader, "Reckless Teen Driving Rattles Adults," *Denver Post,* March 10, 2003, A1.

3. Tom Condon, "Limit Teens' Driving," *Hartford Courant,* December 22, 2002, B1.

4. "America on Wheels," Public Broadcasting System, June 11, 1996.

5. U.S. Department of Transportation, National Highway Traffic Safety Administration, "Traffic Safety Facts 2002: Overview," Washington, D.C., 2003.

6. U.S. Department of Transportation, National Highway Traffic Safety Administration, "Traffic Safety Facts 2002: Children," Washington, D.C., 2003.

7. U.S. Department of Transportation, National Highway Traffic Safety Administration, "Traffic Safety Facts 2002: Alcohol," Washington, D.C., 2003.

8. U.S. Department of Transportation, National Highway Traffic Safety Administration, "Traffic Safety Facts 2002: Alcohol."

9. U.S. Department of Transportation, National Highway Traffic Safety Administration, "Traffic Safety Facts 2002: Alcohol."

10. U.S. Department of Transportation, National Highway Traffic Safety Administration, "Traffic Safety Facts 2002: Alcohol."

11. U.S. Department of Transportation, National Highway Traffic Safety Administration, "Traffic Safety Facts 2002: Young Drivers," Washington, D.C., 2003.

12. U.S. Department of Transportation, National Highway Traffic Safety Administration, "Why Are We Not Seeing a Reduction in Highway Fatalities?" Washington, D.C., 2004.

13. U.S. Department of Transportation, National Highway Traffic Safety Administration, "Why Are We Not Seeing a Reduction?"

14. U.S. Department of Transportation, National Highway Traffic Safety Administration, "Traffic Safety Facts 2002: Speeding," Washington, D.C., 2003.

15. U.S. Department of Transportation, National Highway Traffic Safety Administration, "Traffic Safety Facts 2002: Alcohol."

16. U.S. Department of Transportation, National Highway Traffic Safety Administration, "Safety Belt Use in 2003—Demographic Characteristics," Washington, D.C., 2004.

17. U.S. Department of Transportation, National Highway Safety Traffic Safety Administration, "Traffic Safety Facts 2002: Young Drivers."

18. Wright, "Lax Parents Giving Teen Drivers a License to Kill."

19. Hugo Martin, "Calling in Bad Teen Drivers," *Los Angeles Times*, March 19, 2002, B1.

20. Condon, "Limit Teens' Driving."

21. John Rosemond, "Putting the Brakes on Teen Driving," *Houston Chronicle*, December 4, 2002, 11.

22. Jeanne Wright, "'Black Boxes' Can Monitor Teen Drivers," *Los Angeles Times*, January 29, 2003, G1; Jeanne Wright, "Teens Not Sold on Use of Seat Belts," *Los Angeles Times*, October 15, 2003, G1.

23. Jordan Rau, "Teen Drivers Could Face Ban on Use of Cellphones," *Los Angeles Times*, April 25, 2004, B1.

24. U.S. Department of Transportation, National Highway Traffic Safety Administration, "Traffic Safety Facts 2002: Overview."

25. C. W. Nevius, "Son on the Road to Independence," *San Francisco Chronicle*, February 16, 2003, E2.

26. U.S. Department of Transportation, National Highway Traffic Safety Administration, "Traffic Safety Facts 2002: Young Drivers."

27. Schrader, "Reckless Teen Driving Rattles Adults."

28. U.S. Department of Transportation, National Highway Traffic Safety Administration, "Safety Belt Use in 2003."

29. Editorial, "When Bad Choices Are Fatal," *Los Angeles Times*, March 2, 2003, B18.

30. U.S. Department of Transportation, National Highway Traffic Safety Administration, "Traffic Safety Facts 2002: Young Drivers." Lexis-Nexis search on the terms *drunk driving* and *killed* or *fatal* yielded fifty-two stories from January 1, 2004, to June 30, 2004.

31. U.S. Department of Transportation, National Highway Traffic Safety Administration, "Traffic Safety Facts 2002: Young Drivers." As of this writing, 2002 is the most recent data available.

32. Average word count for stories about teen drivers was 511; when the driver was older than nineteen, the average length was 359 words.

33. Meredith Goldstein, "Clancy Targets Teen Drinking," *Boston Globe*, February 8, 2004, 1. The number of words was 872, compared with 401, the overall average length of all drunk-driving fatality stories.

34. Goldstein, "Clancy Targets Teen Drinking."

35. Lisa W. Foderaro, "Program Battles Drinking Long before Drinking Age," *New York Times*, March 25, 2004, B5.

36. Joanna Massey, "Tragedy Spurs Couple to Help Teens Avoid Deadly Mistakes," *Boston Globe*, May 20, 2004, 1.

37. Emily Sweeney, "Driven to Make a Difference," *Boston Globe*, March 29, 2004, B3.

38. Anthony Lonetree, "Charges Filed in Deadly Crash," *Star Tribune* (Minneapolis), March 2, 2004, 5B; Tillie Fong, "Liquor Store Loses Crash Suit," *Rocky Mountain News*, February 27, 2004, 22A.

39. Ryan Kim, Pamela J. Podger, and Peter Fimrite, "Widespread Ripples Extend from Fatal Crash," *San Francisco Chronicle*, April 19, 2004, B1.

40. Charlie Goodyear, "Bicyclist Killed," *San Francisco Chronicle*, April 20, 2004, B4.

41. Michael Perlstein, "Death Reopens DWI Case," *Times–Picayune*, January 7, 2004, 1.

42. Bernie Miklasz, "If Little Is Guilty, He Shouldn't Get Another Chance," *St. Louis Post–Dispatch*, April 29, 2004, D1.

43. Heather Ratcliffe, "Little's Refusal to Take Breath Test Helped Him in Trial," *St. Louis Post–Dispatch*, April 3, 2005, E3.

44. John Crumpacker, "Swim Star Regrets Getting into Car That Fateful Night," *San Francisco Chronicle*, February 4, 2004, A1.

45. Alan Gathright, "Swimmer Gets Olympic Nod," *San Francisco Chronicle*, April 10, 2004, B1.

46. Sports Digest, *St. Louis Post–Dispatch*, December 14, 2005, D2.

47. Margaret Zack, "Drunken Driver Gets Probation," *Star Tribune* (Minneapolis), June 23, 2004, 2B; Margaret Zack, "Drunk Driver Whose Mother Died in Crash Gets Probation," *Star Tribune* (Minneapolis), April 17, 2004, 3B.

48. Bill Bryan, "Little Could Face Felony Charges," *St. Louis Post–Dispatch*, April 26, 2004, B1.

49. Henry K. Lee, "Nanny Pleads Not Guilty," *San Francisco Chronicle*, May 15, 2004, B5.

50. Henry K. Lee, "Driver Convicted For '01 Fatal Chase," *San Francisco Chronicle*, May 21, 2004, B5.

51. Trisha L. Howard, "Man May Face Prison again for DUI," *St. Louis Post–Dispatch*, June 8, 2004.

52. U.S. Department of Transportation, National Highway Traffic Safety Administration, "Traffic Safety Facts 2002: Speeding."

53. Michelle Morgante, "New Street-Racing Death Has San Diego Officials Warning Parents," Associated Press News and Wire, November 27, 2002.

54. Ray Huard, "More Legal Street Racing Options Sought," *San Diego Union–Tribune*, December 8, 2002, B1.

55. John Wilkens, "Street Racing's Deadly Finish," *San Diego Union–Tribune*, October 13, 2002, A1; Angela Lau, "Tapping the Breaks," *San Diego Union–Tribune*, July 1, 2002, B1.

56. Wilkens, "Street Racing's Deadly Finish."

57. Alex Roth, "Two Street Racers to Stand Trial on Murder Charges in Fatal Accident," *San Diego Union–Tribune*, January 31, 2003, B1.

58. Letters, *San Diego Union–Tribune*, "He Left Street Racing in Rear-View Mirror," October 12, 2002, B9.

59. Letters, *San Diego Union–Tribune*, "He Left Street Racing."

60. Morgante, "New Street-Racing Death."

61. Ray Huard, "Extended Racing Hours Being Sought for Qualcomm Strip," *San Diego Union–Tribune*, December 12, 2002, B4.

62. Bill Center, "Nowhere to Run," *San Diego Union–Tribune*, January 9, 2003, D2.

63. Wilkens, "Street Racing's Deadly Finish."

64. "Drag Racing," *Modern Marvels*, A&E Television Network and the History Channel, 2001.

65. U.S. Department of Transportation, National Highway Traffic Safety Administration, "Traffic Safety Facts: 2001," Washington, D.C., 2002. The year 2001 represents the most recent data available from the U.S. Department of Transportation.

66. Matthew Everett, "2 Fast 2 Last," *Riverfront Times*, May 28, 2003.

67. Letters, "Scaring Street Racers—and Spectators—Won't Help," *San Diego Union–Tribune*, October 26, 2002, B9.

68. Rosemond, "Putting the Brakes on Teen Driving."

69. Associated Press, "License Laws Cut Teen Driver Deaths," *Los Angeles Times*, February 19, 2003, A15.

70. Hugo Martin, "Fewer Teens in Crashes, Study Finds," *Los Angeles Times*, September, 22, 2002, B8.

71. John Berger, "Skills, Not Ages, Determine Driver Safety," *Hartford Courant*, December 28, 2002, A8.

72. Wright, "'Black Boxes' Can Monitor Teen Drivers."

73. Martin, "Calling in Bad Teen Drivers."

74. Wright, "'Black Boxes' Can Monitor Teen Drivers."

Conclusion

The Business of Youth Phobia

Fear Sells

Although our fears of risk-taking teens and our many other anxieties about kids today tend to be out of proportion, it has not been my intent to minimize their seriousness in any way. It is only natural for parents to hear about dangers and worry about their own children's safety. Certainly kids are sometimes abducted by strangers, shot at school, or sometimes fall prey to substance abuse. We of course want to prevent these things from happening, and if they do happen we need to deal with them aggressively. Obesity, drunk driving, and early pregnancy are real public health concerns. By putting these very real problems into perspective, my goal is not to suggest that we stick our heads in the sand and deny that any such trouble exists. Instead, I am trying to put these concerns in context and most importantly, to demonstrate that kids today are not necessarily headed for disaster.

But parents and other adults who work with young people may feel it's better to be safe than sorry, better to worry and protect a little more than necessary if it means keeping kids safe and healthy. I am certainly not suggesting that parents and people concerned about children abdicate their responsibilities to kids, only that we not overlook the more mundane and most common challenges by focusing on rare but catastrophic occurrences.

Fears do not arise in a vacuum. I have incorporated a lot of quotes from various news sources, but I do not want to suggest that our disproportional anxiety about young people is the product of sensational news coverage alone. This news only reinforces our existing concerns and legitimizes these fears by providing sometimes misleading or even wrong information that bolsters our foregone conclusion that things are worse for kids today than ever before.

It is true that coming of age in the twenty-first century provides unique opportunities as well as new challenges. Within the industrialized world, young people have a multitude of ways for finding entertainment, communicating, and accessing information. This scares a lot of adults, especially parents, who may wonder whom their kids may be talking to and what they may learn. In many respects, adults have far less control over young people's knowledge today than at any time in history.

Kids living in industrialized nations also have fewer economic responsibilities overall, and are largely expected to remain out of the labor force until eighteen, twenty-one, or even older. This, coupled with a surplus economy and the designation of young people as consumers rather than as producers as they were in the past, has created an atmosphere of leisure for the young. While not all young people are free from work, marketers want us to believe that being young means having fun, and that the way to have fun is to consume.

Challenges have always been part of growing up, and this generation faces obstacles too. Until the early twentieth century, physical survival was a universal challenge for the very young; epidemics knew no class or ethnic barriers, and children of the wealthy as well as the poor succumbed to diseases such as typhoid and yellow fever. Today in the United States, challenges are more stratified by class. As I discussed in chapter 2, children in poor minority communities are more likely to be obese and to face a lifetime of complications from cardiovascular disease and type 2 diabetes. Our advances in medicine are increasingly out of reach for the young and poor in America, where one child in eight has no health insurance.[1] These kids are also more likely to live in areas plagued by violence and to attend schools that are overcrowded and in disrepair, as we saw in chapter 3. Make no mistake, not all American kids have the luxury of being spoiled today, nor is their biggest threat coming from playing video games or watching television.

Navigating the challenges of sex, drugs, or alcohol is never easy for teens, but it is much harder if the adults in their lives are irresponsible themselves. While drug experimentation may peak in the early twenties, older adults' drug use probably has far more serious consequences than that of young recreational users. Kids today are also more likely to be the product of a teen pregnancy than to have one themselves. Many of the struggles that young people face are the direct result of the poor choices that the adults in their lives have made.

Although complaints about the young span the centuries, youth phobia intensifies at certain times. Times of flux and change create generalized uncertainty, and young people symbolize that uncertainty about the future. Older adults may feel that the world is an unrecognizable place compared with what they once knew and may look at young people as representative of those changes. As we get older, we may recognize the fact of our aging with remorse and may then see young people as usurpers taking our place, the cause rather than the effect of change. Young people have increasingly been valued over older adults as consumers, as marketers seek young customers and audiences even though older people have more money. The "cool" factor resides in youth, not in experience, at least for the moment.

Finally, we often see the social problems that affect young people and blame the kids themselves for causing the problems. We redirect the health-care crisis to blame lazy kids who don't take care of themselves; education problems are blamed on violent, disruptive, and ignorant students; and ongoing substance-abuse problems in the adult population are blamed on risk-taking teens. We focus our concern for STDs on promiscuous spring-break goers and partying teens. Blaming kids means that we think we have found the answer to our problems in individuals who make bad choices, rather than by looking at the complexities of what causes these problems. Issues like lack of economic opportunity, continued inequality, and policy decisions that have had unintended negative consequences are easily overlooked because it seems we have found the source of the problem. It is far easier to blame individuals—especially if they can't vote—than to look at the often hidden causes of social problems.

And fearing youth is profitable. Business tends to thrive on our notion that we can reduce our anxiety by purchasing its products. Youth phobia is a burgeoning industry, with a variety of products and services geared to address our fears of and fear for young people. But while these industries may capitalize on our fear, they are not necessarily devoid of good intent. Wanting to help ensure the safety of young people is an admirable goal, and it can also be profitable. However, the products sold often do more to alleviate adult anxieties than to actually protect kids. In the following sections, I will discuss various business opportunities that have been carved out of our fears of and for kids today.

SELLING KIDNAPPING FEARS

In its oldest forms, kidnapping was a way to make money through ransom. Historian Paula Fass discusses how children of the wealthy were the most common targets of kidnappers in the nineteenth and early twentieth centuries.[2] Today kidnapping for ransom is still a threat to people of all ages in parts of the world experiencing political and economic instability. In some countries, business executives and other wealthy individuals purchase kidnapping insurance, which covers expenses like paying ransom and funding a rescue mission.[3] Companies like the renowned Lloyd's of London and American insurance giant American International Group (AIG) currently offer such policies.

While selling kidnap insurance policies for American children is not a common practice, the technology industry has been developing products and services for parents to allow them to keep track of their children electronically. Talk of implanting Big Brother–like microchips in kids, as we can for pets, may come up as a hypothetical solution after a high-profile kidnapping blankets the airwaves, but other types of products are already on the market to tap into a parent's worst nightmare.

In the 1980s, it was not altogether uncommon to see a child in a mall or airport tethered to a parent's leash. The practice drew a great number of debates about the merits of child safety versus humiliation and the obvious parallel between children and pets. Today the leashes are still there, but they are invisible and electronic.

For instance, a product called Gotcha supplies parents, at a cost of $79.95, with a pager that goes off if their child is more than seventy-five feet away.[4] The Urban Tracker II K allows a 500-foot radius, but the cost for this longer "leash" is significantly higher at $695. On the lower end of the price spectrum, the Kid Safe Alarm emits a deafening sound when a pin is pulled, presumably to ward off would-be kidnappers, for $19.99. More ominously, a Life Lynx Child Safety key will store vital information about a child, information that can be quickly transmitted to the company's website for media and law-enforcement access in case of an abduction. Currently being tested for free in Columbus, Ohio, the product normally retails at $35.[5] This product crosses the line from prevention of to preparing for a kidnapping—as though kidnapping is inevitable. This may make parents feel better prepared, but it is probably less than reassuring to kids.

Additionally, radio frequency identification (RFID), though currently used primarily in tracking products, is available at a European Legoland.[6] Parents there can buy a bracelet for their child to wear during their visit so the child can be tracked anywhere in the park. This again may make parents feel safer, but RFID also opens up a lot of surreptitious marketing-research opportunities for the company. Fear of missing children can even be sold to schools. A charter school in Buffalo, New York, also uses RFID for attendance purposes at a cost of $25,000 for the system and $3 per tag for each child.[7] And a Houston-area school utilizes a different tracking system, requiring kids to swipe a barcode as they get onto the school bus to ensure that they are on the right bus.[8]

Global positioning system (GPS) technology is also being used to track kids. A product by Wherify, a Silicon Valley–based company, includes GPS technology in a watch that also includes a pager and downloadable games for $199 and a $20 per month fee for the locator service.[9] Quik Trak, a British company, has marketed devices for kids to carry so that their whereabouts can be monitored online.[10] Cell phones are beginning to include GPS technology, mainly to locate people making emergency calls, but the technology can also be used to track kids.

Cell phone services marketed to families have also increased in recent years. In March of 2004, *Investor's Business Daily* noted that "cell phone companies in general are benefiting from child safety concerns," and that the typical age for a child's first cell phone has declined from sixteen to twelve.[11]

As with any new technology, the price of a new product is usually cost-prohibitive for most consumers, but as prices come down we may see more young people monitored electronically by their parents and school administrators. While knowing where kids are is a good thing, if parents feel compelled to buy a product out of fear, it could serve to needlessly elevate anxiety and divert families from using their money more productively, such as for paying down consumer debt or saving for a child's education. Electronic monitoring may also seem like a substitute for old-fashioned parental involvement.

If parents are reluctant to spring for high-tech equipment to track their kids, an afternoon at a community safety fair may be a cheaper alternative. Safety fairs sometimes provide a lot of information about fighting off stranger abductions, but also include useful advice about protecting ourselves and children against other more likely threats to safety, such as fires and traffic accidents. Local police and firefighters often get involved, and the fairs also include fun activities for families, including martial-arts demonstrations, face painting, and inflatable moon bounces. In fact, to honor what would have been Danielle Van Dam's eighth birthday, her family invited community members to a safety fair in her honor.[12]

Raising awareness about safety is an excellent way of turning a high-profile tragedy into a form of community service. It is also a great opportunity for corporate sponsors to get good publicity. Several Clear Channel radio stations sponsored the Van Dam family event. Then there are the companies that market "pre-abduction" child identification kits—which include digital fingerprints and pictures of the child, as well as vital statistics and in some cases a DNA sample—to be distributed at fairs like this. The kits are customizable so that corporations can put their logos and contact information on the outside. Kinderprint, a company that produces such a kit, touts its product on the company website as a way for corporations to "generate good will" and "build name recognition."[13] In addition to corporations distributing the kits at safety fairs, some banks have given out free kits to people opening new accounts, replacing the toaster of yesteryear.

By drawing on preexisting parental fears, corporations with no connection to law enforcement can associate their brand with the protection of children, using adult anxiety as a marketing opportunity. It is unclear whether these products are actually effective at making kids any safer, or whether they really help parents feel less afraid of an extremely unlikely event.

On a darker note, electronic monitoring, which is common for adults under house arrest, if adapted for monitoring other individuals, might send a message of fear to young children and of mistrust to teens. The technology could also be abused by those who want not just safety, but excessive control—and not just over kids, but over other adults as well. Abusers who fear losing control over children or romantic partners could create more dependence by using such devices. The same or similar technology, intended to prevent abuse, can actually make it harder to escape abuse. For example, an abusive foster mother in Milwaukee allegedly used a baby monitor to make sure that two girls, aged two and four, held their arms up indefinitely while she was in another room.[14]

PROFITING FROM OBESITY

Stoking fears about child obesity also creates business opportunities. As I noted at the end of chapter 2, food is big business, and so is the diet industry. But while food manufacturers have long been successful at reaching the youth market, the diet industry has thrived more by addressing anxious adults, particularly mothers. Low-sugar cereals, yogurt treats, and other healthier snacks appeal to parents concerned about their children's weight.

Kids who have money in their pockets may spend it on vending machine snacks, but they are a tougher market for the diet industry to reach. Typically, parents are the targets of marketing campaigns for weight-loss programs aimed at helping kids lose weight. The fear that children will be rejected by their peers is perhaps a more powerful selling point than the long-term health risks of obesity, as is the guilt that parents (especially mothers) may feel about how they are feeding their children.

For this reason, most books sold about child and teen weight loss are addressed to the parents, not the kids. An Amazon.com search yields dozens of hits for books written for concerned parents, with titles like *Helping Your Overweight Child, How to Get Your Kid to Eat But Not Too Much*, and *Rescuing the Emotional Lives of Our Overweight Children*. These titles speak directly to parents' anxieties about their kids' emotional well-being, and they provide parents with a sense that they can control childhood weight problems through the tools offered in the books. Several books offer parents suggestions about the sorts of meals, snacks, and activities that they can use to help their kids lose weight. Weight loss is hard enough to accomplish, but it is even harder when the reader is trying to get someone else to lose weight. Just as with products that address parental fear of abduction, it's hard to know how effective these books actually are in helping parents help kids lose weight.

Weight-loss camps are certainly not new on the scene, but they also use our concerns about child obesity to sell their programs. Camp brochures quote obesity trends, oftentimes overstating them, just as news reports sometimes do, in an attempt to market their product. While many camp programs are sponsored by nonprofit organizations, even those may be cost-prohibitive to the poorest and often heaviest kids. For instance, a nonprofit camp in Illinois costs $3,190 per month to attend.[15] For wealthier kids, private boarding schools like the Healthy Living Academy boarding school in Aspen, Colorado, provide summer and year-round programs for the overweight.[16]

In addition to healthy eating and exercise, live-in weight-loss programs promise fun and bully-free experiences for kids accustomed to being teased. But campers told a *New York Times* reporter in 2005 that the teasing continues even in these environments.[17] Rather than a feeling of unity, the weight hierarchy is just recalibrated so that the least obese sometimes torment the heaviest campers. Further, the long-term success of summer weight-loss programs is unclear. Once kids return home they often resume unhealthy habits and must deal with the same emotional contexts that may have created their eating problems to begin with. With Americans getting progressively heavier, camps for families are also starting, such as one in La Jolla, California, selling the concept of a weight-loss vacation.[18]

The fitness industry has started to focus on young people as an untapped market. In 2003 the Wellbridge company, whose press release describes it as "the leading operator of premier athletic clubs, spas, and fitness/wellness centers," announced that it would be entering the kids market, opening what it called "innovative fitness programs for children K–12" in ten states across the country.[19] "Obesity levels in teens twelve to nineteen years has grown by a staggering ten percent," the release continues, adding urgency to its new programs, which include "jumping jacks, parachute play, Funky Hokey Pokey and jump rope games." Sports training is also available for kids who may be too old for the hokeypokey.

Exercise is certainly an important part of a healthy lifestyle. What companies like Wellbridge are packaging, however, is the sort of play that need not come from a gym membership. For parents who don't want their kids to play outside or for communities where kids don't know each other, purchasing playtime may be better than nothing for those who can afford it. But typically, the kids whose families can afford gym memberships are the ones who live in places where they can play outside and ride bicycles with the neighbors without a surcharge. The more affluent school districts that these kids probably attend are also more likely to have gym class and recess and healthier food choices for lunch. Gym memberships, sports leagues, dance classes, and martial-arts lessons are other ways to stay healthy, and are also often unavailable to low-income kids who need it most.

SELLING SCHOOL SAFETY

School security is a growing segment of law enforcement because many districts have their own school police, contract with police departments, or hire private security services. Security consultants often seek out schools, offering to write grants for their districts and to get them a piece of the federal spending on education and even homeland security. Schools may purchase cameras, metal detectors, and X-ray machines to try and make their buildings and grounds safer. In Biloxi, Mississippi, every classroom has a surveillance camera, although every camera is not necessarily monitored.[20] Unmonitored cameras are not uncommon; it is quite costly to pay people to actually watch the feeds, but the cameras can be used to view recorded incidents after they have happened. According to a U.S. Justice Department report, schools may use this footage to help themselves reduce their liability or to convince parents in denial that their kids really are causing trouble.[21] In Connecticut, one school considered installing security cameras as a preventative measure, at an estimated cost of $50,000. Citing concerns over the 1999 Columbine High School shooting in Littleton, Colorado, a security officer noted that it is "better to be safe and take measures to stem violence before it starts."[22] Ironically, a cheaper alternative—having parents and other visitors wear special identifying badges—was dismissed after some parents found wearing nametags "intrusive."

Watching students more seems like a good idea, but it does nothing to prevent violence. Columbine High School had surveillance cameras, which provided grainy images of the shooters' brief reign of terror, but clearly the cameras did not make students safe that day. Keeping students safe should be a primary goal of schools, but the question is how to best accomplish school safety. Given schools' limited budgets, we must tailor our solutions to the actual threat, not the most remote fear. It is easy to lose perspective in an age of anxiety.

Our fears of school violence have clearly commingled with our fears about terrorism. An Associated Press story noted that school security "is only part of the work needed to keep [kids] safe in a time of terror and mass killings."[23] In 2003, the National Association of School Resource Officers (NASRO), an organization of school-based law-enforcement officials, called on Congress to enact an Education Homeland Security Act in order to "prevent school terrorist attacks," arguing that school security officers are on the "front line" of terrorism.[24] In response, a Department of Education official said that schools are "not [a] likely target for terrorists," and that the department had issued $38 million in security grants in 2003.[25] The Department of Justice also funds the Secure Our Schools Initiative (not accidentally referred to as SOS), which provides matching grants for schools to buy metal detectors and other security equipment and training. Nonetheless, a February 2003 *USA Today* article began with the ominous warning that "the nation's public schools are a prime target for terrorists."[26]

The 2004 terrorist attack on a Russian school in Beslan, where over three hundred were killed, increased concerns about terrorists striking American schools, in spite of widely published reports that police at roadblocks were bribed to allow the terrorists and their arsenal of weapons to enter the area. Tragedies like the one at Beslan make school security a very emotional issue, one where questions of proportion seem to be lacking.

Similarly, concerns about privacy in schools have taken a backseat to the push for more surveillance and security. A story about adding cameras in a Quincy, Massachusetts, school noted that privacy concerns "are becoming futile as the world seems less safe."[27] Yet it remains unclear whether surveillance cameras, although widely used in school districts across the country, actually make schools any safer. It is likely that parents feel safer, and of course security companies' profits are safer too. Students, on the other hand, may not feel any more secure with the addition of cameras. "Having someone watch me all the time made me feel untrusted [sic] when I didn't do anything wrong," a Bismarck, North Dakota, high-school senior told the Associated Press.[28]

In a time of limited resources, questions about how we spend money on security need to be asked. In the Washington, D.C., public schools, a private security company allegedly overbilled the district by $8.8 million—after another company was accused of overcharging the district by $11.4 million.[29] The district considered swapping thousands of dollars out of its equipment and supplies budget to pay part of the security contract, but the plan met with strong opposition from the mayor's office. Then an investigation following the shooting death of a student uncovered that many of the district's school guards were not well-trained and some even had criminal records.[30] The district continues to vastly outspend several comparable urban districts on security costs per student.

Other districts have had problems financing their high-priced security as well. In order to cover the costs of school security officers, one Illinois district considered charging students a $25 security fee, much as travelers are charged for airport security. Students receiving subsidized lunches would have been exempt, and no family would have had to pay more than $50, but the proposal was rejected after numerous complaints. School principals in the area criticized the move as well, asking for more counselors rather than more funding for a security force.[31]

Amid fears about school shootings and terrorist attacks, the need for quality school counselors has been largely ignored in our concern for school safety. In the meantime, schools across the country facing budget cuts often reduce their counseling staffs, and the poorest districts with the greatest needs are less likely to have a sufficient number of counselors per student. The president made no request in his Fiscal Year 2006 proposed budget to fund counseling for K–12 education, after spending $34.7 million in 2005 (Congress included another $34.7 million for 2006). By contrast, the Safe and Drug-Free Schools program request was for $268 million. Instead of investing in helping young people manage the obstacles they may face, we have turned schools into fear zones.

While buying expensive security systems seems to make us feel that our schools are protected, it is unclear how effective the systems are in actually making schools safer. But they do represent a growing business opportunity. Companies like CameraWATCH, featured on ABC's *Good Morning America*, promise to provide "cameras that keep an unblinking eye on troubled teens." But schools need to do more than capture events on video for prosecution. They need to do more for the troubled teens who scare schools into purchasing cameras in the first place. A real sense of security doesn't come from surveillance cameras or even school police, but from dealing directly with the conditions that cause violence, both within schools and in the communities that surround them.

SELLING FEARS OF CYBERBULLIES

Trying to get kids to be nice to each other also presents business opportunities. If surveillance systems are sold to schools for safety, they can also be used to capture bullying, when it happens, on tape. And workshops, books, and games with titles like "The Self Control Patrol" and "Stop Being So Mean" can be sold to parents, teachers, and school administrators who may fear school violence or lawsuits.[32] While it is uncertain how effective these short-term interventions may be, they are cheaper and easier to employ than making schools and classrooms smaller and hiring more counselors. But even if classrooms and schoolyards are made safe, many kids now interact online, leading to concerns about *cyberbullying*—rude, even threatening communications via e-mail, instant messaging, or websites. Couple this concern with fears of online predators and sexual content, and we now have a market for parents who want to try to regulate this virtual space as best they can.

A variety of products, often called *spyware*, are sold to allow parents to monitor their kids while they are using computers. One product, curiously named Kid Defender, allows parents for $39.95 a year to read their kids' instant messages from another computer.[33] Sentry Remote Monitoring, on the other hand, costs $9.95 per month, and lets parents view (via another computer) their child's computer screen, and will even place a call to a parent if their child uses "inappropriate" language online.[34] Other products with names like X-Detect, Spy Agent, and IamBigBrother conjure up cold war–era spy games that parents may have played as children themselves, while promoting the idea that spying on kids is not only morally and ethically acceptable, but worth the subscription fees too.

Surveillance products like cameras and tracking software and devices are attempts to assert adult control remotely, that is, without adults necessarily having to be present in their kids' lives. Aside from the very good questions critics have asked about the effect of these products on privacy and trust, these products are marketed under the premise that adult virtual supervision of a child is just as good if not better than the adult's actually being there with the child. Marketers of technological tools realize that parents may not be able (or want) to disrupt their lives to further monitor their kids, and surveillance serves to reduce the guilt of not being there.

Certainly one of the most anxiety-provoking issues for twenty-first-century parents is their inability to completely control their child's environment, and the products discussed thus far are attempts to curtail the perceived freedoms that young people have, a curtailment supposedly for young people's own safety. Parents of course need to monitor their kids at age- and situation-appropriate levels. But kids also need to gradually earn responsibility and trust, establish personal boundaries, and build the confidence that they can handle themselves in the world. Our biggest danger is raising kids so protected from life that they grow up unprepared for life's most basic challenges because we were too scared to let them.

SELLING FEARS OF TEEN DRIVERS

Surveillance can be profitable beyond school property. Teen drivers are not only a business opportunity for the insurance companies that can charge parents higher premiums, but also an opportunity for the high-tech industry to sell tracking devices based on parental fears. As I discussed in chapter 6, several types of monitoring products are on the market for parents who are anxious about their teen's driving and are willing to spend the money trying to alleviate their concerns.

Data from SafetyTrac, a device that monitors a car's location, speed, and length of time stopped, can be accessed from the company's website or via automatic e-mails sent to the subscriber for an initial cost of $899. One parent described how he installed SafetyTrac in his teen daughter's BMW, initially without her knowledge. When he received several e-mails indicating that she was driving at least eighty miles per hour, he let her know about the device. "She rarely goes over eighty now," he told the *Chattanooga Times Free Press*. The company president added that the product gives parents "peace of mind."[35]

I'm not sure how much peace of mind a parent should have knowing that his teen daughter only *occasionally* drives over eighty. There are low-tech solutions that parents can employ that don't involve an $899 fee, such as restricting their child's access to a vehicle, especially if they know he or she has driven with excessive speed. Parents have a responsibility to protect not only their son or daughter's safety, but the safety of the general public as well. If parents are concerned about how their teen is driving, then they don't have to provide them with their own car. No technology can take the place of a parent setting appropriate limits, monitoring new and young drivers themselves, and not leaving that responsibility up to a device. But as SafetyTrac's president told the *Wisconsin State Journal*, "It's not an issue of trust. It's an issue of fear."[36] Fear that she hopes will encourage affluent parents to buy her company's product rather than simply taking away the keys when necessary.

Cheaper products like Teen Arrive Alive cost $14.99 a month for a cell phone–based tracking device that monitors speed and location, with an alarm that sounds if the carrier of the phone is going faster than a preset speed. A spokesperson for ULocate, a similar product that uses GPS technology in a phone for $10.95 a month, boasts that "it can really give a parent a little more peace of mind," even though the device doesn't work inside buildings to track kids once they are out of the car.[37]

While the parents who buy these products may feel more in control, it is unclear whether their kids are really any safer or even better drivers. Sure, the knowledge that their parents are playing Big Brother may deter some kids from driving too fast. But it doesn't teach young people how to make tough choices based on their own judgment. It doesn't help them become safer drivers, and instead may make just kids who fear punishment instead of maturing young people who can make their own decisions about right and wrong. An internal moral and ethical compass lasts a lot longer than the threat of being punished. The goal for young people should be to become self-regulating, and not simply to respond to (or rebel against) authority figures. A tracking device may also instill an artificial sense of confidence in both teens and their parents—after all, teens are far from the only problem drivers on the road. No monitoring device can make someone a good defensive driver.

Just as driving is a privilege, the selling of fear-based products depends on a market of privileged members of the middle and upper classes who can afford both the product and a separate car for a teen driver's use. If driving seems more like a right to some people, it's because many parents treat it like one. It is much easier to regulate new and young drivers if they have only limited access to vehicles, but this may inconvenience parents who may not want to share their own car, or who may feel the need to maintain an image of affluence by purchasing a car for their child as a gift. The fact that some parents have the money for an additional car certainly does not mean that every teen should have their own, or in some cases even access to one.

As we have seen, tracking devices allow busy parents to be someplace else but to feel like they are supervising their kids. In the not-so-distant future, however, all new cars may have tracking devices. LoJack, a tracking system installed to track cars if they are stolen, has been in business since

1987, and many new cars now come with incident data recorders that are part of the vehicle's central computer system. While drivers may not want to be tracked or even to think that they can be, the insurance industry loves devices like these because they cut down on thefts and help assess liability in accidents.[38] The auto industry could also benefit in product-liability cases, and try to save on lawsuit payouts, by using the data from these devices to try to demonstrate that driver error caused an accident. Emergency responders using the same devices may also have an easier time finding accident victims. But the issue of privacy looms large with this technology. Just as kids may be surreptitiously monitored by their parents, we may all someday be monitored and tracked without even knowing about it.

SELLING FEARS OF RISK-TAKING

General fears about teen risk-taking also create business opportunities. Besides monitoring kids' Internet use or driving, dozens of other products allow parents to monitor their child's bloodstream at home. Products like Drug Busters, Drug Test Your Teen, and Meditests are available online and in some drugstores as well. Following the passage of the Safe and Drug-Free Schools Act in 1994, in-school drug testing began in hundreds of schools. A study sponsored by the Robert Wood Johnson Foundation in 2003 found that two highly touted methods of in-school drug testing, mandatory testing for athletes and random testing for all students, did not serve to prevent or inhibit drug use.[39] But drug testing remains a popular idea with many parents and politicians, reinforcing the notion that the war on drugs can be effectively fought in schools, in spite of the fact that the real battles are elsewhere.

Beyond testing and monitoring, fears about teen risk-taking provide millions of dollars each year in government-funded research. While research is vitally important, the research questions and the projects that government agencies and private foundations fund can limit the scope of our knowledge about young people's behavior. For instance, in doing research for this book, I often found it difficult to locate data on adult drinking and drug use, which pose an equal or greater threat to public health than teen substance use. Data on sexual activity, condom use, and frequency of drug and alcohol use is much easier to find for teens and young adults than for the population as a whole. This lack of research and reporting on results may make it appear as though these are only teen problems, because teen research results often make news without the adult context, helping us maintain our assumption that teens are inherent risk-takers and much more trouble than adults.

As sociologist Joel Best discusses in his book *Damned Lies and Statistics: Untangling Numbers from the Media, Politicians, and Activists*, activist groups and nonprofit organizations work to raise awareness and funds for their cause. In the process they may exaggerate the extent of the problem or encourage the public to believe that the problem is growing. For instance, programs set up to help teen substance-users may dramatize the problem in order to frighten the public and policy makers into providing more funding for the programs' cause. While no one disputes the good intentions most of these organizations have, the organizations also have a vested interest in making specific problems seem as scary as possible.

Research almost always has ideological foundations, if not that of the researchers themselves, who want to demonstrate that funding their work is important, then that of the groups that fund the research. This doesn't necessarily mean that research on teen risk-taking is compromised or without utility. But research that challenges the conventional wisdom about young people often goes unfunded, preventing us from reconsidering the way we think about young people, risk, and danger. Science is an attempt to get closer to understanding our world, but it is often based on our preconceptions about the way the world works. If we weren't so collectively concerned about teen drinking or teen sex, researching them might seem pointless, much as we don't tend to worry that too much reading could contribute to obesity. Likewise, fears about adult risk-taking in general are minimal. Thus less research, and less knowledge, is produced in response.

We do tend to look at risk in so-called problem populations: the poor, ethnic minority groups, immigrants, homosexuals, or young people, who have been defined as "other." Studying risk in these groups tacitly promotes methods of control and restriction, which privileged groups evade. We focus our attention on the risk-taking of the groups that we think are causing problems, often without recognizing how the disempowered status of these groups may contribute to the problems themselves.

KIDS THESE DAYS

On a very basic level, the news media also benefit by telling us emotional stories about the trouble that kids may find themselves in, whether it be by the kids' own doing, the fault of other kids, or the result of feared dangers of the outside world. These scary stories serve as cautionary tales, modern-day fables about what can happen to kids who are too bold or who stray too far from control. Bad news about kids is good for ratings because it reaches audiences on a visceral level and in a way that little else can. Bad news about kids encapsulates our fears for the future, gives them a face and a presence, and seems to suggest a solution.

Bad news about kids today does more than boost ratings. It sets up part of the population as the cause of trouble, and often encourages us to act in ways that don't best serve young people or society's best interests. It's not just our personal opinions that are shaped by this perception that kids today face or cause ever-increasing danger. Public policy decisions are regularly made based on misperceptions about young people. For instance, young people are effectively limited from appearing in public in many municipalities. Curfew laws, which are often selectively enforced to target youths of color from low-income families, determine when and where young people can be, legislating what should be parental decisions. A comprehensive study of curfew laws in several cities found that they do not necessarily reduce crime—in fact, in some cases, crime increased *after* a curfew was enforced—but they feel good to the voting public, so they remain popular.[40]

Another program that makes many people feel like they are helping kids and reducing crime is D.A.R.E. (Drug Awareness Resistance Education). Who could oppose antidrug education? But a 2001 article in *Contemporary Pediatrics* noted that "the program's effects are minimal and wear off by the time kids are high school age."[41] Disproportionate fears about drugs and violence led to zero-tolerance policies, as discussed in chapter 3. Like curfews, these policies have created new opportunities to make minor infractions serious law violations and to give some otherwise well-behaved kids criminal records. Rules like these create an atmosphere of disdain for authority if a kid is suspended for bringing aspirin to school.

Contempt for young people, especially other people's children, runs rampant and has made us more likely to favor trying juveniles in adult courts and to feel that rehabilitation in juvenile court means being "soft" on crime. Bad kids seem like a good reason to reduce funding for educational opportunities, especially if the kids do not perform well on standardized tests.

We have a love/hate relationship with kids. Certainly people love their own kids and want the best opportunities for them to succeed and to be happy. But other kids often make people nervous, especially if they look or speak differently. In part, fearing young people comes from a racial and ethnic shift that we have been experiencing in the United States. It also reflects an economic shift, by which the poorest segment of the population has fallen further behind, even with the boom years of the 1990s. Additionally, it has been harder for young people, when they do come of age, to match their parents' standard of living, and young adults today are more likely to be saddled with debt than young adults of a generation ago. Americans typically like to view economic success or failure as the product of individual effort. When young people do struggle, it is easier to think of their challenges as their own fault, or maybe their parents' fault, rather than the result of the host of complex factors that shape our lives.

We hear so much about things like teen sex and substance use, or youth violence and child obesity, that it is hard to see the connections between the individuals and their larger social environment. Issues like poverty, the most serious and pressing childhood problem in the United States, do not grab headlines like stories of kids setting themselves on fire.

Child poverty contradicts the prized American Dream that those who are deserving will have what they need. Poor children, and kids without adequate health care or educational opportunities, don't make us feel so good about ourselves. There is no simple target of blame, no easy solution. These kids represent America's dirty little secret, that amid wealth and plenty, hard work is not always enough to provide for our children. Whether we vilify their parents or not, far too many young people in this country are not getting their basic needs met.

Parents are not blameless in creating problems for kids today. Child abuse, neglect, and substance use often go hand in hand and are serious problems impacting many children. Violent and substance-using kids may command more of our attention, but their parents' problems are often the central cause.

The social problems that affect young people today deserve our attention, but we need to start by more clearly understanding reality and by being able to distinguish the facts from the fictions we often worry about. Kids today aren't the problem any more than we were in our time, or our parents or grandparents were in their time, but instead are in need of adults' support, guidance, and understanding.

NOTES

1. Children's Defense Fund, "Key Facts about American Children," Washington, D.C., August 2004.

2. Paula S. Fass, *Kidnapped: Child Abduction in America* (New York: Oxford University Press, 1997).

3. Kevin O'Grady, "Covering the Risks of the Kidnap Boom," *Business Day* (South Africa), July 13, 2004, 3.

4. David Porter, "Child Security Devices Becoming More Common," Associated Press, October 3, 2003.

5. Holly Zachariah, "Device Could Be Key to Finding Kids Who Are Lost or Abducted," *Columbus Dispatch*, September 13, 2004, 3B.

6. Ann Bednarz, "Legoland Uses RFID for Finding Lost Kids," *Network World*, May 3, 2004, 14.

7. Ann Bednarz, "RFID Everywhere: From Amusement Parks to Blood Supplies," *Network World*, May 3, 2004, 1.

8. Jason Spencer, "Spring ISD Tests Bus Tracking System," *Houston Chronicle*, February 28, 2004, A29.

9. Patrick Seitz, "Makers of Child-Tracking Technology Find Big Potential Market," *Investor's Business Daily*, March 1, 2004, A5.

10. Emma Nash, "Child Tracking System Put to the Test," *Computing*, December 5, 2002, 23.

11. Seitz, "Makers of Child-Tracking Technology."

12. "Family: For the Fridge," *San Diego Union–Tribune*, September 21, 2002, E1.

13. From the Kinderprint website, www.ob4vending.com/kinderprint.htm (last accessed January 5, 2006).

14. Jim Stingl, "A Sad Twist to Use of Baby Monitor," *Milwaukee Journal Sentinel*, February 18, 2004, 1B.

15. Harry Jackson, "New Weight-Loss Camp for Kids Is Set Up," *St. Louis Post-Dispatch*, May 17, 2004, 2.

16. "Aspen Education Group Therapeutic Boarding Schools Opened for Over-weight, Obese Youths," *Law and Health Weekly*, April 10, 2004, 28.

17. Abby Ellin, "For Overweight Children, Are 'Fat Camps' a Solution?" *New York Times*, June 28, 2005, F1.

18. Sandra Hughes, "Camp La Jolla Teaches Entire Families How to Fight Obesity," *The Early Show*, CBS News, August 20, 2004.

19. "Wellbridge Athletic Clubs Nationwide Introduce Kids' Fitness Options," PR Newswire, June 23, 2003.

20. Mike Kennedy, "Providing Safe Schools," *American Schools and University*, January 1, 2004, 5.

21. Mary W. Green, "The Appropriate and Effective Use of Security Technologies in U.S. Schools," U.S. Department of Justice, Office of Justice Programs, National Institute of Justice, Washington, D.C., September 1999.

22. Andrew Brophy, "Security Flunks Test at School in Fairfield," *Connecticut Post*, April 30, 2003.

23. Janet McConnaughey, "Keeping Schools Safe in a Time of Terror Focus of New Orleans Talk," Associated Press, February 20, 2003.

24. "Nation's School-Based Police Officers Call for Education Homeland Security Act to Protect Schools from Terrorist Threat," U.S. Newswire, February 10, 2003.

25. Harvey Simon, "Education Department Disputes Survey on School Security," *Aviation Week's Homeland Security and Defense*, August 27, 2003, 4.

26. Greg Toppo, "Group Says Schools Need Anti-terrorism Training," *USA Today*, February 10, 2003, 6D.

27. Jessica Van Sack, "Cams Monitor School Halls," *Patriot Ledger*, September 11, 2004, 1.

28. "Bismarck Considers School Security Cameras," Associated Press, July 28, 2004.

29. Jim McElhatton, "Funds Eyed for School Security," *Washington Times*, August 6, 2004.

30. Jim McElhatton, "School Security Costly in D.C.," *Washington Times*, April 27, 2004, A1.

31. Leah Friedman, "Board Rejects Assessment of Student Security Fees," *State Journal Register*, January 21, 2004, 9.

32. From the Childswork catalog, www.childswork.com (last accessed January 5, 2006).

33. Mackenzie Carpenter, "Spying Appeals to Worried Parents," *Pittsburgh Post-Gazette*, February 15, 2004, A1.

34. Cindy Krischer Goodman, "High-Tech Devices Can Spy on Kids 24/7, But What About Trust?" *Miami Herald*, October 26, 2004.

35. Clint Cooper, "Tracking Teens," *Chattanooga Times Free Press*, February 11, 2003, E1.

36. Fred McKissack, "What Are the Ethical Implications?" *Wisconsin State Journal*, March 16, 2003, 11.

37. Krischer Goodman, "High-Tech Devices Can Spy."

38. Salley Shannon, "Witness on Board," *Los Angeles Times Magazine*, July 17, 2005, 14–16, 32–33.

39. R. Yamaguchi, L. D. Johnson, and P. M. O'Malley, "Drug Testing in Schools: Policies, Practices, and Association with Student Drug Use," *YES Occasional Papers*, no. 2, 2003.

40. Kenneth Adams, "The Effectiveness of Juvenile Curfews at Crime Prevention," *Annals of the American Academy of Political and Social Science* 587 (2003): 136–59. See also Mike A. Males, *Framing Youth: Ten Myths about the Next Generation* (Monroe, Maine: Common Courage, 1999), 71–79.

41. Judith Asch-Goodkin, "D.A.R.E. Redux," *Contemporary Pediatrics* 3 (2001): 13. See also "GAO Literature Review Reiterates Ineffectiveness of Original D.A.R.E.," *Alcoholism and Drug Abuse Weekly* (January 27, 2003), 1–3.

Selected Bibliography

Anderson, Mark et al. "School-Associated Violent Deaths in the United States, 1994–1999." *Journal of the American Medical Association* 286 (2001): 2695–2702.

Ayers, William, Bernardine Dohrn, and Rick Ayers, eds. *Zero Tolerance: Resisting the Drive for Punishment in Our Schools.* New York: New Press, 2001.

Berliner, David C. and Bruce J. Biddle. *The Manufactured Crisis: Myths, Fraud, and the Attack on America's Public Schools.* New York: Addison-Wesley, 1995.

Best, Joel. *Damned Lies and Statistics: Untangling Numbers from the Media, Politicians, and Activists.* Berkeley: University of California Press, 2001.

———. "Monster Hype: How a Few Isolated Tragedies—and Their Supposed Causes—Were Turned into a National 'Epidemic.'" *Education Next* 2 (2002): 51–55.

Biddle, Bruce J. and David C. Berliner. "What Research Says about Unequal Funding for Schools in America." *Policy Perspectives* (2003).

Brückner, Hannah and Peter Bearman. "After the Promise: The Consequences of Adolescent Virginity Pledges." *Journal of Adolescent Health* 36 (2005): 271–78.

Campos, Paul. *The Obesity Myth: Why America's Obsession with Weight Is Hazardous to Your Health.* New York: Gotham Books, 2004.

Critser, Greg. *Fat Land: How Americans Became the Fattest People in the World.* New York: Houghton Mifflin, 2003.

Curwin, Richard L. and Allen N. Mendler. "Zero Tolerance for Zero Tolerance." *Phi Delta Kappan* 81 (1999): 119–20.

de Becker, Gavin. *The Gift of Fear: Survival Signals that Protect Us from Violence.* New York: Little, Brown, 1997.

Donovan, Frank R. *Wild Kids: How Youth Has Shocked Its Elders—Then and Now!* Harrisburg, Pa.: Stackpole Books, 1967.

Fass, Paula S. *Kidnapped: Child Abduction in America.* New York: Oxford University Press, 1997.

Flegal, Katherine M. et al. "Prevalence and Trends in Obesity among U.S. Adults, 1999–2000." *Journal of the American Medical Association* 288 (2002): 1723–27.

Glassner, Barry. *The Culture of Fear: Why Americans Are Afraid of the Wrong Things*. New York: Basic Books, 1999.

Gunderson, Gordon W. *The National School Lunch Program: Background and Development*. Washington, D.C.: GPO, 1971.

Higonnet, Anne. *Pictures of Innocence: The History and Crisis of Ideal Childhood*. London: Thames and Hudson, 1998.

Hine, Thomas. *The Rise and Fall of the American Teenager: A New History of the American Adolescent Experience*. New York: Perennial, 1999.

Hulbert, Ann. *Raising America: Experts, Parents, and a Century of Advice about Children*. New York: Vintage Books, 2003.

Hyman, Irwin A. *Reading, Writing, and the Hickory Stick: The Appalling Story of Physical and Psychological Abuse in American Schools*. Lexington, Mass.: Lexington Books, 1990.

Jones, Gerard. *Killing Monsters: Why Children Need Fantasy, Super Heroes, and Make-Believe Violence*. New York: Basic Books, 2002.

Kimm, Sue Y. S. et al. "Race, Socioeconomic Status, and Obesity in 9- to 10-year-old Girls: The NHLBI Growth and Health Study." *Annals of Epidemiology* 6 (1996): 266–75.

Kozol, Jonathan. "Malign Neglect: Children in New York City Schools Are Being Shortchanged—Again." *The Nation*, June 10, 2002.

Lamb, Sharon. *The Secret Lives of Girls: What Good Girls Really Do—Sex Play, Aggression, and Their Guilt*. New York: Free Press, 2001.

Males, Mike A. *The Scapegoat Generation: America's War on Adolescents*. Monroe, Maine: Common Courage Press, 1996.

———. *Framing Youth: Ten Myths about the Next Generation*. Monroe, Maine: Common Courage Press, 1999.

———. *Kids and Guns*. Monroe, Maine: Common Courage Press, 2004.

———. "Dumping on Girls: Now That's Mean," *Los Angeles Times*, May 30, 2004, M3.

Milner, Murray Jr. *Freaks, Geeks, and Cool Kids: American Teenagers, Schools, and the Culture of Consumption*. New York: Routledge, 2004.

Mokdad, Ali H. et al. "The Spread of the Obesity Epidemic in the United States, 1991–1998." *Journal of the American Medical Association* 282 (1999): 1519.

Nasaw, David. *Schooled to Order: A Social History of Public Schooling in the United States*. New York: Oxford University Press, 1979.

———. *Children of the City: At Work and At Play*. New York: Anchor Press, 1985.

Nuwer, Hank, ed. *The Hazing Reader*. Bloomington: Indiana University Press, 2004.

Ogden, Cynthia L. et al. "Prevalence and Trends in Overweight among U.S. Children and Adolescents, 1999–2000." *Journal of the American Medical Association* 288 (2002): 1728–32.

Paeratakul, S. et al. "The Relation of Gender, Race, and Socioeconomic Status to Obesity and Obesity Comorbidities in a Sample of U.S. Adults." *International Journal of Obesity* 26 (2002): 1205–10.

Palladino, Grace. *Teenagers: An American History*. New York: Basic Books, 1996.

Remez, Lisa. "Oral Sex among Adolescents: Is It Sex or Is It Abstinence?" *Family Planning Perspectives* 32 (2000).

Simmons, Rachel. *Odd Girl Out: The Hidden Culture of Aggression in Girls*. New York: Harcourt, 2002.

Skiba, Russell J. and Reece L. Peterson. "The Dark Side of Zero Tolerance: Can Punishment Lead to Safe Schools?" *Phi Delta Kappan* 80 (1999): 373.

Skiba, Russell J., Reece L. Peterson, and Tara Williams. "Office Referrals and Suspension: Disciplinary Intervention in Middle Schools." *Education and Treatment of Children* 20 (1997): 316–35.

Stearns, Peter N. *Anxious Parents: A History of Modern Childrearing in America.* New York: New York University Press, 2003.

Sternheimer, Karen. *It's Not the Media: The Truth about Pop Culture's Influence on Children.* Boulder, Colorado: Westview Press, 2003.

Strauch, Barbara. *The Primal Teen: What the New Discoveries about the Teenage Brain Tell Us about Our Kids.* New York: Doubleday, 2003.

Tanenbaum, Leora. *Slut! Growing Up Female with a Bad Reputation.* New York: Perennial, 2000.

U.S. Department of Transportation, National Highway Traffic Safety Administration. "Traffic Safety Facts 2002: Overview." Washington, D.C., 2003.

Wang, Youfa. "Cross-National Comparison of Childhood Obesity: The Epidemic and the Relationship between Obesity and Socioeconomic Status." *International Journal of Epidemiology* 30 (2001): 1129–36.

Zimring, Franklin E. *American Youth Violence.* London: Oxford University Press, 1998.

Index

161

About the Author

Karen Sternheimer teaches in the Department of Sociology at the University of Southern California and is a research consultant for the Center of Media Literacy. She is author of *It's Not the Media: The Truth About Pop Culture's Influence on Children* (2003). Her commentary has been published in the *Los Angeles Times, Newsday*, and the *San Jose Mercury News*. Additionally, her work has been discussed in *Variety, Child* magazine, *Ladies' Home Journal*, the *Los Angeles Times*, and other major newspapers. She has appeared on CNN, *The O'Reilly Factor*, the *Fox Morning News* and numerous radio programs.